100 THINGS
SYRACUSE FANS
SHOULD KNOW & DO
BEFORE THEY DIE

100 THINGS SYRACUSE FANS SHOULD KNOW & DO BEFORE THEY DIE

Scott Pitoniak

TRIUMPH
BOOKS

No part of this publication may be reproduced, stored in a retrieval system, or transmitted in any form by any means, electronic, mechanical, photocopying, or otherwise, without the prior written permission of the publisher, Triumph Books LLC, 814 North Franklin Street, Chicago, Illinois 60610.

Library of Congress Cataloging-in-Publication Data has been applied for.

This book is available in quantity at special discounts for your group or organization. For further information, contact:

Triumph Books LLC
814 North Franklin Street
Chicago, Illinois 60610
(312) 337-0747
www.triumphbooks.com

Printed in U.S.A.
ISBN: 978-1-60078-988-5
Design by Patricia Frey
Photos courtesy of AP Images unless otherwise indicated

To my bride, Beth; my children, Amy and Christopher; my granddaughter, Camryn Marie; and everyone who has taken the time to read my stuff through the years.

Contents

Foreword

A wise man once suggested that you can't go home again. Well, I'm here to tell you that man was wrong. In 2011—44 years after I graduated from Syracuse University—I accepted athletic director Daryl Gross' offer to return to my alma mater as his special assistant, and I couldn't be happier. In fact, this is my favorite job ever, and that's saying something because I had some pretty good careers before this one. I spent nine seasons playing running back for the Denver Broncos and wound up making it into the Pro Football Hall of Fame. And after I hung up the helmet and shoulder pads, I spent 32 years as a dealer for Ford, Lincoln-Mercury, and Mazda. But this latest job has been the most rewarding because every day I get an opportunity to motivate and inspire young student-athletes. I get a chance to help them make their dreams come true—to develop not only as athletes but as people.

My office contains a lot of photographs and memorabilia from my life, including pictures of me with prominent Syracuse alumni such as Vice President Joe Biden, famed running backs Jim Brown and Larry Csonka, and ESPN sportscaster Mike Tirico. There's also a large sign on one of the walls that reads: SUCCESS IS A JOURNEY, NOT A DESTINATION. I think it's really cool that my journey has brought my life full circle.

I have so many fond memories of SU. It's a place that certainly changed my life. As you'll read in further detail in this book, I came really close to attending West Point and playing football for Army. They wanted me so badly that they had General Douglas MacArthur heavily recruit me when I was at Bordentown Military Academy in New Jersey. I joke to people that I could have beaten Colin Powell to the punch and became the first African American general had I accepted West Point's offer. But I wound up going to Syracuse because I had given my word to Ernie Davis, the legendary SU running back who was the first African American to win the Heisman Trophy. The shocking day Ernie died of leukemia—May 18, 1963—I remembered the promise I had made to him. To me, a man's word is the most valuable thing he has, so I picked up the phone and told Coach Ben Schwartzwalder I was coming to Syracuse. It wound up being one of the greatest decisions of my life.

I was blessed to wear the same jersey number my predecessors Ernie and Jim Brown wore—No. 44. Those two men set the bar awfully high, but I'd like to think that I did my share to add to the legacy they started. I was fortunate enough to be able to break most of their records and become the first Orangeman in six decades to earn All-American honors three times. But I'm just as proud of the fact that I earned my degree. I truly believe in the concept of the student-athlete—in that order. Student, then athlete. Academics did not come easily to me at first, but I kept working at it and working at it and working at it. The concepts I learned at Syracuse helped me fulfill my goal of not only earning my undergraduate degree but also of earning a law degree from the University of Denver during my off-seasons with the Broncos. Those concepts also helped me become a successful entrepreneur when my football days were over.

In the pages that follow, you'll have an opportunity to read about the people, moments, and traditions that have helped make Syracuse University one of the most historic and best-known collegiate athletic programs in the world. From football, basketball, and lacrosse All-Americans to Olympic gold-medal winners to pioneers who broke down barriers to famous sportscasters, SU certainly has made its mark. I couldn't be more proud to have contributed to that legacy, and, hopefully, I can help current and future Orange men and women add to that legacy.

Appropriately enough, 44 years after graduating from Syracuse, I came home again and couldn't be happier.

Enjoy these essays and Go Orange!

—Floyd Little
Special assistant to the Syracuse University
athletics director and member of the College Football
Hall of Fame and the Pro Football Hall of Fame

Acknowledgments

A book is always a team effort, and I had some great teammates assisting me with this one. This is my fifth book published by Triumph, and each experience has been a good one. Thanks to Noah Amstadter, Mitch Rogatz, and Tom Bast for entrusting me with this subject, and thanks to Karen O'Brien for her meticulous and thoughtful editing.

The folks at Syracuse University were extremely helpful, especially Sue Edson, Pete Moore, Susie Mehringer, and Mike Morrison from the sports information department; Jay Cox and David Marc from *Syracuse University* magazine; SU archivist Mary O'Brien; and Falk School professor Rick Burton. And a special thanks to my longtime friend, SU SID emeritus Larry Kimball, who is a walking encyclopedia of Syracuse sports history.

It's an honor and a thrill to have one of my boyhood heroes, Floyd Little, write the foreword to this book. I can't think of a better person to set the tone than Little, who wore Syracuse's famed No. 44 football jersey with distinction and has always been a class act, on and off the field.

The works of those who've covered the Orange through the years also made my job easier. They include Mike Waters, Bud Poliquin, Bob Snyder, Sean Kirst, Donna Ditota, Pete Thamel, David Ramsey, Donnie Webb, Dave Elfin, John Kekis, John Pitarresi, Tom Batzold, Frank Bilovsky, Matt Park, and Steve Bradley.

I've covered scores of players and coaches at SU. It would take several pages to mention all of them. Let me just say thank you to all of you for your cooperation, and thanks for providing me with so many memorable performances to write about.

I'm indebted to the editors from the various newspapers and magazines that have employed me for giving me the opportunity to cover the people and events I've written about on the pages that follow.

I'd like to thank all the readers who have purchased my books and read my stuff in newspapers, magazines, and online through the decades. None of this happens without you.

Lastly, I'd like to thank my home team—my bride, Beth; our children, Amy and Christopher; our new granddaughter, Camryn Marie; and our aptly named cat, Sassy. Your love and support is my most treasured gift.

— Scott Pitoniak

Introduction

The list of unfinished business was a mile long. There was a 12-page American history term paper to write, a chapter of introductory economics to read, an interview to conduct for a journalism class, and a take-home psychology exam to complete.

All due in just a few days.

My sophomore year at Syracuse University was winding down, and I fully intended to sequester myself in Bird Library on March 22, 1975, so I could dig my way out of the avalanche of school work, but the basketball team forced a change in plans. A few days earlier, the Orangemen had set the sports world on its ear by upsetting mighty North Carolina in the 1975 NCAA East semifinals in Providence, Rhode Island, and now they were just one game removed from reaching the Final Four for the first time…ever. My roommate, Ed Shaw, gave me an earful about the historical significance of that day's game against Kansas State. He warned me this opportunity might never come again and that I would absolutely hate myself if I missed it. His arguments were quite convincing. Long story short, I didn't make it to Bird that Saturday afternoon. But I did make it to hoops heaven.

Several of us gathered to watch the game on our small-screen, black-and-white TV in a Skytop apartment on south campus. Our reaction to what transpired was similar to the reaction of announcer Jack Buck watching Kirk Gibson of the Los Angeles Dodgers hobble to the plate and smack a walk-off homer in the 1988 World Series. Upon seeing the home run, Buck bellowed incredulously into his microphone, "I don't believe what I just saw!" In our case, the Syracuse basketball team, featuring a center who looked like a bouncer recruited from a tavern and a speedy little guard who inexplicably wore sunglasses 24/7 in a city where the sun rarely shines, was a motley crew of hoopsters who managed to upset Kansas

State in overtime in the East Region finals. The Orangemen were headed to San Diego to play Kentucky in the Final Four, and we were headed to Marshall Street for one of the biggest parties the Hill had ever seen.

The streets on campus were paralyzed with cars and people. Along fraternity and sorority row, music blared from speakers and a flood light brightened the night sky. Every bar along the M-Street and Crouse Avenue strip was stuffed to the gills. We managed to shoe-horn our way into the Varsity, the pizza joint that's been serving SU students fast food since the Great Depression. Inside, the patrons chanted "Let's Go Orange!" before belting out the lyrics to the Beach Boys' "California Girls." Spud Dellas, one of the Varsity's owners, told me he hadn't seen a celebration like this since the Syracuse football team won the national championship in 1959, when thousands snake-danced through the streets like New Orleans revelers during Mardi Gras. I awoke the next morning with a severe case of laryngitis and a mild hangover. It was a small price to pay.

The campus was electric during the days leading up to the Final Four. The frat houses were draped with banners. People were smiling more. Total strangers began speaking to one another. The sun even made a few appearances. For a week, anyway, sports were a unifying force on campus. For the first time, many of my classmates and I experienced true school spirit. What you need to understand is that SU basketball was decent in those days but nowhere near the juggernaut it has become. We were kind of like the Gonzagas and Butlers and Virginia Commonwealths of that era, an up-and-coming program trying to prove it could play with the big boys. To be honest, those were kind of lean days for the sports program in general, especially football. We'd go to games at dilapidated Archbold Stadium and watch Penn State and Pitt toss us around like blocking dummies, and we'd fantasize about what it must be like to be at a school where the sports teams were really,

really good. Well, that March we finally got to sample what that was like. It was pretty cool.

No, it did not end the way we would have liked. The Orangemen got trounced by Kentucky in the semifinals, then they lost to Louisville in overtime in the consolation game. (Yes, back in the day, the semifinal losers played a consy game.) But that didn't matter. Just reaching the Final Four was a destination beyond our wildest expectations. Nearly 40—egads!—years later, my roommate and I still occasionally reminisce about that seminal moment in SU basketball and sports history. I tell him that he was right, for the one and only time in his life, on that day when he talked me out of going to Bird Library.

You'll read more about that first Final Four appearance in the ensuing essays. I've been following Syracuse sports since the early 1960s when sublime running back Floyd Little was gobbling up football real estate at Archbold and gravity-defying guard Dave Bing was teaming with a gangly, bespectacled backcourt mate by the name of James Arthur Boeheim to start a half-century run of unabated success by the Orange hoops program that continues to this day. As you turn the pages, you'll find the expected cast of characters—Jim Brown, Ernie Davis, Gary and Paul Gait, Carmelo Anthony, Ben Schwartzwalder, and Coach Mac, just to name a few. But you'll also read about the special places (Manley Field House, the Carrier Dome, Archbold), traditions ("Let's Go Orange!" "Down, down the field," Varsity pizza), rivalries (Georgetown, Penn State, Colgate), games (Pearl's half-court shot, Michael Owens' season-saving two-point conversion, the six-overtime contest in the Big Apple), pioneers (Wilmeth Sidat-Singh, Kathrine Switzer, Oren Lyons), and mascots (Vita the Goat, the Saltine Warrior, Otto the Orange). You'll also be treated to a number of stories about athletes with Syracuse ties who you've either forgotten or didn't know about (SU baseball player turned acclaimed novelist Stephen Crane, football-wanna-be Ted Koppel, and National League Most Valuable Player Jim Konstanty).

As someone who has followed the Orangemen for nearly a half-century and written about them as a sportswriter and author for nearly four decades, it never ceases to amaze me how rich and textured the history of Syracuse University sports truly is. Believe me, it was a daunting task keeping this list to 100. Hopefully these essays and vignettes will enlighten and entertain and give you a greater appreciation of SU's sporting past. And if it stirs a little debate, well, that's okay, too.

Enjoy.

— Scott Pitoniak

1 Jim Boeheim

His father had mailed in the non-refundable $100 deposit check after Jim Boeheim had been accepted to Colgate University in the spring of 1962. But the elder Boeheim might as well have taken a match to the money because his son, over his old man's vehement objections, had designs on playing basketball at Syracuse University. And that was that, as far as Jim was concerned. His mind was made up. And when his mind was made up, you could forget about it, because he could be as stubborn as the mule that tugged the Erie Canal boat that brought his German-born ancestors to upstate New York in 1853.

Like one of his early sports idols, Jim Brown, Boeheim was determined to become an Orange man. So he showed up on the SU campus that September, and more than a half-century and 1,100 victories later (as a player, assistant, and head coach), he's still stubbornly churning out 25-win seasons and NCAA tournament appearances. "When I think of Syracuse basketball, two words come immediately to mind—Jimmy Boeheim," said longtime ESPN basketball guru Dick Vitale. "The 'Cuse and Boeheim are inseparable. They go together perfectly, like spaghetti and meatballs."

Through the years, larger schools and the NBA courted Boeheim with financial offers that dwarfed what he was making at SU. But the guy who grew up in the small canal town of Lyons, just 45 minutes west of campus, was never drawn to the big-city lights. By deciding, in the words of his former assistant Rick Pitino, "to become a nester rather than a nomad," Boeheim was able to build a hoops juggernaut in his own backyard. After racking up the second-most wins in men's college basketball history, he has become to Syracuse what Bear Bryant was to Alabama, what John Wooden was to UCLA, and what Mike Krzyzewski is to Duke—a legend in his adopted hometown, the face of not only a program but a university.

And it could be argued quite cogently that Boeheim's ties to his school run even deeper than the aforementioned because he played at SU, too. He's been around for 52 of the 114 years the school has been dribbling, passing, and shooting basketballs on Piety Hill and he has had a hand in more than 60 percent of the Orangemen's wins.

"I guess I've always viewed things a little differently than most people," Boeheim said, when asked about his longevity at his school. "Most people believe the grass is greener on the other side. But I guess I was fortunate enough early on to appreciate the greenness of the grass on my side of the fence."

The funny thing is that few expected Boeheim to last a semester, let alone 52 years. Even head SU coach Fred Lewis had his doubts about the scrawny, bespectacled, physically underwhelming kid, which is why Boeheim arrived on campus sans scholarship. Lewis promised Boeheim the opportunity to walk on and earn one. But it was a similar promise, Boeheim later came to find out, that the smooth-talking Lewis had made to at least three other freshmen who had been star high school players.

Boeheim would eventually win over Lewis and his teammates with his toughness, smarts, and scoring ability. Not only would he receive his scholarship, he would receive Lewis' undying appreciation for teaming with All-American Dave Bing to help revive a program that had lost 27 games in a row the two seasons before their arrival.

"If you play the game, sometimes you go against somebody who doesn't look like they can do it," Lewis said of Boeheim, who converted 57 percent of his shots and averaged 14.6 points per game his senior year. "You think, *This will be an easy game. I'll kill*

Jim Boeheim, head coach of the Syracuse Orange during their game against the Indiana Hoosiers during the NCAA Regional Final on March 28, 2013, at the Verizon Center, Washington, D.C.. Syracuse won the game 61–50 to get to the Final Four. (AP Photo/Bruce Schwartzman)

this guy. And by the end of the game, he's beaten your brains out. That was Jim. He had a tremendous advantage. People looked at him and thought every step would be his last, but that last step never came."

Boeheim tried out for the NBA, and he was one of the final players cut by the Chicago Bulls at their training camp in 1966. He then returned to Syracuse to work on his master's degree. Though he continued playing professionally on weekends for Scranton in the old Eastern League, he began his coaching career at his alma mater, first as a graduate assistant and then as a full-time assistant. Under head coach Roy Danforth, Boeheim helped the 1974–75 Orangemen make the school's first trip to the Final Four. When

Boeheim Superlatives

- Inducted into the Naismith Basketball Hall of Fame in 2005
- Won a national championship in 2003
- Coached the Orange to an NCAA-record 36 20-win seasons in 38 years
- Holds record as second-winningest coach in NCAA men's basketball history
- Assistant on two Olympic gold-medal teams (2008 and 2012)
- Appeared in four Final Fours (1987, 1996, 2003, 2013)
- Appeared in 31 NCAA tournaments
- Holds a record of 1,139–398 at Syracuse, combining his won-lost record as a player (52–24), assistant (139–55), and head coach (948–319)
- Holds record for most wins at one school (948)
- Averaged 9.8 points and 2.3 rebounds per game as a player for the Orange
- Played six years of minor-league basketball for Scranton, Pennsylvania, in the Eastern League, averaging 17 points per game while leading his team to two titles
- Earned two varsity letters in golf, going 6–6–2 in match play during his career
- Coached the SU varsity golf team to an 18–13–1 record in six seasons before the sport was dropped in 1972.

Danforth left the following season, Boeheim applied for the head coaching vacancy. A search committee, headed by athletics director Les Dye, dragged its feet before finally offering the job to Boeheim, who was about to accept a similar position with the University of Rochester.

Thanks to the recruitment of center Roosevelt Bouie and forward Louis Orr, the Orangemen got off to a fast start, going 26–4 in Boeheim's first season. The "Louie and Bouie Show" went 100–18 with four consecutive NCAA tournament appearances. "Those two launched the ship," Boeheim said. "They laid the foundation for all the success we've enjoyed since."

The excellence of the program over such a long stretch may be unparalleled in college basketball. Boeheim has never experienced a losing season, and only twice in 38 seasons have the Orangemen failed to win at least 20 games. During this era, they've made 31 NCAA tournament appearances and have reached the Final Four four times—including 2003 when they won it all. On September 9, 2005, Boeheim was inducted into the Naismith Basketball Hall of Fame in Springfield, Massachusetts. His presenter at the ceremony was his former teammate and roommate, Dave Bing, who had been inducted 15 years earlier. "He's created a program that year-in, year-out demands excellence, and that's not easy to sustain in the dog-eat-dog world of college basketball," said former Georgetown University coach John Thompson of his longtime nemesis and friend. "Most programs hit a rut at some point, and it's tough for them to get out of it. Jim's program has never been in a rut for any prolonged period of time, and that's a tribute to him."

2 Jim Brown

In retrospect, it's difficult to fathom that the greatest all-around athlete in Syracuse University history, and perhaps American history, didn't receive a scholarship until his sophomore year.

At Manhasset High School on Long Island, Jim Brown had earned 13 varsity letters in three years in four different sports, and he had attracted dozens of offers from colleges, including several Big Ten and Ivy League schools. Fortunately for SU, a prominent alum—Manhasset-based attorney and judge Kenny Molloy—helped raise money so Brown could attend Syracuse. Brown would go on to earn All-American honors in football and lacrosse and letter in four varsity sports for the Orangemen, but his journey to stardom at Syracuse would be rocky, filled with run-ins with coaches and accusations of racial prejudice.

"I've made peace with Syracuse—I like the direction the university is heading," Brown said in a 2008 return to campus for the premiere of *The Express*, the film about his friend and Syracuse successor, Ernie Davis. "But it took me a long time to heal the wounds. I've now reached a point where I can look back with pride at what I did here and put the other stuff to the side."

On several occasions, Brown was ready to leave school, but thanks to the friendship and mentorship of Malloy and SU lacrosse coach and football assistant Roy Simmons Sr., Brown was convinced each time to stick it out. What he wound up accomplishing athletically remains the stuff of legend.

A chiseled 6'2", 212-lb. Adonis with sprinter's speed, Brown started the legend of No. 44 at Syracuse with his exploits on the football field, where he became an unstoppable, indestructible force. He came into his own during his senior year when he rushed for a school record 986 yards in just eight games, caught five passes, completed three passes, scored 14 touchdowns, kicked 22 extra points, and intercepted three passes on defense.

In a mid-season battle against Eastern powerhouse Army in 1956 in front of 40,053 at Archbold Stadium—the largest football crowd in upstate New York history to that point—Brown gained 125 yards on 22 carries and set up the only score of the game on a 36-yard run to the Cadets' 4-yard line. Jim Ridlon ran it in from there, and Brown kicked the PAT. Late in the fourth quarter, Brown helped preserve the 7–0 victory by making three tackles during a goal-line stand. Afterward, Army coach Earl Blaik paid Brown high praise, comparing him to former Cadets and Heisman Trophy winners Doc Blanchard and Glenn Davis. "He has the speed and power to be Mr. Inside and Mr. Outside combined," Blaik said, referring to the nicknames that sportswriters had pegged on Blanchard and Davis.

With a bowl bid on the line in the season finale, Brown ran wild in a 61–7 thrashing of overmatched Colgate. Nearly 40,000 fans looked on at Archbold as Brown scored an NCAA-record 43 points (since surpassed) on touchdown runs of one, fifteen, fifty, eight and one yards. He also kicked seven extra points and, for good measure, intercepted a pass and caused a fumble while playing defense, thwarting two Colgate scoring drives. "He probably could have scored 10 touchdowns without too much additional effort," Val Pinchbeck, the late SU sports information director, noted that day. Brown finished with 197 yards on 22 carries—a remarkable eight yards per carry—and also caught two passes for 13 yards. The record-shattering performance put an exclamation point on the Orangemen's 7–1 season and earned them an invitation to the Cotton Bowl. The Monday after the Colgate victory, Brown was named first-team All-America, the first time an SU running back was ever accorded that honor.

Halfback Jim Brown was named "Back of the Week" by Associated Press on November 21, 1956. Brown scored 43 points and gained 197 yards rushing in Syracuse's game against Colgate. (AP Photo)

As good as his effort was against Colgate, Brown's performance against Texas Christian University in the Cotton Bowl that followed may have been even better. Though the Horned Frogs won 28–27, Brown rushed for 132 yards and scored 21 points.

"The headlines should have read, 'TCU 28, Jim Brown U 27,'" said Ron Luciano, an All-American lineman on that Syracuse team who went on to become one of the most famous umpires in Major League Baseball history. "Jim was a one-man wrecking crew that day. The rest of us were just along for the ride."

Brown, of course, would go on to become arguably the greatest running back in National Football League history, leading the league in rushing eight of his nine seasons with the Cleveland Browns and playing a role in convincing Davis, the 1961 Heisman winner, to follow in his footsteps at SU. As great as he was in football, Brown might have been even better in lacrosse, where he earned All-American honors his senior year after scoring 43 goals and leading the Orangemen to a 10–0 season. Brown was also superb in basketball where he lettered twice and averaged 13.1 points per game his junior year. Some have surmised that if Brown played hoops his senior year, SU might have upset the North Carolina Tar Heels and faced Kansas and its 7'1" superstar center, Wilt Chamberlain, in the national championship game.

Brown also ran track & field and once competed in two varsity sports in the same day at Archbold Stadium. He wound up finishing first in the high jump and discus and second in the javelin to account for 13 points in a track-and-field victory vs. Colgate. Then he put on his lacrosse gear and scored the winning goals against Army.

"That was just Jim," said Roy Simmons Jr., a teammate of Brown's who went on to coach SU's lacrosse team to six national championships. "He was just a natural at anything he did. Hard as it might be for football people to believe, I still think lacrosse might have been his best sport. He was just unstoppable. I should know

SU Players in the Pro Football Hall of Fame

Player	Year Inducted
Jim Brown	1971
Jim Ringo	1981
Larry Csonka	1987
Al Davis	1992
John Mackey	1992
Art Monk	2008
Floyd Little	2010

because I had to go against him every day in practice. I joke that nobody has been knocked down more by Jim Brown than me."

Kevin Conwick, a former All-American lacrosse player for Colgate, recalled a game where he witnessed the scary velocity of Brown's shot. "We had just put new nets on the field for a game with Syracuse," he said. "The first time Jimmy came down the field, he fired the ball so hard that it tore right through the net. Our goalie spent the rest of the day trying to keep out of his way."

Brown concluded his college lacrosse career by scoring five goals and assisting on two others as the North upset the South 14–10 in the annual All-Star game. "He only played half the game," Roy Simmons Sr. said in the book, *The Syracuse Football Story*, by Ken Rappoport. "They had to take him out of the game to make a contest out of it. He was that good."

Brown retired from the Cleveland Browns at age 30 despite having, in his estimation, "at least six more good seasons of football in me." He went on to have a successful movie career, acting in more than 40 movies and numerous television dramas while establishing himself as Hollywood's first black action hero. He promoted racial economic equality through a variety of programs he founded, including the Amer-I-Can company. A former gang member himself, Brown has worked with gang members in Los

Angeles in hopes of channeling their energies into more positive endeavors.

His life has not been without controversy. He has been accused several times of domestic violence, though he's never been convicted. In 1999, Brown was charged with a misdemeanor for vandalizing his wife's car, and he served several weeks in jail after refusing to participate in domestic violence counseling, community service, and probation programs.

"I think Big Jim is a complicated individual, as we all are, with some good and some bad," Simmons Sr. said in an interview in the late 1980s. "He's a fiercely proud individual with strong beliefs. He isn't going to back down. That's part of what made him a great athlete. He ran the football with conviction. He shot the lacrosse ball with conviction. I always got along with the guy. I think he respected the fact that I tried to understand what he was going through. I think he's done a lot more good than bad in his life. Whether you like him or not, there's no disputing that Big Jim left quite a legacy at Syracuse. People around here will be talking about him forever."

The Legend of 44

The legend began innocently enough when longtime equipment manager Al Zak tossed football jersey No. 44 to sophomore Jim Brown in the summer of 1954. There was no real significance as to why Zak chose to give him that number, other than Zak had been told by the SU coaching staff that the kid was a running back so he had to have a number under 50.

Fifty-two years and three College Football Hall of Fame induction ceremonies later, the No. 44 jersey had become so famous in Syracuse that a large replica of it was hoisted to the Carrier Dome rafters several years ago, signifying that it would never be worn again. Twenty-five SU football players have tugged it over their shoulder pads through the years, but it was the trio of Brown and fellow All-Americans Ernie Davis and Floyd Little who made it unique. Here are 44 tidbits about the most famous number in Syracuse University history:

1. On November 12, 2005, No. 44 became the first football number retired at SU.
2. Brown was the first player to make it famous. He earned All-American honors during his senior season in 1956, scoring a then-NCAA record 43 points in a single game while leading SU to a Cotton Bowl berth. He would have scored 44, but he missed one of his extra-point attempts.
3. Davis followed in Big Jim's footsteps, helping the Orange win a national championship in 1959. Two years later, Davis became the first African American to win the Heisman Trophy.
4. Little was the next great No. 44. He broke most of his predecessors' records while becoming only the second Orangeman to earn All-American honors three times.
5. Brown, Davis, and Little are all members of the College Football Hall of Fame. Brown and Little are also enshrined in the Pro Football Hall of Fame.
6. In 1985, the University's zip code was switched from 13210 to 13244
7. In 1988, the University's phone exchange was switched from 423 to 443.
8. Twenty-five football players have worn No. 44 at SU.
9. Halfback Gifford Zimmerman wore it first, in 1921.
10. Fullback Rob Konrad wore it last, in 1998.

11. Larry Csonka was offered the number before his senior year in 1967 but he declined, sticking with No. 39.

12. Joe Morris, the school's all-time leading rusher, was also offered the jersey before his senior season (1981) but stuck with No. 47.

13. Damien Rhodes, a highly recruited running back from suburban Syracuse, was offered it for his freshman season (2001), but he chose No. 1 instead.

14. Davis ultimately chose SU over Notre Dame because of the opportunity to follow Brown and wear his old number.

15. Little decided to accept Syracuse's scholarship offer the day Davis died of leukemia.

16. Tom Stephens wore the number for the two seasons between Brown and Davis.

17. William Schoonover wore the number for the two seasons between Davis and Little.

18. Little and Michael Owens are the only No. 44s to rush for more than 1,000 yards in a single season.

19. The number remained in mothballs from 1970 until 1976 when Mandel Robinson, a highly touted recruit from North Syracuse, was given the jersey. The pressure proved too much and he transferred to Wyoming, where he wound up having a 1,000-yard rushing season.

20. Other football numbers honored by SU include Csonka's 39, John Mackey's 88, Don McPherson's 9, and Donovan McNabb's 5.

21. Derrick Coleman's No. 44 has been retired in basketball. John Wallace also wore No. 44 in hoops, and his number is expected to be retired, too.

22. For several years there was a popular campus bar named 44's that was located on Marshall Street, better known as M Street.

23. Retiring football's No. 44 was the brainchild of athletic director Daryl Gross.

24. Brown was cool with the idea of retiring the number.

25. Little wishes the number was still available to prospective recruits.

26. No. 22—half of 44—is the most famous number in SU lacrosse history, having been worn by All-Americans Gary Gait, Charlie Lockwood, Casey Powell, Ryan Powell, and Michael Powell.

27. John Mackey, the superb tight end who wore No. 88 during the early 1960s, liked to joke that he was twice the player No. 44 was.

28. Brown's No. 32 was retired by the Cleveland Browns.

29. Although he never played for the Browns because he was stricken with leukemia, Davis' No. 45 was retired by the team.

30. Little's No. 44 was retired by the Denver Broncos.

31. Davis was the first overall pick in the NFL and the fourth overall pick in the AFL in 1962. The Buffalo Bills actually offered him more money than the Browns, who acquired him in a trade with the Washington Redskins.

32. Brown was the sixth pick overall in the 1957 NFL draft.

33. Little was the sixth pick overall in the 1967 NFL draft.

34. Davis still holds the SU record for highest average yards per carry for a game (15.7), season (7.8), and career (6.63).

35. Little had three punt returns of more than 90 yards in his SU career.

36. Brown had seven 100-yard rushing games in 1956 and averaged 123 yards per game that season.

37. Rob Konrad was the only fullback to wear the number.

38. Clarence Taylor (1925), Henry Merz (1933), and Rich Panczyszyn (1967–69) were the only quarterbacks to wear No. 44.

39. Three two-way linemen—Francis Mazejko (1939), Richard Ransom (1940), and Jack O'Brien (1945)—wore No. 44.

40. Brown also lettered in lacrosse, basketball, and track & field.

41. Davis played one year of varsity basketball.
42. Little ran track.
43. While looking for a successor to Davis, SU assistants offered the number to three different high school running backs at the same time. Jim Nance, Billy Hunter, and Nat Duckett arrived on campus in the summer of 1961 expecting to receive No. 44 once Davis graduated. Head Coach Ben Schwartzwalder's solution was to put the famous jersey back into storage.
44. Nance led the Orange in rushing his senior season and went on to become the all-time leading rusher for the New England Patriots. Hunter, a three-year letterman, became the longtime head of the NBA's player union. Duckett also earned three varsity letters.

Ben Schwartzwalder

Despite the urgings of a longtime mentor, Ben Schwartzwalder initially refused to apply for the vacant Orange head football coaching job following the 1948 season.

"I'm not interested in Syracuse," said Schwartzwalder, who was enjoying considerable success coaching football at Muhlenberg, a small college football powerhouse in Allentown, Pennsylvania. "Syracuse is a graveyard for coaches."

His reluctance to toss his cap into the ring was understandable. The Orangemen were coming off a 1–8 campaign, extending their streak of consecutive losing seasons to five. Schwartzwalder figured he was better off staying put at a school he had guided to a national title and a sterling 25–5 record in three seasons. Bigger and better opportunities would eventually come.

But the rising young coach had a change of heart a few weeks later after the president of Muhlenberg reportedly called him into his office and told him that he was doing too good of a job and that other schools in the Mid-Atlantic Conference were complaining about it. Schwartzwalder said the president told him, "You can't win over half your games. So if you want to stay at Muhlenberg, we don't want you to win over half your games." Just to make sure his ears weren't deceiving him, Schwartzwalder asked the president to repeat himself, so he did. Suddenly the SU job didn't seem like such a bad option after all.

So Schwartzwalder applied and was hired, and the fans and media appeared underwhelmed. In an interview years later, the droll Schwartzwalder joked, "The alumni wanted a big-name coach, and they wound up with a long-name coach."

They also wound up with a Hall of Fame coach, one who would resuscitate a moribund program that had mustered just 11 wins in its previous 41 games. The peak, of course, came in 1959 when the Orangemen scaled college football's Everest and won the national title with an 11–0 record. During Ol' Ben's 25-year reign, SU went 153–91–3 and made seven bowl appearances. His teams recorded 22 consecutive non-losing seasons and churned out a long line of outstanding running backs, including Jim Brown, Ernie Davis, Jim Nance, Floyd Little, and Larry Csonka.

A paratrooper in World War II, Schwartzwalder earned a Bronze Star, a Silver Star, and a Purple Heart for his heroics during the D-Day invasion of Normandy and the Battle of the Bulge. Over time, the laconic coach with the trademark crew cut and stern countenance built the program in his tough image. "When you think of a hard-nosed, old-school football coach, you think of Ben Schwartzwalder," said Dick MacPherson, who eventually followed in Schwartzwalder's cleat steps and performed a similar football revival job in the 1980s. "He was right out of central casting."

Success came slowly for Schwartzwalder at SU. It took him a while to convince school administrators that if they truly wanted to field a successful team they would need to increase the number of scholarships they offered so they would be on par with competitors such as Penn State and Pittsburgh. After going 14–14 in his first three seasons, the Orange enjoyed a breakthrough campaign with a 7–2 record and the school's first bowl appearance. Though SU was crushed 61–6 by Alabama in the Orange Bowl on January 1, 1953, the program was finally pointed in the right direction.

By the late 1960s and early 1970s, Syracuse's football fortunes sagged once more. Several black players accused Schwartzwalder of being racially insensitive and staged a boycott. That incident, along with the continued deterioration of outdated Archbold Stadium and a reduction in support from the administration, resulted in a severe talent drain and a 2–9 record by Schwartzwalder's final team in 1973. Despite the sad ending, he departed as the winningest football coach in school history. Syracuse wound up being a launching pad rather than a graveyard for his coaching career.

5 2003 NCAA Basketball Champs

As the final frenetic seconds of the 2003 NCAA basketball championship game wound down in the Louisiana Superdome, Jim Boeheim couldn't help but flash back briefly to the Nightmare on Bourbon Street he had experienced 16 years earlier in this very same building.

It seemed as if history was about to repeat itself and Syracuse was going to get nipped at the end again, the way it had in 1987 when Indiana's Keith Smart hit that dagger-in-the-heart jumper to deny the Orangemen their first NCAA hoops title.

This time Kansas, which had trailed by as many as 18 points, had shaved the lead to three. Momentum appeared to be on the Jayhawks' side.

"I'm not thinking good thoughts when Kansas is bringing the ball down the court on that final possession," Boeheim recounted in the book, *Slices of Orange*. "We had just missed a few free throws—just like '87—and I looked to the corner and I saw [Michael] Lee open, just like Keith Smart was."

But this time, thanks to a marvelous heads-up play by SU defender Hakim Warrick, Lee's shot ended up in the stands instead of the basket. Warrick, a 6'9" forward with elastic arms, came over to the corner and swatted away Lee's potential game-tying 3-point attempt with 1.5 seconds remaining.

"It actually worked out for us because we had our centers out and we had put Hakim in at center," Boeheim said. "We didn't do it for defensive reasons but rather because I wanted to have our best ball-handlers and shooters on the floor. If we had our centers in, it is doubtful one of them would have come out to contest Lee. But Hakim was thinking like a forward, so he went out there. It was an incredible play on his part. I still don't know how he got to that ball."

After the block the Jayhawks inbounded the ball and were way off with their final desperation shot. The Orangemen had an 81–78 victory and the school's first NCAA hoops title. The ghost of Keith Smart had been exorcised. There was a new signature play in SU hoops history and a more joyous one—Warrick's block.

"Same building, same part of the court, similar situation," Boeheim marveled. "If that shot had gone in…they probably wouldn't have let me back in town." Instead, he became the toast of the town.

Syracuse players react after winning the championship game 81–78 against Kansas at the Final Four on Monday, April 7, 2003, in New Orleans.
(AP Photo/Ed Reinke)

While Warrick's block was *the* play of the game, two precocious freshmen were *the* players of the game. Forward Carmelo Anthony, whose back was so stiff he had difficulties tying his sneakers before the game, finished with 20 points, 10 rebounds, and seven assists, while guard Gerry McNamara hit a championship-game-record six three-pointers in the first half to build SU's sizable cushion. Senior captain Kueth Duany contributed 11 points, while reserves Josh Pace and Billy Edelin combined for 20 points, six steals, 10 rebounds, and four assists.

"The excitement this team has brought, the attitude of never giving up and continuing to play hard is a life lesson for every kid who lives in the Syracuse area, and for the adults, too," said Boeheim, whose team erased second-half deficits 15 times while compiling a 30–5 record. "This team showed that you can be behind, you can be struggling, you can do some silly things sometimes, but you can still overcome all that. If you keep playing and keep working together all the time, anything's possible."

The college basketball prognosticators had low expectations for Syracuse heading into the season. Few believed the team would be more talented than its predecessor, which had lost eight of its final 12 to wind up in the NIT. Anthony, whose incandescent smile reminded many of a young Magic Johnson, was everybody's preseason choice for college basketball's Rookie of the Year. McNamara was a Pennsylvania high school hoops legend who had been recruited by the likes of national champion Duke. And Edelin had been the point guard for the nation's top-ranked high school team while playing for Oak Hill Academy in Virginia. But none of the pundits believed a team that started two freshmen and two sophomores could make the quantum leap from missing the NCAAs one year to winning it all the next.

However, sometimes talent trumps experience, and sometimes youth is not wasted on the young. That clearly was the case with the 2002–03 Orange.

SU's Other National Basketball Champions

In 1936, Paul Helms and Bill Schroeder formed the Helms Athletic Foundation in Los Angeles with the idea of remembering some forgotten sports history. Among their early projects was the formation of a panel of experts to retroactively choose All-Americans and national champions in college basketball, dating back to 1901. There wasn't an NCAA postseason tournament at the time, and Helms and Schroeder believed this would acknowledge the sport's pioneering players, teams, and coaches. They also selected players and coaches for a Hall of Fame.

This was good news for the Syracuse Orangemen, as both their 1917–18 and 1925–26 teams were voted national champs. SU's first title team was coached by Edmund Dollard and went 16–1, its only loss coming by one point in the season finale against Penn. The star of the team was Joseph Schwarzer, a Helms All-American selection at guard who served as the squad's captain.

Lew Andreas coached the 1925–26 team that went 19–1. The Orangemen's only loss that season was to Penn State 37–31 on February 24, 1926. Led by three-time All-American guard Vic Hanson, Syracuse avenged that defeat with a 17-point victory against the Nittany Lions nine days later. Andreas wound up coaching the Orange to 358 wins in 26 seasons and is second only to Jim Boeheim on the school's all-time victory list. Hanson was named the Helms National Player of the Year for 1927. Hanson, Andreas, and former Orange star Lewis Castle, who was an All-American in 1912 and 1914, were also named to the Foundation's Hall of Fame.

SU's other Helms basketball All-America selections included Leon Marcus (1919), Billy Gabor (1946, 1947), John Kiley (1951), Vincent Cohen (1957), and Dave Bing (1965).

The foundation's panel continued to vote on national champions until 1982. Some historians have disputed its choice of champions, but a few years ago the NCAA began listing them in its records and facts book. The NCAA tournament began three years after Helms started selecting champions. Though the Helms choices are regarded as mythical champions, the selection process is really no different than the one that's been used by college football for more than a century.

So the next time someone asks you how many national basketball championships the Orangemen have won, tell 'em three—two Helms and one NCAA.

"I guess we wound up defying the conventional wisdom that says you can't win without experience," said Duany, the only senior scholarship player on the team and the recipient of the Big East Conference's Sportsmanship Award. Duany, known to his teammates as "Gramps," saw something special in this group the first day of practice in Manley Field House.

"I think Melo and G-Mac and Billy Edelin were in so many pressure games in high school and in AAU leagues that the pressure didn't bother them," Duany said. "They arrived here with a big-game mentality. I had to keep reminding myself these guys are only freshmen and sophomores. There are times when they play like seniors, and sometimes they play like grad students. It's interesting to note that they ended their first practice of the season by huddling up and chanting in unison, 'Final Four.'" Talk about a good omen.

Though they lost their season opener to Memphis at Madison Square Garden on November 14, 2002, notice was served as Anthony scored 27 points, at the time a school record for freshmen, and McNamara added 14. The Orangemen then reeled off 11 consecutive victories, including a 76–69 win over 11th-ranked Missouri. They continued to open eyes by storming back from double-digit deficits to defeat second-ranked Pittsburgh and ninth-ranked Notre Dame in the Carrier Dome in February. But it wasn't until the Orangemen came away with victories at three of the toughest venues in college basketball—Michigan State, Notre Dame, and Georgetown—that outsiders began taking them seriously.

After losing to Connecticut in the Big East Tournament semifinals, the Orangemen received an NCAA bid and were sent to Boston where they defeated Manhattan in the opener before coming back from a 17-point deficit to defeat second-round opponent Oklahoma State. From there they went to Albany for the East Regionals. The Pepsi Civic Center became like a mini Carrier Dome as SU escaped with a surprisingly close victory against Auburn before trouncing Oklahoma to reach the Final Four. In the semis in New Orleans they continued to impress with an 11-point victory vs. Texas. That set the stage for the title game between Boeheim and Roy Williams, two coaches who had never won a national championship.

Thanks to Warrick's block, the Orange prevailed. Surrounded by family and players past and present on the Superdome court following the victory, Boeheim shed a tear as he peered at the scoreboard to make sure this wasn't all a dream. Later, he and his wife, Juli, led a procession of hundreds of adoring Syracuse fans, Pied Piper–style, through New Orleans' French Quarter. Before calling it a night, a fan presented Juli with an orange velour cowboy hat that her husband wound up wearing at several functions honoring the team in Syracuse, showing a humorous side he hadn't always made public.

The nation witnessed Boeheim's self-deprecating personality when he traded barbs with David Letterman on national television and felt his pride when he and Anthony rang the opening bell at the New York Stock Exchange. (The Dow wound up climbing 147 points that day.)

Five days after knocking off the Jayhawks, more than 25,000 fans congregated in the Carrier Dome to say thanks amid an atmosphere that resembled a high-energy rock concert. During the ceremonies, Boeheim emerged from a cloud of smoke holding aloft the championship trophy. The crowd roared its approval. School spirit had never been higher. "This is honestly the coolest thing I've ever lived through," student Tiffany Roy said the day after the title game. "Last night and today were worth every snowy day, every cloud in the sky, every dollar we paid to go here."

6 Ernie Davis

Marie Fleming would occasionally daydream about what might have been had her son, Ernie Davis, not been struck down by leukemia at age 23. She'd start filling in the unfinished chapters of his life, the chapters that a premature death stole from him and her and everyone fortunate enough to have known him.

"It's hard not to wonder at times how things might have turned out for Ernie," she said in a 2003 interview with the Rochester (NY) *Democrat & Chronicle.* "But I'd rather focus on what was rather than on what might have been." She, like others, came to realize that although her son's life was short, it was also incredibly sweet. Twenty-three years may seem like a brief time to spend on this planet, but it proved long enough for Davis to make a profound and lasting impact. "He lived more life in 23 years," she said, "than most people live in 83 years."

That he did. In 1961, Davis became the first Syracuse football player and first African American to win the coveted Heisman Trophy, which ensured him a small measure of sports immortality. But there's much more to the Ernie Davis story than the bronze trophy on display in the atrium of the football complex on the SU campus. The joyful, dignified, courageous way Davis lived his life, especially while dying, still resonates with people several generations later. He clearly lives on in others.

"I reflect on my life and I know it was a whole lot richer, a whole lot better because I was fortunate enough to have known Ernie," said John Brown, a teammate of Davis' at Syracuse and with the Cleveland Browns. "As a direct result of knowing Ernie, I became more community-minded, I treated people with greater care and respect and kindness. Sure I wish he could have grown old with me and others, but I realize I was blessed to have at least known him for as long as I did." Brown's affection for his friend was underscored when he named his first son Ernie Davis Brown. "I told my boy that I wanted to name him after a heroic figure," Brown said. "And that's what Ernie was—a hero in every sense of the word."

Davis was an All-American in football and basketball at Elmira Free Academy. And he was so good in baseball that one National League scout called him "a great prospect, a natural." No one recruited him more heavily than Syracuse football coach Ben Schwartzwalder, who saw Davis as the perfect successor to Jim Brown. Big Jim made several visits to Elmira, too, and he became friends with the young athlete who wound up winning 11 varsity letters in high school.

Orangemen in the College Football Hall of Fame

Player	Year Inducted
Frank "Buck" O'Neill	1951
Howard Jones	1951
Joe Alexander	1954
Tad Jones	1958
Clarence "Biggie" Munn	1959
Lynn "Pappy" Waldorf	1966
Bud Wilkinson	1969
Vic Hanson	1973
Ernie Davis	1979
Ben Schwartzwalder	1982
Floyd Little	1983
Hugh "Duffy" Daugherty	1984
Larry Csonka	1989
Jim Brown	1995
Tim Green	2001
Don McPherson	2008
Dick MacPherson	2009

The persistence of Schwartzwalder and Brown paid off when Davis, at the urging of his high school coach, Marty Harrigan, and close family friend, Tony DiFilippo, chose Syracuse over Notre Dame. Schwartzwalder saw the same football attributes in Davis that he had in Brown, so it wasn't surprising that the coach would issue him Big Jim's No. 44. The player known as "The Elmira Express" did the jersey proud, rushing for 2,386 yards during his three varsity seasons, eclipsing Brown's school rushing record. During his sophomore year, Davis averaged seven yards per carry and scored eight touchdowns to lead the 1959 team to an 11–0 record and the national championship. Despite nursing a severely pulled hamstring, Davis scored two touchdowns—one on an 87-yard reception, one on a one-yard run—and a two-point conversion, plus he intercepted a pass in SU's decisive 23–14 victory against the Texas Longhorns in the Cotton Bowl.

Two years later, Davis concluded his brilliant college football career by winning the Heisman Trophy. Following the award ceremony at the Downtown Athletic Club, President John F. Kennedy asked to meet Davis. "I got to shake hands with him," Davis said later. "That was almost as big a thrill as winning the Heisman."

Not long after, Davis turned down a huge offer from the Buffalo Bills of the American Football League to sign with the Cleveland Browns. The Browns had acquired him from the Washington Redskins, who had selected him first overall in the NFL draft. Davis was thrilled because he was going to get an opportunity to play in the same backfield as his Syracuse predecessor, Jim Brown. "The world was his oyster," John Brown remembered. "He had everything going for him at that time—looks, ability, character, charm, youth. Just about anyone would have traded places with him."

By September 1962, no one would have traded places with Davis. Feeling run-down and noticing lumps on his neck and sores in his mouth, Davis went to the doctor, who diagnosed him with

Syracuse football player Ernie Davis holds his Heisman Trophy at the Downtown Athletic Club in New York on December 6, 1961.
(AP Photo/Jack Harris, File)

leukemia. That fall, his cancer went into remission but recurred in the early months of 1963.

"He would have been justified cursing, 'Why me, God? Why me?'" John Brown recalled. "But I never heard him bemoan his fate. One time I came home from a particularly tough practice with the Browns. I was really down, really worried about making the team. Ernie sat there and listened to me bitch and tried to pick my spirits up. Suddenly, I realized how dumb I had been. I'm complaining about something as insignificant as making a football team in front of a guy battling for his life. That Ernie would listen to my little problems despite what he was facing was so typical of him. He always put the concerns of others ahead of himself."

On May 18, 1963, Davis died at Lakeside Hospital in Cleveland. His death touched a nation. His story transcended sports. About 10,000 people, including most of the members of the Browns team for which he never played, attended his funeral at Elmira's Woodlawn Cemetery, where Mark Twain is also buried. Jim Brown, one of the pallbearers, spoke eloquently about the young man whom he inspired and befriended.

"I've always felt the words 'great' and 'courage' have been overused and abused. I have never been one to take them idly. I say with the utmost sincerity [that] Ernie Davis, to me, was the greatest, most courageous person I've ever met. Though death is sad and often tragic—and these elements were present in Ernie's death—his is not a sad story. He made our lives better, brighter, and fuller because we were privileged to know him. I find it difficult to believe he's gone. Maybe it's because I never heard him complain. The way he acted, he had me believing he'd make it."

Few were as devastated as Schwartzwalder, who had come to regard Davis as a son. "When you talk about Ernie Davis, you're treading on hallowed ground," he said. "We always thought he had a halo around him, and now we know he has."

1959 National Football Champs

Although Ben Schwartzwalder had essentially resurrected Syracuse University football from the dead, patience in the Salt City was starting to wear thin after the Orangemen suffered a 21–6 loss to Oklahoma in the Orange Bowl following the 1958 season.

It was SU's third consecutive bowl loss and there was a growing sentiment, particularly among some sportswriters in Syracuse and beyond, that Schwartzwalder was one of those good but not great coaches who couldn't win the big one. The decorated World War II paratrooper who had survived jumps on D Day and the Battle of the Bulge appeared unfazed by the criticism.

"I don't resent it," he told an assistant. "The writers write what they see."

What the writers and everyone else would see in 1959 would be one of the greatest college football teams of all time. Ol' Ben would finally win the big one, and all the little ones leading up to it. That season the Orangemen dominated college football, winning all 11 of their games and becoming the first team in history to lead the nation in total offense (451.5 yards per game) and defense (96.2 yards per game) in the same season.

Led by their "Sizeable Seven" line and their "Four Furies" backfield, SU atoned for its previous bowl futility and struck a blow for Eastern football with a decisive 23–14 victory against the No. 4-ranked Texas Longhorns in the Cotton Bowl. SU's aggressive defense pitched five shutouts that season, holding four different opponents to negative rushing yardage, including a minus-88 performance vs. Boston University. Led by future Heisman Trophy winner Ernie Davis and a backfield that threw

1959: Game by Game
Syracuse 35, Kansas 21
Syracuse 29, Maryland 0
Syracuse 32, Navy 6
Syracuse 42, Holy Cross 6
Syracuse 44, West Virginia 0
Syracuse 35, Pittsburgh 0
Syracuse 20, Penn State 18
Syracuse 71, Colgate 0
Syracuse 46, Boston University 0
Syracuse 36, UCLA 8
Syracuse 23, Texas 14

a nation-leading 21 touchdown passes, the SU offense did its part, topping college football with a 39 points-per-game scoring average. Syracuse's talent was so abundant that during a nationally televised 36–8 annihilation of UCLA in the Los Angeles Coliseum, football Hall of Famer Red Grange told viewers, "If Syracuse's first team is the No. 1 team in the country, then their second team must to No. 2."

Schwartzwalder had every reason to be optimistic before the season began because the nucleus from a squad that had gone 8–2 was returning. And that veteran core would be bolstered by several promising players from the unbeaten freshmen team—players such as Davis and tackle John Brown. But before preseason workouts began that August, the Orangemen's confidence was shaken when starting quarterback Bob Thomas suffered a severe back injury while working a summer job. Although Syracuse had a talented but inexperienced backup in Dave Sarette, Schwartzwalder decided to shift halfback Gerhard Schwedes to quarterback for the season opener against highly touted Kansas. Schwedes was reluctant, but everything worked out just fine and Sarette was deemed ready to take over for good during the second half of the 35–21 victory vs. the Jayhawks.

The Orangemen pummeled their next five opponents—Maryland, Navy, Holy Cross, West Virginia, and Pittsburgh—by an average score of 36–2, setting up a battle of unbeatens against Eastern archrival Penn State on the road in Happy Valley. The seventh-ranked Nittany Lions made things interesting by blocking a punt and returning a kickoff for a touchdown. They threatened to tie the game at 20 with about six minutes remaining, but Gene Grabosky stuffed running back Roger Kauffman on a two-point conversion attempt. Despite Grabosky's heroics, the victory and SU's dreams of an unbeaten season remained in jeopardy when Davis accidentally stepped out of bounds at the Syracuse 7-yard line on the ensuing kickoff.

"The momentum had clearly shifted Penn State's way," Schwedes recalled. "But we didn't panic. We knew we had a great line, and we knew we could run out those final six minutes."

And that's what they did, imposing their will and methodically moving all the way to the Nittany Lions 1-yard line as time expired, preserving a 20–18 victory.

"Ernie and I received a lot of credit that season, but our line was the heart and soul of the team," Schwedes said, referring to two-way linemen Fred Mautino, Gerry Skonieczki, Roger Davis, Bruce Tarbox, Maury Youmans, Bob Yates, and Al Bemiller, collectively known as the Sizeable Seven. "And as good as those guys were, our second line was nearly as good."

SU steamrolled its next two opponents—Colgate and Boston University—by a combined score of 117–0, then traveled cross country where it trounced 17th-ranked UCLA by four touchdowns.

In those days, the national champion was declared before the bowl games, but the SU coaches and players realized that distinction would ring hollow if they lost their Cotton Bowl showdown with No. 4-ranked Texas. During the first day of pre-bowl workouts, Davis severely pulled a hamstring while fooling around kicking field goals.

"It really was touch-and-go whether he'd be able to play," said Pat Stark, one of SU's assistant coaches. "On game day, it was still really tight, but Ernie wasn't going to miss this game. He would have played with crutches if he had to."

Syracuse won the toss and on its third play from scrimmage, Davis turned a halfback option pass from Schwedes into an 87-yard touchdown. "The funny thing about the play is that Ernie ran the wrong pattern," Schwedes said. "But he wound up in the right place—their end zone." Davis scored again later in the half on a one-yard run. He also scored a two-point conversion and had a long interception return to set up another touchdown.

Sadly, the game was marred by fights after several Longhorn players shouted racial epithets at Davis and SU's two other African American players, John Brown and fullback Art Baker. "It was an unfortunate and ugly thing, but guys like Maury Youmans immediately came to their defense," Stark said. "We were like a family, and I think that made us even closer."

The victory capped SU's perfect season and removed that "can't win the big one" albatross from Ben Schwartzwalder's neck. Nearly 30 years later, *The Sporting News* ranked the 1959 Orangemen as the 10th greatest team in college football history. It was a team for the ages...a team that has stood the test of time.

Dave Bing

No one appreciates Dave Bing's impact on Syracuse basketball more than current coach Jim Boeheim.

"The success we continue to enjoy can be traced directly back to him," said Boeheim, who was a roommate and teammate of Bing's. "Dave's the guy who got things turned around here. He

Orangemen in Naismith Basketball Hall of Fame

Player	Year Inducted
Vic Hanson	1960
Dave Bing	1990
Jim Boeheim	2005

raised this program from the ashes." Or more accurately, he raised it from the dust that once accumulated on the old raised wooden basketball court at Manley Field House, SU's hoops home before the Carrier Dome.

When Bing arrived on campus in the autumn of 1962, football reigned. The Orange gridders were just three years removed from a national championship and just a year removed from Ernie Davis winning the Heisman Trophy. The Orange hoopsters, meanwhile, had become a source of ridicule, with losses in 41 of their previous 47 games.

But during his three varsity seasons (freshmen weren't eligible to play in those days), Bing resuscitated a program on life support, guiding SU all the way to the NCAA East Region finals by his senior year. During that 1965–66 season, the Orange went 22–6 and led the nation in scoring with an average of 99 points per game. Bing was the pace-setter, averaging 28.4 points and 10.8 rebounds per game to become the school's first consensus first-team All-American in basketball since Vic Hanson in 1927. The Orange went 52–24 with two postseason appearances during his three seasons, and Bing's presence had a positive impact on recruiting as top high school players began committing to play at SU.

That the 6'3" guard from Spingarn High School in Washington, D.C., would wind up at Syracuse remains the greatest recruiting coup in program history. Given SU's bottom-feeder basketball status at the time and the fact that 200 schools, including powerhouses

Syracuse basketball player Dave Bing in 1966. (AP photo)

Maryland and UCLA, were hot on Bing's trail, it is truly amazing that coach Fred Lewis was able to lure the high school star known as "The Capitol Comet."

"Syracuse was not even on [David Bing's] list when Fred went down, but he was able to convince David that by coming here, he'd be able to build up the program," Boeheim said. "It was a recruiting miracle in my judgment, to get a kid of that quality to come into your program."

The opportunity to be the guy who elevated a team that had fallen on hard times appealed to Bing. "Coach Lewis convinced me that the Syracuse program had bottomed out and that I could be the catalyst in turning things around," Bing said. "I welcomed that challenge."

Lewis shrewdly scheduled Bing's recruiting visit during May rather than the heart of winter.

"I had no idea about the way it snows and snows and snows in Syracuse," Bing joked. "I'm up there on a sunny, spring day and the students are all over the place, wearing shorts and having a good old time, and I'm thinking to myself, 'Wow, it must be like this year-round.' Nobody told me how bad the winters were."

But the thing that may have sealed the deal was Ernie Davis, who served as Bing's chaperon during his campus visit. "I was clearly awestruck being in Ernie's presence," Bing recalled. "I had a chance to speak to him at length…. He was honest and frank. He told me about the good experiences and the bad experiences he had at SU. I walked away thinking, *What an impressive human being.* And I thought that if SU could help develop a human being like Ernie Davis, then I wanted to go there and try to follow in his footsteps. The way he handled himself on and off the field with such dignity… [he] set a standard, I believe, for everyone at Syracuse to follow. I remember when I was getting ready to leave campus that weekend, he told me I had an opportunity to be the 'Ernie Davis of basketball.' That was the clincher for me."

Bing lived up to those high standards, both on and off the court. Following his SU career, he was drafted second overall by the Detroit Pistons and played 12 years in the NBA, earning All-Star honors seven times. During a December 19, 1981, ceremony in the Carrier Dome, Bing's No. 22 was retired along with Vic Hanson's No. 8, making them the first athletes in school history to have their jersey numbers taken out of circulation. Nine years later, Bing received another prestigious honor when he was inducted into the Naismith Basketball Hall of Fame. In 2005, Boeheim joined him in Springfield, Massachusetts, as they became the first college teammates to be inducted into the Hall.

Floyd Little

General Douglas MacArthur was a huge fan of Army football, so when he heard about the exploits of a star running back at Bordentown Military Academy in New Jersey, he invited the young man to dinner at his suite in the Waldorf Astoria. MacArthur also invited two African American baseball stars—Roy Campanella from the old Brooklyn Dodgers and Elston Howard from the New York Yankees.

"The general put an all-out recruiting blitz on me," Floyd Little recalled in a 2010 interview. "He thought that because I was black I'd be impressed with Campy and Elston being there, and he was right. But I was most impressed with the general himself. He told me how I could follow in the footsteps of Doc Blanchard and Glenn Davis, who had won back-to-back Heismans at West Point in the 1940s.

"You could see why the General had commanded our forces so expertly during World War II. He had a presence about him that all great leaders have. I didn't make any commitments, but I did walk away from that dinner convinced that I was going to wind up at West Point."

That winter, Ben Schwartzwalder and Ernie Davis plowed through a blizzard to visit Little at his family's home in New Haven, Connecticut. They took the recruit to a swank restaurant on the campus of Yale University, and Davis and Little wound up talking alone in the men's room for nearly 45 minutes. At the end of conversation, Little told Davis he would attend Syracuse.

"The strange thing is that when I got back home that night, my mind really hadn't been changed at all," Little said. "As impressive and nice as Ernie had been to me, in my heart I was still going to West Point."

It wasn't until a few months later on May 18, 1963, that Little changed his mind. On that day, just 17 months after hearing the joyous news that Davis had become the first African American to win the Heisman Trophy, Little heard the shocking news that Ernie had died of leukemia at age 23.

"I was like, 'You're kidding me. It can't be true,'" Little said. "I didn't even know that he was sick. At that moment I remembered that I had given Ernie my word that I was going to Syracuse, and a man's word is the most valuable thing he has. So I picked up the phone and called Coach Schwartzwalder to tell him I would be attending Syracuse University. It wound up being one of the greatest decisions of my life."

Little would carry on the No. 44 tradition started by Jim Brown and enhanced by Davis. By the time he graduated in 1967, Little had broken most of his predecessors' records and had become the first three-time All-American in SU football since Joe Alexander had been so honored from 1918 to 1920. Some are convinced Little would have gone four-for-four had he not played during an era when freshmen weren't eligible to play varsity football.

Little's greatness became evident in his second varsity game when he overshadowed legendary running back Gale Sayers in a showdown against the Kansas Jayhawks at Archbold Stadium. Sayers had earned All-American honors in 1963 and would go on to have a brief but spectacular NFL career with the Chicago Bears. However, on this late September day in 1964, the Kansas Comet would be the second-best back on the field. Little wowed the crowd of 28,000 by rushing for 159 yards and five touchdowns on just sixteen carries as the Orangemen crushed the favored Jayhawks 38–6. Little also caught two passes for 47 yards and, tossing in his punt return yardage, finished with 254 yards for the day.

"That was the greatest performance by a back that I have ever seen," Kansas coach Jack Mitchell told reporters afterward—an extravagant compliment, considering Mitchell has been an eyewitness to Sayers' electrifying runs for two seasons. It would not be the last compliment Little would receive from opposing coaches that autumn. After watching SU's latest No. 44 run roughshod against his team, Penn State coach Joe Paterno said, "The best defense against him, I have decided, is to have my old mother in Brooklyn say a novena." Army coach Paul Dietzel called Little "the greatest back in America."

Little went on to rush for 828 yards and score twelve touchdowns that season as SU went 7–3 to earn a Sugar Bowl invitation. "Ol' Jim, then Ernie, now Floyd," Schwartzwalder sighed one day in his office. "I think I ought to pinch myself."

During his junior year, Little became the first Syracuse back to surpass 1,000 rushing yards (1,065) in a season. He also led the nation in all-purpose yardage with 1,990, and he scored 19 touchdowns and 114 points. He completed his college career by rushing for 811 yards and scoring 15 touchdowns. Little finished fifth in the Heisman balloting in 1966 and might have won the trophy had the votes been cast after the bowl games. Teaming with fullback

Syracuse halfback Floyd Little holds the Player of the Year Award presented to him at the 12th annual dinner of the Eastern College Athlete Conference in New York on December 8, 1966. (AP Photo)

Larry Csonka, Little saved his best for last, rushing for 216 yards in an 18–12 loss to Tennessee in the Gator Bowl.

Little spent nine seasons in the NFL with the Denver Broncos. Although he didn't enjoy the success he had at SU, he rushed for 6,323 yards and 43 touchdowns, earned four Pro Bowl invitations, and led the league in rushing in 1971. He was the player who laid the foundation for the Broncos to become one of the NFL's most successful franchises. In 1984, they retired his No. 44 and made him the first inductee into the Broncos Ring of Fame. Little was also inducted into both the college and pro football halls of fame.

After football, he earned a law degree and became a successful entrepreneur, once owning several car dealerships out west. In 2011, Little's life came full circle when he returned to his college alma mater as a special assistant to athletic director Daryl Gross. Occasionally, Little thinks about how different things might have been had he wound up at West Point.

"I might have beaten Colin Powell to the punch," Little said, chuckling. "I might have wound up being the first African American general."

10 Carrier Dome

It has become the most recognizable architectural landmark in upstate New York—a billowy, white mushroom of a building that dominates the Syracuse University skyline, far above Onondaga's waters. At night it glows like some enormous UFO that plopped down on campus. That description seems apt because the impact the Carrier Dome has made on the university and this Rust Belt city has truly been out of this world.

Dome-Field Advantage

The Carrier Dome has provided the Orange with a distinct home-field and court advantage since it opened in 1980. Through the 2014 spring sports season, Syracuse is 507–96 (.841) in basketball, 129–76 (.629) in football, and 203–30 (.871) in lacrosse inside the Dome.

Since the Carrier Dome's opening on September 20, 1980, through the 2014 spring sports season, roughly 25 million spectators have streamed through the wind-blown rotating doors for more than 1,000 SU sporting events, many of which have transformed this concrete building—with its air-supported, Teflon-coated, bubble-topped roof—into the Loud House. They've watched Donovan McNabb raze the Miami Hurricanes. They've seen Pearl Washington heave one in from half-court at the buzzer. They've witnessed scores of goals by lacrosse legends such as Paul and Gary Gait and the three Powell brothers. They've congregated to establish numerous on-campus basketball attendance records. They've rocked to Springsteen, Paul McCartney, the Rolling Stones, and Sinatra, and they've listened to Bill Clinton and other luminaries deliver commencement speeches.

"It is one of the truly unique venues in America," said ESPN basketball guru Dick Vitale, who has worked numerous games at the Dome, including a classic overtime contest vs. Duke on February 1, 2014, that drew an on-campus record 35,446 fans. "You'd have to live in a cave not to know about the Carrier Dome. It put Syracuse on the map."

And it helped save the football program. The Dome's predecessor was Archbold Stadium. When it was constructed in the early 20th century, Archbold was an architectural marvel, too—a concrete bowl modeled after the Roman Coliseum. But by the mid-1970s, it had become a crumbling, out-dated eyesore.

Dome-inating Moments

Here is a list of 10 memorable moments from the Carrier Dome:

David Beats Goliath: On September 29, 1984, the SU football team upset top-ranked Nebraska 17–9. The Cornhuskers had beaten the Orangemen 63–7 the previous season and entered the game as 24-point favorites.

A Gem of a Shot: During a 1984 basketball game against Boston College, Pearl Washington heaved in a half-court shot at the final buzzer as the Orange won 75–73.

Perfection Preserved: After tight end Pat Kelly caught a touchdown pass with time winding down during the 1987 regular season finale vs. West Virginia, Michael Owens ran in a two-point conversion to give SU a dramatic come-from-behind 32–31 victory to improve to 10–0.

Taming the Nittany Lions: During the 1987 season, SU snapped its 16-game series losing streak against Penn State with a resounding 48–21 win.

Dome Opener: SU running back Joe Morris christened the Carrier Dome on September 20, 1980, by scoring four touchdowns, including one on a 94-yard kickoff return, as the Orange defeated Miami of Ohio.

"There was no way we could have existed in Division I football without a new facility," said Frank Maloney, the former Orange head football coach who lobbied long and hard for a new stadium shortly after taking over for Ben Schwartzwalder in 1974. "We had arguably the worst stadium in the country. Any time a recruit came to town, we wouldn't take him to the stadium unless he insisted. And that went against the fundamentals of recruiting visits because the stadium or arena where a kid was going to be playing was supposed to be one of the big allures."

It took several years of political wrangling, but thanks to New York governor Hugh Carey, more than $15 million in state funding was allocated for the building of the Dome on the same site as Ol' Archie. Carrier Corporation chipped in $2.7 million

What the Hell's a Hoya?: It's almost impossible to pick just one Syracuse-Georgetown game, but the March 4, 1990, contest may have been the strangest. Hoyas coach John Thompson was ejected after being called for three technical fouls, and SU went on a 10-point run during which Georgetown did not touch the ball. The Orange won 89–87 in overtime.

Triple Play: Leo Rautins' tip-in of a missed free throw in the third overtime enabled Syracuse to defeat Villanova on March 7, 1981, to claim the first Big East Conference tournament crown.

Downing Duke: As witnessed by 35,446 fans, the largest on-campus crowd in college basketball history, C.J. Fair and Jerami Grant combined for 52 points as the Orange defeated Duke 91–89 in overtime on February 1, 2014. It was the first ACC meeting between the schools, and the win improved top-ranked SU's record to 21–0.

Razing 'Cane: Donovan McNabb rushed for three touchdowns and threw for two more as Syracuse flattened the Miami Hurricanes 66–13 in the quarterback's final game in the Dome in 1998.

Do the Hokey-Pokey: McNabb threw a 13-yard touchdown pass to Stephen Brominski in the final seconds of a 1998 game as the Orange knocked off Virginia Tech 28–26.

for the naming rights, and the university raised the remaining $6 million for a no-frills facility that included 38 luxury boxes and three decks of aluminum bleacher seats.

One of the unusual things about the building was that the 220-ton roof was supported by cables and air generated from 16 different 5' fans located in mechanical rooms in the north and south ends of the stadium. It was the first building of its kind in the Northeast, and it took 18 months to build. "Now we had something we could be proud of showing the recruits," said Maloney, who went on to become the director of group ticket sales for the Chicago Cubs after leaving SU following the 1981 season. "And weather was no longer a factor."

The Dome was officially christened on September 20, 1980, as Joe Morris scored four touchdowns in a 36–24 victory against Miami of Ohio in front of a still-record crowd of 50,564. Interestingly, most of the spectators left the building that night bathed in sweat. Despite being named for the world's largest manufacturer of air conditioners, the climate-controlled Dome was not air-conditioned. The building proved to be not only warm but also noisier than most stadiums because of the roof. "The noise doesn't escape," Maloney said. "It hits the roof and comes right back at you."

Although it was built in hopes of reviving the football program—which it did—the Dome also wound up having a huge impact on the basketball program. SU hoops coach Jim Boeheim was adamantly opposed to the move from the cozy confines of Manley Field House (with a maximum capacity of 9,500) to the cavernous Dome, and with good reason. In Manley, the fans were right on top of the action, and that gave the Orange a huge home-court advantage, as evidenced by win streaks there of 57 and 38 games.

"As a coach, you never want to give up any advantage you have, and we had a great home-court advantage at Manley," he said. "Plus, I didn't think we'd draw that many more people." Neither did former athletic director Jake Crouthamel, who initiated the change of basketball venues. "I thought we'd max out at about 14,000 for basketball," Crouthamel said. "Fortunately, I wound up being way off with that projection."

Thanks to the arrival of basketball superstar Dwayne Pearl Washington in 1984, the rapid evolution of the Big East into a power conference, and the formation of intense rivalries with Georgetown, St. John's and Villanova, basketball games at the Dome became a spectacle. SU wound up drawing crowds in excess of 30,000, with many spectators seated so far away from the action that they needed binoculars. Through the 2013–14 season, SU had attracted 77 crowds of 30,000 or more and had led the nation in attendance 14 times. The peak occurred during the 1989–90 season when SU averaged an NCAA-record 29,919 fans per game, 3,400 more than it averaged in 2013–14. "It's truly amazing when you think about it," said current SU athletic director Daryl Gross. "A sellout at Madison Square Garden [at 19,812] would be perceived as a bad crowd here."

11 Vic Hanson

Old-timers might argue that Vic Hanson deserves to be several notches higher on this list—maybe even 11 notches higher—and they might be right. You can make a strong case that the guy, known as the "Black Menace" for his jet-black hair, was the best all-around athlete in Syracuse University history.

Hanson was a three-time All-American in basketball and football, and he was good enough at baseball to sign a minor league contract with the New York Yankees following his graduation in 1927. He captained all three sports he played at SU and was named the Helms Foundation's National Player of the Year in basketball his senior year. He guided the Orange hoopsters to a 19–1 record and the national championship in his junior year, and he established school records for most points in a game, a season, and a career that stood for two decades. As a two-way end in football, he helped the Orangemen go 23–5–3 in his three varsity seasons. He is the only person to have been inducted into both the Naismith Memorial Basketball Hall of Fame (1960) and the College Football Hall of Fame (1973). He is also the only athlete selected to both SU's All-Century teams in basketball and football.

In 1952, famed sportswriter Grantland Rice named Hanson to his All-Time, All-American basketball team (along with George Mikan, John Wooden, Bob Kurland, and Hank Luisetti), calling Hanson "the best all-around athlete Syracuse ever had." On top of all that, Hanson did a pretty fair job in his seven years as SU's head football coach, guiding his alma mater to a 33–21–5 record before resigning. His only sin as a coach was that he couldn't beat archrival Colgate, which was a fireable offense in those days.

Hanson's reputation as a phenomenal athlete was established even before he arrived at SU. He starred in football, baseball, basketball, and track at nearby Manlius Academy. Although the Syracuse campus was only a few miles down the road, he seriously considered attending Yale or Harvard.

"In that particular period, the Ivy League ruled the roost and had big teams," said Hanson in the book, *The Syracuse Football Story*, by Ken Rappoport. "Their representatives came and saw me at Manlius, and I had gone down to Yale. I had several other offers, including Michigan."

But the persuasive powers of SU coach Chick Meehan proved too hard to resist. Hanson excelled on Syracuse's freshman teams in the three major sports on campus, and he became the only sophomore to make the varsity football squad. Although he was just 5'10" and 174 lbs., Hanson was extremely strong and quick, proving to be a punishing tackler on defense and a glue-fingered receiver on offense. He was also extremely intelligent. Formations and positions were different back then. There wasn't a quarterback per se as there is today, and ends would often call out instructions on offense. "He had terrific speed and a great pair of hands," said Lew Andreas, who coached Hanson in both football and basketball. "In this modern passing game, he'd be a knockout. He'd make these modern football teams just as he did in his day."

Andreas, the second-winningest basketball coach in SU history, was even more impressed with Hanson's hardwood prowess.

Retired SU Hoops Jerseys

No.	Player
22	Dave Bing
8	Vic Hanson
31	Dwayne "Pearl" Washington
20	Sherman Douglas
19	Wilmeth Sidat-Singh
44	Derrick Coleman
4	Rony Seikaly
30	Billy Owens
17	Billy Gabor
15	Carmelo Anthony

"He was probably the finest basketball player we ever had," said Andreas, who coached the Orange from 1924 to 1950 and also served as athletic director. "He was a wonderful competitor, a very skillful and guileful player, but most of all, a fine team leader."

Hanson was SU's primary scoring threat. During that era of designated free throw shooters he took nearly all of the Orangemen's foul shots. In perhaps the best game of his entire career, he scored 25 points in a 30–25 overtime victory at Pennsylvania on December 29, 1925. Hanson scored four of SU's five points in OT and helped the Orangemen hold Penn scoreless in the extra session.

"It was one of those nights when everything went right," Hanson said in the book, *Syracuse Basketball: 1900–1975*. "I felt good, and I was running, and I had the touch. A long shot would drop in. Sometimes they rimmed, but everything went in. That was a great night."

SU's only loss that season came at Penn State, when they had to play without starter Gotch Carr, who was declared academically ineligible, and without Andreas, who was recovering from a severe case of tonsillitis. The loss snapped the Orangemen's 15-game win streak, but they avenged the loss a few weeks later by clobbering the Nittany Lions 29–12 in Syracuse. There were no postseason tournaments in those days, but years later the Helms Foundation decided SU, with its 19–1 record—including impressive victories over Eastern League champion Penn and Big 10 champ Michigan—was title-worthy. Though he had frequently been double-teamed, Hanson set a school record that season with 282 points, a 14.2-points-per-game average, which would be the equivalent of an average in the mid–30s in today's game.

Although much was expected from the Orangemen during Hanson's senior year, they stumbled at the start, losing their first three straight after winning the first four games before rebounding to win 11 of their final 12. Hanson missed breaking his single-season record by five points, but his per-game output jumped to 14.6 as the Orange played one less game. For the third consecutive year, he earned All-America honors, and Helms named him the National Player of the Year.

The Yankees had scouted Hanson on the ball diamond and invited him to a tryout, which was witnessed by sluggers Babe Ruth and Lou Gehrig. Hanson was signed to a minor league contract, but his inability to hit the curve ball ended his professional baseball career after just one season. He returned to Syracuse where he formed a professional basketball team made up of former SU players. The Syracuse All-Americans held their own, beating some of the nation's best teams of the day, including the original Boston Celtics and the New York Renaissance, better known as the Renns.

In 1930, at age 27, Hanson was named varsity football coach at his alma mater, making him one of the youngest head coaches in the United States. After resigning the position in 1936, he became a prominent insurance counselor. On December 19, 1981, SU officials retired Dave Bing's No. 22 and Hanson's No. 8.

"The two great, great basketball players in Syracuse University history are Vic Hanson and Dave Bing," Boeheim said at the time. "Syracuse might not retire any more numbers in the future, but these two guys deserve it more than anybody else."

Sportscaster U

There's a good chance that if you turn on your television on any given night and begin surfing the sports channels, you'll hear the voice of someone who studied at Syracuse University's Newhouse School of Public Communications.

Few colleges in the country have become more closely associated with a profession than Newhouse has with sports broadcasting. *Sports Illustrated* magazine called it the "incubator" of American sportscasters, lauding SU's "dazzling record" of turning out not only the most but the best in the business.

Of the hundreds of Newhouse alumni currently in the field, none has become more recognizable, more decorated, or more popular than Bob Costas. The winner of 25 Emmy Awards and an unprecedented eight Sportscaster of the Year awards from the National Sportswriters and Sportscasters Association, Costas has pretty much done it all, from play-by-play to reporting to anchoring. One publication wrote, "When he arrived on the scene in the early '80s, Costas essentially reinvented sports broadcasting by imparting levels of articulation, intelligence, polish, insight, and wit that were unseen since the retirement of Howard Cosell. But unlike Cosell, Costas projected a congenial aura and probed effectively, without grating."

A native of Queens, Costas attended Syracuse in the early 1970s. While there, he worked part-time as a sports anchor and reporter for WSYR-TV and radio. He also did occasional play-by-play broadcasts of Syracuse Blazer hockey games in a league that was the basis for *Slap Shot*, the cult comedy movie starring Paul Newman. Costas left SU before graduating in order to call American Basketball Association games for KMOX in St. Louis. In

1980, he began work for NBC and has been with the network ever since. His most visible assignments have been as the anchor for the network's Olympic coverage. The 2014 Winter Games in Sochi was Costas' 10th Olympics as anchor and 11th Olympics overall.

While Costas might be the most famous of the sportscasters SU has produced, Marty Glickman is generally regarded as the father of SU sportscasting. An Olympic sprinter and football All-American while at Syracuse in the late 1930s, Glickman went on to make a name for himself as a New York City broadcaster. Like Costas, Glickman did a little bit of everything—including radio play-by-play of the New York Knicks and football Giants, pre- and postgame shows on New York Yankees and Brooklyn Dodgers broadcasts, and anchor work on several Big Apple television stations.

"He had a way of making you feel like you were inside Madison Square Garden," recalled Hank Greenwald, a Newhouse alum who became the long-time voice of the San Francisco Giants. "When you listened to Marty, you could smell the cigar smoke wafting up to the ceiling. In a medium like radio, where you can't see what's happening, he gave you the word picture you needed."

Glickman began his sportscasting career at SU, hosting a sports review show on WSYR radio for $15 a week. His descriptions became so vivid that he once was asked to broadcast a circus to the blind. He gladly accepted the assignment and became the eyes for those who could not see the elephants, clowns, or people on the flying trapeze. One critic called Glickman "the Michelangelo of play-by-play broadcasting." He was that—and the Pied Piper, too.

Glickman would eventually inspire and mentor other SU sportscasters who came after him, including Costas, Marv Albert, Dick Stockton, and Len Berman, who in turn would inspire and mentor another generation of microphone men and women, including Mike Tirico, Sean McDonough, Ian Eagle, and Beth Mowins. This great lineage has been a huge factor in SU becoming

Sportscaster U. But the Newhouse faculty and state of-the-art facilities have also contributed greatly, as has the opportunity to cover major college sports for the student-run station, WAER, and local television and radio stations.

"We have been particularly fortunate that the athletics department has permitted WAER the right to broadcast SU's football, basketball, and lacrosse games in competition with the commercial stations that carry them," former Newhouse dean David Rubin said in a 2002 interview with *Syracuse University Magazine*. "They didn't have to do that; most schools don't. But as a result, our students get chances to broadcast college athletics at the highest level. No Ivy League school can give you the opportunity to broadcast a Final Four NCAA basketball game or a major college football bowl game. We can, and we do."

In the summer of 2013, the Newhouse School presented the first Marty Glickman Award for Leadership in Sports Media to Costas.

13 Archbold Stadium

When it opened in 1907 it was touted as the greatest athletic arena in America. Designed after the Roman Colosseum and the modern Olympic stadium in Athens, and built into a natural hollow on the southwestern side of campus, Archbold Stadium was indeed an impressive edifice, one worthy of superlatives.

"Athletic contests may come and go, but the recently completed concrete stadium of Syracuse University will last forever," gushed Dr. Charles Burrows of *Technical World* magazine, upon viewing the stadium in 1909 for the first time.

As it turned out, the concrete bowl lasted 71 years before being torn down with wrecking balls to make room for the Carrier Dome. But what a 71 years it was.

The arena with the castle-like, twin-towered entrance was christened with a 28–0 victory against Hobart College on September 25, 1907, and closed with a 20–17 upset of 18th-ranked Navy on November 11, 1978. The Orange would enjoy a decided home-field advantage there, going 265–112–20. From Marquis "Big Bill" Horr, who was named SU's first football All-American in 1908, through Joe Morris, who rushed for 203 yards in the stadium's swan song, the place that came to be known as Old Archie would witness some of the greatest players and games in the history of college football.

As one of only three concrete stadiums in the country at the time, Archbold was the fulfillment of one man's dream to make SU into a world-class university in both academics and athletics. Oil tycoon and SU board of trustees president John D. Archbold approached then-chancellor James Roscoe Day about building a stadium that would enable the Orangemen to compete with national championship programs such as Yale, Michigan, and Pennsylvania. Day, a Methodist minister who had been recruited by Archbold to lead SU, was all for it.

Archbold, who would become arguably the most influential benefactor in Syracuse history, donated $600,000 for the stadium's construction, at the time the largest gift ever given to an American university. Archbold's donation may have been historically significant for another reason, too. It's believed to represent the first-ever naming gift for a fully encircled stadium. Archbold would wind up donating more than $4 million—an enormous sum in those days—to pay off the young university's debt and construct several academic buildings. But his greatest gift may have been the 6.5-acre stadium that laid the groundwork for SU to become a major player in collegiate athletics.

The stadium was designed by SU architecture professors Frederick Revels and Earl Hallenbeck, and it was built by a construction firm out of New York City. Its original seating capacity was 20,000, but as football grew in popularity, particularly under Coach Ben Schwartzwalder in the 1950s and '60s, grandstands were added that increased capacity to about 40,000. That number was later reduced to about 27,000 because of fire code regulations.

In its later years, Old Archie really showed its age—to the point where SU football coaches stopped showing prospective recruits the stadium for fear they would immediately cross off Syracuse from their lists. After exploring a number of new stadium options, including tracts of land on the southern part of campus and at the New York State Fairgrounds northwest of the city, university officials decided the best course of action was to build a new domed arena where Archbold stood. That meant the Orange would have to play the entire 1979 season on the road while the old place was torn down and a new one was constructed.

A sell-out crowd of 26,429 showed up for the stadium finale against powerful Navy. The 1978 Orangemen had lost each of their four home games and were in danger of becoming the first team in the stadium's history to go winless at home in a season. However, thanks to Morris' huge day, two field goals by Dave Jacobs, and a dropped pass by a Navy receiver on the game's final play, SU was able to escape with a three-point win.

"When that final pass was in the air, I said, 'Please, God, don't let him catch that,'" said Morris, who on that day became the first SU freshman running back to exceed 1,000 rushing yards in a season. "I didn't want us to close this place on a sour note. I think on that day, at that moment, God bled a little Orange."

After the game, fans stormed the field and tore down the wooden goal posts and toppled the scoreboard. Many people took home clumps of sod and railings and pieces of the scoreboard. Three-time All-American Floyd Little attended the game and gave a farewell speech at halftime. "It may have been dumpy, but I always loved that place," Little said. "Running out of that tunnel and onto that field is a feeling none of us who ever played there will ever, ever forget."

14 The Color Orange

Orange fans owe a huge debt of gratitude to Frank Marion and his fellow students from Syracuse University's class of 1890. Had they not raised a stink about the school's colors, current SU fans might be chanting "Let's Go Pink!" instead of "Let's Go Orange!"

According to research by the university's archivists—and they're not making this up—the school's original colors were pink and pea green. A year later, in 1873, the colors were changed to rose pink and azure blue. Orange wasn't adopted until 17 years later, and it came about as a result of the embarrassment and frustration Marion and his classmates experienced on the train ride back from a track meet at Hamilton College. During his 50th reunion in 1940, Marion, a motion picture pioneer, described how the switch came about:

"A number of us went along to cheer our team. We wore high collars, right up to our chins—cutaway coats, baggy trousers, and rolled-brim derby hats. On our canes we had ribbons of the college colors, pink and blue. Much to our surprise, we won the meet, and on the train coming home from Utica we tried to 'whoop it up.' What kind of 'whoopee' can be made with pink and blue, the pale kind you use on babies' what-do-you-call-thems? It just couldn't be done!

"So on Monday morning a lot of us went to see the chancellor in his office and told him our tale of woe. Chancellor [Charles]

Sims was a kindly old gentleman, a real father to us all, and he was sympathetic. He agreed that pink and blue were not very suitable colors.

"Professor J. Scott Clark was named chairman of a committee to find new colors. I recall that we seniors had a sneaking idea that we might put over the class colors, orange and olive green. Professor Clark consulted Baird's manual, then the authority on college matters, to see what combinations of orange had already been taken. Orange and blue were the most popular, but orange alone apparently was not claimed by any school and was Syracuse's for the taking. It was adopted unanimously by the committee, the faculty, the Alumni Association, and finally the trustees."

Not long after the color's adoption, people began referring to the school's teams as the Orangemen, and the nickname started appearing in newspaper accounts. As the years progressed, blue became an unofficial secondary color. The nickname Orangemen stuck until the school shortened it to Orange in the 1990s so it would be gender neutral.

Roy Simmons Sr.

During Thanksgiving break of his freshman year at the University of Chicago in 1920, Roy Simmons went to watch his high school alma mater, Hyde Park, play the Michigan champs in Lansing. The story goes that he became so frustrated with his old school's lackluster performance that he suited up at halftime, even though he obviously had no eligibility left. Simmons rushed for 85 yards and the touchdown that enabled Hyde Park to leave Lansing with a 7–7 tie.

"It was a crazy thing to do," Simmons recalled 64 years later in an interview with *Sports Illustrated*. "And it changed my life." His life—and the course of Syracuse University sports history. When Simmons got back to Chicago, news of him being a high school ringer was splashed across the front pages of all the newspapers.

"Son, you're the only boy who would do a thing like that," a chagrined University of Chicago coach Amos Alonzo Stagg told him. "You've got too much school spirit." School administrators immediately expelled the young man.

Undeterred, Simmons soon stowed away on an eastbound train in search of a school that could use his services. His primary destination was Philadelphia and the University of Pennsylvania campus because he had heard that Quakers coach Pop Warner was very interested in him. But he also remembered how a Syracuse alum had suggested he visit Orangemen coach Chick Meehan. So he got off at the Salt City. Not long after arriving on campus, Simmons put on a helmet and pads and made numerous tackles for the freshman team in its scrimmage against the varsity that day. After the long session ended, Meehan pulled the young man aside and asked, "What's this about you and Penn? What have they got in Philadelphia that you don't have right here?" The more Simmons thought about it, the more he agreed. He decided to enroll at Syracuse.

Nicknamed the Hobo Quarterback, Simmons wound up having one of the most fascinating playing and coaching careers in Orange annals. From 1922 to 1924, he helped SU's football team compile a 22–4–3 record, which included two victories against the Nebraska Cornhuskers, the only team to defeat Notre Dame's vaunted Four Horsemen. After going 8–1 in 1923, SU received a bid to the Rose Bowl, but the chancellor turned it down.

During his undergraduate years, Simmons also took up lacrosse. He knew nothing about the sport until he was walking

Orangemen in Lacrosse Hall of Fame

Player	Year Inducted
Laurie D. Cox	1957
Irving Lydecker	1960
Frederick Fitch	1961
Victor Ross	1962
Roy Simmons Sr.	1964
Glenn Thiel	1965
Victor Jenkins	1967
William Ritch	1972
Louis Robbins	1974
Stewart Lindsay Jr.	1976
William Fuller	1981
Jim Brown	1983
Ron Fraser	1987
Roy Simmons Jr.	1991
Oren Lyons	1992
Dick Finley	1999
Brad Kotz	2001
Gary Gait	2005
Paul Gait	2005
Pat McCabe	2006
Tom Marechek	2008
Todd Curry	2009
Roy Colsey	2012
Tim Nelson	2012

across campus one day and saw some students tossing a ball with funny netted sticks that he surmised were meant to be used for crabbing. He stopped to inquire and before you knew it, he was whipping the ball around and he was hooked. Simmons proved to be a natural from the start, and the rugged defenseman helped coach Laurie Cox's Orange stick men win national titles in 1924 and 1925.

Simmie, as he came to be known, also started a boxing program as an undergraduate in 1925, and he quickly established himself as a tough pugilist who often fought several weight classes above his weight. He eventually coached the team through 1955 before the school dropped the sport. His teams ruled the region, winning 14 Eastern titles and one national title (1936).

After graduating, Simmons began assisting the football team as a coach, a job he held for 41 seasons, including SU's national championship year (1959). He took over the lacrosse program from Cox following the 1931 season. From that point until 1970, he would guide the Orangemen to a 253–130–1 record, the highlight being the 10–0 squad in 1957 that featured All-Americans Jim Brown, Oren Lyons, Jim Ridlon, and Simmons' own son, Roy Simmons Jr. Incidentally, Simmie's other big contribution to the lacrosse program was his son, who would succeed him as coach and lead Syracuse to six national championships. Simmie's many contributions to the game would be recognized in 1964 when he was inducted into the National Lacrosse Hall of Fame.

Simmie was also credited for his pioneering efforts to break down racial and cultural barriers that had kept many minority athletes off the playing field. "If a guy was a good person and a good athlete, that was all that mattered to Roy," said former SU football player, coach, and administrator Joe Szombathy. "He gave people a chance," added Lyons, a Native American who was an All-American goalie for the Orange. "He understood what the quality of a person was, rather than the color of a person…. In order to do that, he had to challenge the administration." Simmons developed a friendship with Brown, an African American multi-sport superstar who refused to back down from the bigotry he occasionally faced during his SU years. Brown still calls Simmons his "favorite coach of all-time, a true father figure."

Simmons' positive impact was felt beyond campus and beyond sports. The man who fought with the marines in World War I and the navy in World War II served several terms on the Syracuse Common Council and was briefly the city's acting mayor. Even after he was done coaching, he remained a strong presence at his alma mater's sporting events, particularly football and lacrosse games, and he became known, along with Ben Schwartzwalder, as one of the patriarchs of SU sports. Simmie's son often joked that he had to keep his feisty father off the sidelines and up in the stands because "he was known to be a little rough on the refs."

Following Simmons' death at age 92 in 1994, Lyons said, "It's clear he was much more than a coach...he was a father figure. He was an excellent person who had a genuine concern for the people he was involved with." Arnie Burdick, a former SU lacrosse player who would become a longtime sports editor and columnist for the *Syracuse Herald-Journal*, wrote, "Of all the alumni at Syracuse University, he is number one because of his contributions to the community and university as a whole."

Simmie said in numerous interviews later in his life that getting off the train in Syracuse back in 1921 was one of the best things that ever happened to him. Turns out it was one of the best things that ever happened to SU sports, too.

Pearl Washington

There have been scores of great athletes in Syracuse University history, but no one was more hyped or anticipated than Dwayne "The Pearl" Washington.

A playground and high school hoops legend from New York City, Washington dazzled with Harlem Globetrotter–like moves and a flair for the dramatic. By age 10, the precocious guard was dribbling past the likes of NBA stars World B. Free and Sly Williams in pickup games on the city's asphalt courts. Larry Costello, who had won an NBA championship as a player with Wilt Chamberlain and as a coach with Kareem Abdul-Jabbar and Oscar Robertson, called Washington "a miniature Oscar Robertson. He can do anything he wants to on the basketball court. You just can't guard him one-on-one." SU assistant coach Brendan Malone, a New York City native, called Washington "the best guard I've ever seen coming out of the city. Pearl can penetrate a crowded, rush-hour train in Manhattan and come out of the car without picking up a foul." And Boeheim, not one prone to hyperbole, could barely contain his enthusiasm when talking about the charismatic Washington: "He doesn't disappoint. People come in with enormous expectations about him, and they always leave happy."

During a halftime interview of a nationally televised college basketball game on February 20, 1983, Pearl told NBC's Al McGuire that he had chosen Syracuse from the more than 300 schools that had recruited him. His decision had an immediate impact on SU's athletic coffers as 2,000 additional season tickets were sold, guaranteeing that Washington would play in front of a record six crowds of more than 30,000 fans in the Carrier Dome his freshman season.

His first of many indelible moments came in his 15th game as a collegian when he heaved in a half-court shot at the buzzer to beat Boston College 75–73. "That shot made me a permanent part of Syracuse basketball," Washington said nearly three decades later. "I had so many great moments during my playing days there, but that one's hard to top."

Boeheim agreed. "That was a historic moment for our program," he said. "The instant that thing went through, there was an explosion in the building. As long as they play basketball at Syracuse, people will always talk about that shot." It was, said Washington's teammate, Sean Kerins, the moment the Pearl "officially arrived."

The victory would prompt an enterprising vendor to begin producing and selling T-shirts that read, "And on the eighth day,

Dwayne Washington makes a breakaway layup as Earl Kelley of the University of Connecticut tries to stop him during a game in Hartford, Connecticut, on January 19, 1984. Syracuse won 95–68. (AP Photo/Bob Child)

God created the Pearl." It also enabled the Orangemen to crack the top 20 the following week. They would remain there the rest of Pearl's career.

Almost a year later at the Dome, Washington would work his late-game magic again, hitting a 15' jumper with eight seconds to go as SU nipped second-ranked Georgetown by a point. During his junior season, in 1985–86, Washington literally put the team on his shoulders after star teammate Rafael Addision was injured. Washington averaged 17.3 points per game as the Orange went 23–4 in the regular season.

"And then," said Boeheim, "he took it to another level when we went to the Big East tournament that year."

After disposing of Boston College 102–79 in Madison Square Garden, SU found itself once more matched up against the hated Hoyas. The teams had split their regular-season series, and much was made in the New York tabloids about the bad blood that had developed between Washington and Georgetown center Patrick Ewing during the 1985 semifinals. In that game, the two exchanged elbows to the ribs, prompting Ewing to throw a roundhouse right that barely missed Pearl. The two were assessed technical fouls but were allowed to remain in the game, and the riled-up Hoyas went on to beat the Orangemen by nine.

This time, however, Washington would deliver a knock-out punch of a different kind, scoring 21 points as SU defeated Georgetown 75–73 in overtime. "What you have to remember," Boeheim said, "is that Georgetown team played suffocating defense. There were teams that struggled to score 40 or 50 points against them, and there's Pearl scoring 21 on them and just dominating them from start to finish. They had no answer whatsoever for him. It was one of those nights where he was unstoppable."

Despite being spent from that performance, Washington put on another show in the finals against fifth-ranked St. John's the following night and was unstoppable until his attempted

Attendance Champions

Syracuse reclaimed the national basketball attendance crown from Kentucky during the 2013–14 season by drawing 518,143 fans in 18 games at the Carrier Dome, a 26,523 per-game average. The Orange attracted four crowds of more than 30,000, including a new on-campus record of 35,446 for the Duke game on February 1, 2014. It marked the first time since 2004–05 that Syracuse has led the nation in attendance. The Orange have been the biggest draw in college basketball 13 times and have finished in the top four every year since they started playing basketball in the Dome in 1980.

game-winning shot was blocked by Walter Berry. Although his team didn't win the crown, Washington was voted tournament MVP.

The next day, the NCAA tournament selection committee presented Pearl and his teammates a gift, placing the eighth-ranked Orangemen in the Carrier Dome for the opening-round games. Some in the national media squawked about this obvious home-court advantage. (A few years later, the NCAA would change the rules to prohibit tournament teams from playing on their home courts.) But nobody in Syracuse was complaining. It appeared the Orangemen had been given a free-pass into the Sweet Sixteen. After annihilating Brown 101–52, though, SU wound up being manhandled by a Navy team they had manhandled during the regular season. Future NBA star center David Robinson beat the Orangemen singlehandedly. Not long after that stunning defeat, Washington announced he was going to skip his senior season and turn pro.

The New Jersey Nets drafted him 13th overall, and everyone believed Pearl would become a huge NBA star. But the magic he had displayed on the playgrounds, in high school, and at Syracuse disappeared. He spent just three seasons in the NBA, averaging 8.6 points and 3.8 assists per game. "I kind of lost my love for the game when I turned pro," he said. "It wasn't fun anymore." Years later, at Boeheim's urging, Washington returned to SU and finished the 31 credit hours he needed to complete his degree. He also became the third SU basketball player to have his jersey retired.

Though he never guided the Orangemen to a Big East title and had only limited success in his three NCAA appearances, Washington made a lasting impression on the program. He averaged 15.7 points and 6.7 assists per game as Syracuse went 71–24. But his impact transcended the numbers. Pearl's decision to play at SU transformed the Orangemen from a regional to a national program and had a magnetic effect on recruiting, enabling them to lure blue-chip prospects who wouldn't have considered them before.

Washington turned the Dome into The House That Pearl Filled. During his sophomore and junior seasons, SU led the nation in basketball attendance. By the time he left, the Orangemen were averaging 26,255 fans per game, a jump of nearly 6,000 fans per game from the year before his arrival. In his three seasons, he played in front of crowds in excess of 30,000 thirteen times. "Pearl's the reason there was that guy in line waiting to buy that 31,000th seat," Boeheim said.

And Washington was the reason that SU basketball became such a ratings success on national television. "Everybody says Patrick Ewing and Chris Mullin made the Big East, but I think Pearl made the league," Boeheim said. "They were the best players, but Pearl was the player that people turned out to see and turned on their TVs to watch. We had the highest-rated games every year because Pearl was here."

Coach Mac

Dick MacPherson became so popular in Syracuse that the Onondaga Republican Party recruited him to run for political office after his coaching career ended in 1993. The man who revived the SU football program politely declined. Coach Mac had no desire to become Mayor Mac. The native of Old Town, Maine, was clearly flattered by the offer but also somewhat amused by the dramatic transformation that had occurred in the public's perception of him. The garrulous, highly personable MacPherson smiled as he remembered a time when many Syracuse fans were more concerned about running him out of town than watching him run for political office.

After the Orangemen opened the 1986 season with four consecutive losses, angry fans formed a "Sack Mac Pack." The only membership requirement was a staunch belief that MacPherson should be fired. There was a growing sentiment that the coach had been given more than enough time to turn things around; up to that point, MacPherson had produced just a 25–34–1 record in 5½ seasons. The program appeared to be stuck in mediocrity. Time to move on, advised the critics. Fortunately for MacPherson and SU football, athletic director Jake Crouthamel didn't listen to them. "Jake was an old football coach, so he could see that we were on the verge of getting this thing turned around," MacPherson said in that familiar R-dropping, New England accent of his. "I'll always be grateful for him sticking his neck out for me."

Members of the soon-to-be-defunct Sack Mac Pack ended up being grateful, too. Led by their promising junior quarterback, Don McPherson, the Orangemen rebounded to win five of their

Former Syracuse and Massachusetts coach Dick MacPherson during the announcement of the 2009 College Football Hall of Fame class at NASDAQ Marketsite in New York on Thursday, April 30, 2009. MacPherson was one of two coaches and 16 players named by the National Football Foundation to the 2009 class. (AP Photo/Kathy Willens)

final seven games in 1986 to finish 5–6 and set the stage for one of the most memorable seasons in SU history.

In 1987, the 'Cuse went 11–0–1 and finished fourth in the final polls, their highest ranking since winning the national championship 28 years earlier. The string of victories included a thrashing of Penn State, which snapped a 16-year losing streak to the Nittany Lions, and a last-second, one-point victory against West Virginia when running back Michael Owens scored on a two-point conversion run. The only blemish was a 16–16 tie with Auburn in the Sugar Bowl when the Tigers opted to kick a field goal at the end instead of going for the win.

Coach Mac received national Coach of the Year honors for resurrecting the program following a long dry spell. "That was such a special group of young men and such a special season," MacPherson said. "Just about everything fell our way. It put an exclamation point on the fact we were back."

They were back all right—with a vengeance. The '87 campaign began a string of 15 consecutive winning seasons that saw the Orangemen make 12 bowl appearances (8–3–1).

Athletic director Jake Crouthamel clearly made the right decision by hiring and then not firing MacPherson. When Frank Maloney resigned following the 1980 season, Crouthamel believed he needed to find a proven coach with a dynamic personality to breathe new life into the program. While working as the head football coach at Dartmouth College in the 1970s, Crouthamel's teams played the University of Massachusetts teams coached by MacPherson and the two men struck up a friendship. Mac was coaching the linebackers for the Cleveland Browns when SU's AD came calling.

"They were down when I got there, and then the university made a huge commitment to turn things around," MacPherson said. "There were a lot of things in place. The Dome was brand new, and that really helped recruiting. And Syracuse had such a great tradition that we could sell to young people."

Success came slowly. After guiding SU to 4–6–1 and 2–9 records his first two seasons, MacPherson's rebuilding efforts gained traction as the Orangemen went 6–5 in both 1983 and 1984, then finished 7–5 with a Cherry Bowl appearance in 1985. But the putrid start the following year got the natives restless. "I knew it was going to take some time to make the situation better," said MacPherson, the third-winningest coach in SU history with a 66–46–4 record. "And thank God I had a guy in my corner who was willing to be patient."

Following a 7–4–2 season in 1990 that was capped with a 28–0 victory against Arizona in the Aloha Bowl, MacPherson left to coach the New England Patriots for two seasons. His stint as an NFL coach did not go well; the Pats won just eight of 32 games and Mac was fired. Not long after coming back to the Salt City, he was approached about that political run.

Death, Taxes, and Syracuse Making Extra Points

On November 18, 1978, Dave Jacobs missed an extra point after Syracuse had scored its fourth touchdown in a 37–23 victory at Boston College. He converted one on SU's final touchdown of the day, and nobody gave it a second thought. Who could have known that successful PAT would kick-start an NCAA record streak that would span 12 years and 262 consecutive extra points? But that's what transpired. Jacobs started it. His successor Gary Anderson then went 72-for-72 the next three seasons. His successor, Russ Carpentieri, was 17-for-17 in 1982. Don McAulay then went 62-for-62 the next three years, followed by Tim Vesling's 71 straight in 1986–87 and Kevin Greene's 37 straight in 1988.

All good things must come to an end, and so it was with SU's PAT streak. On September 9, 1989, John Biskup missed his third attempt in the opener against Temple and the run was over. But the record still stands—262 extra points in a row.

"To be mayor of Syracuse, New York, would have been a fascinating job, but I realized me and politics would not have been a good match," said MacPherson, who has instead spent two decades providing commentary on SU football broadcasts. "Even though you know you've made the right decision, you've got to convince a council or other people that it's right. All of a sudden you are not the head coach. You become a mediator, and I don't feel I ever was a good mediator. I wouldn't want to run anything where people run me and tell me how to run my business."

Although he never became an elected official, Coach Mac did become an elder statesman and goodwill ambassador for the university and its football program. His achievements at UMass and SU were recognized in 2009 when he was inducted into the College Football Hall of Fame.

Roy Simmons Jr.

He literally grew up in the Syracuse program, tagging along with his father the coach, Roy Simmons Sr., from the time he was knee-high to a lacrosse stick. Roy Jr. would later go on to box and play lacrosse for his dad at SU, earning All-America honors as an attackman and ranking among the nation's top scorers in both his junior and senior seasons (1957 and 1958). Upon graduation, he joined the family business, so to speak, coaching the Syracuse freshmen lacrosse team while assisting his father with the varsity. And when it came time to name a replacement for Simmons Sr. following his retirement in the summer of 1970 after a 40-year, Hall-of-Fame coaching career, SU athletic director James Decker didn't have to venture very far. Simmons Jr. appeared well-prepared to carry on where his father left off.

His first team went 9–4, but during the next three seasons there would be a steady decline. By 1974, the program had been so badly ravaged by budget cuts that Simmons had no scholarships to offer, and the team stumbled to a 2–9 record. After an embarrassing 27–4 thrashing by Cornell, in which Simmons put two men in goal in order to hold down the score, people began to grumble that Junior wasn't half the coach his old man had been. "I was so low I had to reach up to touch bottom," he recalled. "People were saying this was a clear case of nepotism; that the only reason I got the job was because of my father and I wasn't worthy. Those were some dark times for me."

Thanks to strong support from several prominent alumni, the man nicknamed "Slugger" pulled himself up and slowly but surely revived the program. Simmons helped cultivate a revival in high school lacrosse in Central New York, and soon scholastic powerhouses such as West Genesee began churning out players that would help the Orangemen become the New York Yankees of their sport. The breakthrough moment came in 1983 when SU stormed back from a seven-goal deficit to upset Johns Hopkins 17–16 in the NCAA title game, giving the Orangemen their first national championship since Simmons Sr. was a player in 1925.

During the next 15 years, Simmons Jr. would lead SU to 15 more trips to the Final Four and five more NCAA titles. He would also mentor 130 All-Americans and four national Player of the Year winners. By the time he retired after a 28-year head coaching career following the 1998 season, he had led the Orangemen to a 290–96 record, which computed to a .751 winning percentage, exceeding the records compiled by his father (253–130–1, .660) and the school's original lacrosse coach, Laurie Cox (116–40–15, .722). This clearly was a case where the son also rises. As Sean Keeley wrote in his thoroughly entertaining book, *How to Grow*

Simmons and Sons

There has been a Roy Simmons involved with Syracuse lacrosse every season since the Herbert Hoover administration. Simmons Sr., who played lacrosse at SU during the 1924–25 seasons and earned All-America honors, got the ball rolling when he took over for Laurie Cox in 1931. He held the post through the 1970 season when he was replaced by Simmons Jr. The son guided the Orangemen the next 28 years before passing the torch to John Desko. But Desko's hiring didn't break the link because Roy Simmons III returned to SU for his third stint as one of Desko's assistants in 1999.

As head coaches, Simmons Sr. and Jr. combined for 543 wins, 226 losses, one tie, and six NCAA titles. One of those titles—the 1990 championship—is not recognized by the NCAA because Gary Gait was ruled ineligible following an investigation. The NCAA tournament didn't begin until 1971, so there are some who believe SU's unbeaten 1957 squad, featuring Jim Brown, would have won a matchup with Johns Hopkins, which was awarded the top spot in the writers' poll. SU was ranked second.

an Orange, "If Roy Simmons Sr. built the house, Roy Simmons Jr. turned it into a 24-room mansion."

But to fully appreciate Junior's impact on the sport of lacrosse and the young men he coached, you have to go beyond the numbers. As Damian Andrew wrote in the October 2009 issue of *Inside Lacrosse* magazine, "Simmons was more than a coach. He was a teacher, an intellect, an artist. He was someone who wanted his players to understand that there is more to life than lacrosse. As important as winning was to him, it never defined him."

"I feel like that's how I really won in lacrosse," Simmons said. "I won by what happened later, not by what happened that day. You win when a kid comes back and wants to introduce you to his wife and kids. The scoreboard, yeah, that's history, that's memories, nothing wrong with that. What comes out of being with those kids on a 48-hour trip is more meaningful to me than berating them because they didn't win or threw the ball over the cage."

An accomplished sculptor whose works have been displayed at prestigious art museums, Simmons saw similarities between creating in a studio and on a lacrosse field. He allowed his players tremendous latitude. He often referred to "dreams and fantasies." Once the players crossed midfield and went on offense, it was time for their dreams and fantasies to become reality. "If that led to a Syracuse player's passing behind his back and throwing the ball away, so be it," wrote Bill Tanton of *Inside Lacrosse* magazine. "Roy never scolded a player for that."

Simmons allowed transformative players like Gary and Paul Gait and Powell brothers Casey, Ryan and Mike to experiment with new moves and shots and passes. "Others," wrote Tanton, "may have criticized him for his reckless style, but he believed the way to promote the game was to allow great talent to express itself. His players loved him for that." Simmons' run-and-gun style produced a record number of goals and victories, and that style appealed not only to players but to fans. "He allowed a game that was formerly defensive to become offensive," said Gary Gait, who's regarded by many people to be the Michael Jordan of lacrosse. "He really was a visionary. He changed the way the game is played and viewed. He's the reason lacrosse is the fastest growing sport in America."

Simmons' coaching extended beyond the lacrosse field. On trips to road games, he would occasionally take his team to museums or historical sites. His most famous trip was when he took his team to Lockerbie, a year after the 1988 terrorist attack on Pan Am Flight 103, which exploded over that Scottish village, claiming 270 lives, including 35 Syracuse students returning from a semester abroad. Simmons and his players staged car washes and bake sales and other fund-raisers to pay for the trip. SU players stayed in family homes while there and staged youth lacrosse clinics and handed out equipment that was donated by American sporting goods manufacturers. "It was one of the most meaningful experiences of my life," Gait said. "And it told you a lot about Coach Simmons' priorities. He wanted to win as badly as the next guy, but he also believed he had a responsibility to coach us in life as well as lacrosse."

One of the most emotional and gratifying moments in Simmons' life occurred when he was inducted into the National Lacrosse Hall of Fame on February 8, 1992. His 91-year-old father was there and he was beaming. "It's the proudest day of my life to see him make it," Simmons Sr. said. "It's a hell of an achievement."

Simmons Jr. retired following an 11–10 loss to Princeton at the NCAA semifinals in 1998. Though he turned over the reins to John Desko, the Simmons lacrosse legacy at SU continues. Roy Simmons III, who played and coached under his dad, is now in his 24th year as a Syracuse assistant, and his son, Ryan, is a freshman midfielder for the Orange.

Donovan McNabb

On November 28, 1998, Donovan McNabb was introduced a final time as the starting Syracuse University quarterback in the Carrier Dome. The Orangemen were about to play Miami in a contest to determine the Big East Conference champion, and the ovation the celebrated signal-caller received from the 49,521 spectators was so thunderous that the folks monitoring the Richter scale had to wonder if the SU campus was the epicenter of a mild earthquake.

There would be many more stadium-shaking tremors that afternoon as the most beloved SU athlete since 1961 Heisman Trophy winner Ernie Davis gave the Dome denizens a parting gift they would always treasure. McNabb rushed for three touchdowns and threw for two more as the Orange crushed the Hurricanes

66–13. When Syracuse coach Paul Pasqualoni mercifully took his All-American quarterback out of the game with just more than 11 minutes remaining, McNabb stood on the bench and doffed his helmet to the crowd to thank them for their support.

Fifteen years later, McNabb rocked the Dome again when the greatest quarterback in Syracuse and Philadelphia Eagles history returned to have his No. 5 jersey retired. Many memories stampeded through his head as he watched the unveiling of his number near the stadium's ceiling. Foremost among those memories was that evisceration of Miami, a team that had tossed around the Orangemen like a bunch of rag dolls until Donovan arrived on campus.

"To be received the way I was [during the Miami game], that was something special for myself and my parents," he recalled. "That was a memorable event. It's second to none. It's something that I never expected to happen." It was the high point of a marvelous career that saw McNabb establish seven school records and five conference records, earn Big East Offensive Player of the Year honors an unprecedented three times, and lead SU to a 35–14 mark and four bowl appearances.

But McNabb's legend extended beyond the football field and into the classroom and the community. He graduated with a degree in speech communications with a minor in African American studies in four years. No small feat when you consider that, in addition to his extensive football commitments, he also spent two

SU Football's Retired Jerseys

No.	Player(s)
44	Jim Brown, Ernie Davis, Floyd Little
39	Larry Csonka
88	John Mackey
5	Donovan McNabb
9	Don McPherson

seasons as a valuable reserve on Jim Boeheim's basketball team. McNabb provided a spark off the bench in a memorable victory against Georgetown and was a member of the 1996 Orange hoops squad that played Kentucky in the NCAA championship game. Each of the football players in McNabb's class also graduated on time, a laudable achievement that doesn't happen often in big-time college football programs. McNabb was also heavily involved in the Syracuse community, tirelessly appearing at schools and rec centers to speak to kids about the importance of setting positive goals and being a good person.

In retrospect, his most meaningful run in his Dome finale occurred after the game and away from the field. After removing his pads and slipping on a Big East championship T-shirt, McNabb made a beeline through the stands to a handicap area where he high-fived a dozen people seated in wheelchairs. As we came to find out, that was just Donovan being Donovan.

"The community has shown great, great admiration and love for this kid," Pasqualoni said at the time. "And this kid has given it back to the community. I mean, he's been perfect. He's been a role model for every kid in New York and a tremendous representative of Syracuse and a tremendous representative of Division I football. The guy came in humble. He doesn't have a selfish bone in his body."

He credits his parents, Sam and Wilma McNabb, and his older brother, Sean, for keeping him grounded. Former SU offensive coordinator George DeLeone recalled how Donovan was doing dishes each time he made a recruiting visit to the family home on the south side of Chicago. "Here's one of the best high school quarterbacks in the country, and each time I'm there he's scrubbing pots and pans and drying forks and spoons and plates," DeLeone said. "That showed me that he wasn't a big shot and he wasn't spoiled. It showed me that his family had given him a solid foundation."

Donovan's athletic prowess and penchant for improvisation was evident at an early age. People remember the time he was sprinting toward home plate in a Little League game. Rather than bowl over the catcher, McNabb leaped over him to score the run. He loved the Chicago Bears and legendary running back Walter Payton, but he didn't want to follow in Payton's cleatsteps. "From the seventh grade on, I knew I wanted to be a quarterback," he said. "I wanted to take Jim McMahon's job, not Walter's."

Despite starring at quarterback at Mt. Carmel, a national high school football power that has produced scores of NFL players through the years, only a handful of college recruiters saw McNabb's future behind center. Most schools wanted to move him to running back or wide receiver or even defensive back. But Nebraska and Syracuse envisioned McNabb as a QB, and he initially leaned toward the Cornhuskers because he was intrigued by the prospect of playing for legendary coach Tom Osborne. The 'Cuse eventually won out because it had the No. 1 communications program in the country. "I really wanted to be acknowledged as a student first," McNabb said. "That was very important to me and my family."

McNabb's emergence as an SU football legend began not long after he beat out Kevin Johnson and Keith Downing for the quarterback job. McNabb set an NCAA freshman record for passing efficiency as the Orange went 9–3 and destroyed Clemson 41–0 in the Gator Bowl. It would be more of the same over the next three seasons, as McNabb not only put up impressive stats but turned in indelible highlights. He could throw the ball 70 yards, was strong enough to bench-press 325 pounds, possessed Houdini-like escape abilities, and was super cool when the game was on the line. "It was almost like you had to defend 12 guys instead of 11 because of Donovan," said former Rutgers and Virginia Tech defensive coordinator Rod Sharpless. Added long-time West Virginia coach Don Nehlen, "You can do everything right and he can still beat you."

Quarterback Donovan McNabb scrambles by Miami's Dan Morgan (44) during the first quarter at the Carrier Dome in Syracuse, New York, on Saturday, November 28, 1998. (AP Photo/David Duprey)

Some of McNabb's greatest moments came during his senior season, in 1998. He completed 22-of-28 passes for 300 yards and two touchdowns and also ran for a score in a near-upset of eventual national champion, Tennessee, in the opener. The next week, he threw for 233 yards and two scores and rushed for 60 yards and another score (in which he lost his shoe but kept on running) as the Orange built a 31-point lead en route to a 38–28 victory at Michigan.

"Donovan was incredible," said New England Patriots legend Tom Brady, who started at quarterback for the Wolverines that day. "Every time they snapped the ball, it was like 10 yards. That was probably the worst defeat I've ever had."

Later that season, McNabb erased a 21–3 deficit and beat Virginia Tech with a 13-yard touchdown pass to Stephen Brominski as time expired in the Dome. That scintillating win was followed by the aforementioned Miami game.

McNabb clearly had all the physical attributes you look for in a quarterback, and then some. But it was his mind and his leadership skills that set him apart. At the Senior Bowl All-Star game following McNabb's senior season, North squad coach Jon Gruden gave the young quarterback 40 plays to memorize for the next day's practice. Gruden, now ESPN's *Monday Night Football* analyst, was astounded the following day as he watched McNabb run the plays flawlessly. "A veteran NFL quarterback might struggle with that intense a homework assignment," Gruden said. "But Donovan assimilated everything rapidly. That was pretty darn impressive." The Eagles drafted him third overall, and McNabb delivered. He earned Pro Bowl honors six times, was named NFC Player of the Year in 2004, and guided a Philadelphia franchise that had won just 11 of its previous 40 games to a 101–56–1 record and a Super Bowl appearance.

After retiring as a player, McNabb put his speech communications degree and his wealth of football knowledge to good use as a panelist on *FOX Sports Live* television and as the host of a daily show on NBC Sports Radio. McNabb also continues to be a huge supporter of his alma mater, serving on SU's board of trustees and making generous donations to the school's football facilities. "My time at Syracuse prepared me for everything that has followed," he said.

Following his last game in the Dome, McNabb was asked how he wanted to be remembered. He responded, "Not only as a quarterback who led Syracuse to three Big East championships, but as a caring, responsible individual who can be relied on—a guy who will do whatever it takes to bring a smile to someone's face. I don't consider myself a legend, just a player who was a part of something special."

20 Six Overtimes in the Garden

Jonny Flynn can't remember exactly when he started pleading for divine intervention. Perhaps it was during the fourth overtime. Or maybe the fifth.

"I just recall looking up at the ceiling at Madison Square Garden and saying to myself, 'Lord, just get this game over with. Doesn't matter who wins, let's just get it over,'" the SU point guard recalled of the Big East Conference tournament matchup with Connecticut that tipped off on the evening of March 12, 2009, and didn't conclude until 1:22 AM the next morning. "By that point I was so exhausted I couldn't feel my legs."

As it turned out, Flynn's prayers weren't answered until the sixth overtime as the Orangemen took a lead they would not relinquish, beating the Huskies 127–117 in the second-longest game in college basketball history. Flynn's reputation for being a marathon man was enhanced that night—and morning—as he played 67 of a possible 70 minutes, scoring 34 points, including 26 in overtime.

"The [sellout crowd of 19,375] got their money's worth, and then some," Flynn said. "I don't think anybody left. I think a bunch of them were as gassed as we were."

The game took three hours and 46 minutes to complete. A combined 244 points were scored, 102 of which came after the regulation buzzer sounded. Eight players fouled out. Six players recorded double-doubles—including Flynn, who had 11 assists to go with his game-high point total, and teammate Paul Harris, who had 29 points and 22 rebounds. Remarkably, the Orangemen never led until the final overtime period.

What's forgotten is that the game appeared to be over in regulation when Eric Devendorf swished a jumper at the buzzer after taking an improbable length-of-the-court pass from Harris. Immediately after sinking the 28' shot, Devendorf leaped onto the scorer's table and pounded his chest in celebration. However, after reviewing the shot on courtside monitors, the officials ruled that the ball had not left Devendorf's hand before the buzzer sounded. The basket was waved off, sending the game into overtime.

By the fourth session, 6'7" swingman Kris Joseph had to jump center because SU's post players—Arinze Onuaku, Rick Jackson, and Kristof Ongenaet—had fouled out. When Devendorf fouled out in the fifth overtime, Jim Boeheim had no choice but to insert walk-on Justin Thomas, who had not played a meaningful minute all season. At the end of the fifth OT, Flynn huddled with his teammates and told them, "If we can win one tip, we'll win the game."

With UConn's 7'3" center Hasheem Thabeet fouled out, the Orange finally won a tip and Andy Rautins drained a jumper that gave SU its first lead. Syracuse went on to outscore the Huskies 17–7 in the final OT to make the weary Flynn a prophet.

"If you're a basketball fan, at some point you have to look around during that game and say, 'There's never been anything like this before,'" Boeheim said. "During the fourth overtime, I looked at the guys at the scorers' table and said, 'What in the world are we a part of right now?' I mean, we're down in five different overtimes and come back every time. How incredible is that?" When it was mentioned that the longest game in college basketball history—a 1981 matchup between Bradley and Cincinnati—went seven overtimes, Boeheim astutely pointed out, "Yeah, but that was before the shot clock. Those guys were holding the ball. I would make the case this is something none of us have ever seen or are likely to ever see again."

One of the Big Apple tabloids summed up the game later that morning with the headline, "Six in the City," a clever takeoff on the popular *Sex in the City* television series and movies. By the following week, orange T-shirts with that phrase were being sold on campus.

Just in case Flynn & Co. didn't get their fill of basketball from that game, SU played another overtime in a victory vs. West Virginia in the semifinals. That set up a championship matchup with Louisville. The Orangemen led at halftime, then understandably ran out of gas as the Cardinals copped the title with a 76–66 victory. Flynn, who played an astounding 181 of a possible 195 minutes of basketball in four days, was named the tournament's most outstanding player, and Devendorf, who set a record with 84 points, earned a spot on the All-Tournament team.

Derrick Coleman

Derrick Coleman had no idea when his basketball coach at Detroit's Northern High School introduced him to Dave Bing that the nattily attired, bespectacled man seated behind the big desk had once been a great hoopster.

"The introduction wasn't in a basketball setting," Coleman explained. "It was in the office at the company Dave ran—Bing Steel. The thing that impressed me was that here was this distinguished-looking black man in a really sharp suit who owned his own company. That's what struck me. I thought that was so cool because the only successful black role models I had been exposed to were athletes."

It wasn't until after Coleman began working a summer job sweeping floors and running errands at Bing Steel that he found out that Bing had been one of the greatest basketball players of all time. This discovery was made one day while Coleman was looking around the lobby. A poster caught his eye.

"I see Dr. J, Bob Lanier, and this real skinny guy with a big afro and it said 'Dave Bing' on it," Coleman recalled in the book, *Legends of Syracuse Basketball*, by Mike Waters. "I'd never noticed it. That's when our relationship took off in a basketball sense."

The two began chatting regularly after that, but the conversations rarely touched on basketball. Instead, Bing emphasized the importance of a college education. "Even after Jim [Boeheim], my college roommate, started recruiting him to go to SU, I told Derrick, 'I don't care what college you get your degree from as long as you get one,'" Bing said.

Syracuse had been one of the first schools to recruit Coleman, but after his junior year, the young man's thin body began to fill out and every school was after him. "It ultimately came down to Michigan State and Syracuse," Coleman said. "And I figured if Syracuse University could produce a man with the class of Dave Bing, then that's where I wanted to go. By that time, I had learned all about Dave Bing's records at Syracuse. I joked to him that I was going to go to SU and break his records. He said he didn't care as long as I got a degree."

Coleman made good on his boast. He wound up rewriting the record books before becoming the first Orangeman to be selected No. 1 overall in the NBA draft. By the time the 6'10" forward left campus in 1990, he was the school's all-time leading scorer (2,143 points) and the NCAA's all-time leading rebounder (1,537), averaging a double-double (15 points and 10.8 rebounds per game)

Syracuse's First-Round NBA Draft Choices

Year	Player	Team	Pick No. (Overall)
1966	Dave Bing	Detroit Pistons	2
1978	Marty Byrnes	Phoenix Suns	19
1981	Danny Schayes	Utah Jazz	13
1983	Leo Rautins	Philadelphia 76ers	17
1986	Pearl Washington	New Jersey Nets	13
1988	Rony Seikaly	Miami Heat	9
1990	Derrick Coleman	New Jersey Nets	1
1991	Billy Owens	Sacramento Kings	3
1991	LeRon Ellis	Los Angeles Clippers	22
1992	Dave Johnson	Portland Trail Blazers	26
1996	John Wallace	New York Knicks	18
2000	Etan Thomas	Dallas Mavericks	12
2003	Carmelo Anthony	Denver Nuggets	3
2005	Hakim Warrick	Memphis Grizzlies	19
2008	Donte Greene	Memphis Grizzlies	28
2009	Jonny Flynn	Minnesota Timberwolves	6
2010	Wesley Johnson	Minnesota Timberwolves	4
2012	Dion Waiters	Cleveland Cavaliers	4
2012	Fab Melo	Boston Celtics	22
2013	Michael Carter-Williams	Philadelphia 76ers	11
2014	Tyler Ennis	Phoenix Suns	18

for his career. A three-time, first-team Big East selection and a consensus All-American and national Player of the Year his senior year, Coleman led the Orangemen to 113 victories and four NCAA tournament berths in four seasons.

Coleman's superb rebounding and defensive skills were apparent from the get-go as he averaged a team-leading 8.8 rebounds as a freshman. He hauled down a freshman-record 19 rebounds in the 1987 championship game against Indiana, but he will also be remembered for missing the front end of a one-and-one with about 30 seconds remaining that led to the game-winning jumper by

Keith Smart. That miss still haunts Coleman, nearly three decades later. "We were so close, we had it in our hands," he said. "But we let it slip away. I'd rather lose by 15 or 20 than lose by one shot."

Although he didn't make it back to the title game, Coleman continued to dominate during his next three seasons, showing that he was much more than a rugged rebounder and intimidating shot-blocker. He was able to run the court well and, because he was a deft ballhandler, he was often used to bring the ball up against full-court presses.

"He had a great all-around game, especially for a big man," Boeheim said. "And he could have been an even better scorer than he was, but he was a great team player and he sacrificed some of that because he wanted others to have opportunities. Guys loved playing with him. You won't find a single guy who didn't enjoy being a teammate of Derrick Coleman's."

When he wanted to, Coleman could literally take control of a game and put up scary numbers. During his senior year, he had 16 points and 19 rebounds in a win over Duke; 23 points and 21 rebounds against Providence, and 29 points and 12 rebounds against Connecticut. And in his Carrier Dome finale, he had 27 points and 13 rebounds in an 89–87 victory against the hated Georgetown Hoyas in front of 33,015 spectators.

"Derrick could shoot the ball and handle the ball and rebound the ball," said teammate and fellow SU hoops legend Stevie Thompson. "He was a multi-skilled player. When he came to play—I don't care if it was Alonzo Mourning or Dikembe Mutombo or Jerome Lane—[Coleman] could dominate. Nobody could stop him."

Coleman would leave SU as one of its greatest players…and one of its most controversial. As a sophomore, he was at the heart of an ugly brawl with Cornell. And as a junior, he was involved in a fight on campus and a break-in. He wound up pleading guilty to two non-criminal misdemeanors. As Waters wrote in his book,

Derrick Coleman (44) stuffs one in the basket against Indiana as Sherman Douglas looks on during NIT action at New York's Madison Square Garden on Wednesday, November 23, 1988. (AP Photo/Ron Frehm)

"That's one side of him. But there's another side to this complex person. What other NBA superstar owns a home in the same inner-city neighborhood where he grew up? What other NBA superstar ponied up $2 million of his own money to build a playground in that same neighborhood when the city couldn't find the funds? And what other NBA superstar painted that park blue and orange in homage to his alma mater?"

Coleman enjoyed a very good NBA career, averaging 16.5 points and 9.3 rebounds per game in 15 seasons. But there was always a sense that it could have been so much better had he been more focused and not suffered a number of injuries. A *Sports Illustrated* reporter once wrote, "Coleman could have been the best power forward ever. Instead he played just well enough to earn his next paycheck."

Coleman's legacy at SU, though, is secure. On March 6, 2006, his No. 44 jersey was retired in front of a sold-out crowd in the Dome.

The Gait Brothers

During the spring of 1990, when Gary and Paul Gait were helping Syracuse dominate college lacrosse like it had never been dominated before or since, Coach Roy Simmons Jr. was asked to put the other-worldly play of his identical-twin All-Americans into perspective.

"It's like having Magic Johnson," he said. "Only there's two of him."

It was a great analogy because the brothers from British Columbia, Canada, did for lacrosse what Magic had done for the NBA—they helped revolutionize and popularize their game.

And like Magic, they also helped their team win it all...not once, not twice, but three times. The explosion in interest in lacrosse is directly attributable to the flamboyant, innovative style of play created by the Gaits.

"I came on campus as a freshman [in 1988], and everyone was talking about them," said former SU defender Pat McCabe. "I wondered to myself, 'How good could these guys be?' Well, we get out there on the first day and [I realized] how exceptional they were. They were such an unusual package of everything. You saw big guys, fast guys, guys who handled the stick well, but never did you see guys that were the total package of size, speed, intelligence, and flair like they were."

SU won 51 of the 56 games that Paul and Gary played there, including the last 27, while capturing three national championships. Between them, they combined for seven All-American selections, two national Player of the Year awards, two NCAA Final Four MVP awards, and 319 goals and 146 assists, an average of eight points per game. Gary was the more dominant scorer of the two and still holds or shares school records for most goals in a game (nine), a season (70) and a career (192).

Before the arrival of the Gaits, the Orangemen averaged maybe a few thousand spectators per home game. But the Gaits became a huge "gate" attraction as SU averaged more than 11,000 fans per game by their senior year. "The crowd comes to see the Gaits play," Simmons said in 1990. "Many times the crowd leaves when they realize they're out for the rest of the game." Thanks to the Gaits' exploits, the Orangemen were often up by double-digits by early in the second half, and Simmons would show mercy by pulling them out of the game. "If I hadn't taken them out, they would have established records that never would have been broken, but they were great team players and they understood what was important," Simmons said.

Also to his credit, Simmons didn't try to rein in the Gaits' creativity. He was all for their routine behind-the-back passes and shots because they weren't merely fun to watch, they were extremely effective. Of all the derring-do practiced by the Gaits, none received more publicity than the "Air Gait" shot in a May 28, 1988, NCAA semifinal game against Penn in the Carrier Dome. That's when the inventive Gary leaped through the air from behind the net and stuffed the ball under the crossbar.

"He did something no one had seen before," Simmons said. "Watching that shot was like being there the first time someone slam-dunked a basketball." Added stunned Penn goalie John Kanaras, "I don't know what the hell he was doing. I was amazed." It was such an unbelievable move that it was later outlawed because, the rules-makers argued, it's tough enough for a goalie to stop shots in front of him, let alone behind him.

Initially, few coaches in the United States were aware of these two lacrosse phenoms from Western Canada. The Gaits tried out for the Canadian national lacrosse team in 1984. Although they didn't make it, the coach was so impressed with their skills that he immediately called his old friend, Simmons. The SU coach then began vigorously recruiting the twins, and they made the cross-continent trek to central New York. When the Orangemen lost to Cornell in the NCAA tournament their freshman year, the Gaits realized how disappointed Simmons was. Walking off the field, they vowed to him that he would not be disappointed the next three years—and he wasn't.

After graduating from Syracuse, Paul and Gary played integral roles in popularizing professional indoor and outdoor lacrosse in the United States. Their flashy style of play helped the leagues thrive and would continue to grow the sport at all levels. The twins have received numerous accolades for their impact on the game. They have been inducted into several halls of fame and were named to the NCAA's 25-year Anniversary Team. Gary is back at his alma mater coaching the women's lacrosse team, guiding the Orange to multiple Final Four appearances.

23 Syracuse 17, No. 1 Nebraska 9

Perhaps the season-opening wins against Maryland and Northwestern had made them overconfident. Or maybe they were looking ahead to their next game against top-ranked Nebraska. Whatever the reason, the Orangemen clearly lacked focus in their game against Rutgers in the Carrier Dome on September 22, 1984, turning over the ball eight times in a 19–0 loss to a team they were favored to beat by 10 points. The sloppy upset elicited lusty boos from the home crowd; the great expectations for the SU football season had come to a screeching halt. Before leaving the Dome that night, one of the Orangemen grabbed a marker and wrote "19–0" on the cinder-block wall above his locker. He easily could have written "63–7" next to it as a painful, motivating reminder of how badly the Cornhuskers had clobbered Syracuse in Lincoln, Nebraska, the year before.

There was a feeling in the days leading up to the Cornhuskers' first visit to the Dome that Nebraska might even exceed that margin of victory in the 1984 meeting between the teams. The wizards of odds in Las Vegas had installed No. 1 Nebraska as 24-point favorites, and *Sports Illustrated* splashed a photo of the Cornhuskers on its cover, calling them "The Big Red Machine."

Although his team had won 24 consecutive regular season games, Nebraska coach Tom Osborne was wary of the Orangemen. "We beat them badly last year," Osborne told reporters. "But as I looked at the films, I realized it was one of those situations where the score wasn't indicative of the game. We had more trouble blocking Syracuse than anybody we played all year. What I'm trying to do is convince you that this isn't going to be a pushover. I'd rather be playing a team coming off a win than a loss. I think it will probably bring out the best in Syracuse."

No one seemed to heed Osborne's concerns, nor did anyone seem to be buying the optimism SU coach Dick MacPherson was selling in Syracuse. While speaking to the media, he didn't sound at all like a man being led to the gallows. "The matchups are there," Coach Mac said. "Their good offense against our good defense. Our offense, which has sputtered, against their pretty good defense. Special teams against special teams. Now we'll play the game and see what happens."

What happened was the most remarkable upset in the more than 100-year history of Syracuse football. Playing with a ferocity and precision sorely lacking the week before, the Orangemen totally dominated the No. 1 team on their way to a 17–9 victory in front of 47,280 shocked spectators. Many of the same fans that had booed SU off the field following the Rutgers debacle were so appreciative that they stormed the field and tried to tear down the goal posts. Up in the press box, Ben Schwartzwalder, who had coached the 1959 team to the national championship 25 years earlier, leaped to his feet when the final gun sounded. "I still can't believe it," he said, chomping on an unlit cigar. "This and the Cotton Bowl win over Texas on New Year's Day 1960… That's the only other win I can remember that compares to this one."

Interestingly, the Orangemen didn't rely on any trick plays, funny bounces, or 99-yard kickoff or interception returns to pull off the upset. They merely lined up and beat the stuffing out of their opponent. "They won it up front, both offensively and defensively," Osborne admitted. "We got banged around pretty good. Football is a physical game, and they were flat-out more physical than we were."

The Cornhuskers came to Syracuse averaging 531 yards per game. But Nebraska was unable to move the ball with any consistency that day against a defense led by All-American defensive end Tim Green, and the Cornhuskers finished with just 214 yards. The Orange forced seven punts, caused two fumbles, intercepted a pass, and stopped Nebraska cold on a crucial fourth-and-1. Osborne, to his credit, didn't blame the absence of injured star running back Jeff Smith for the loss. "I honestly can't say it would have been any different if Jeff played," Osborne said.

Running back Jamie Covington rushed for 99 yards, but the unsung hero for the Orangemen was beleaguered quarterback Todd Norley. The week before he had been jeered off the field after fumbling three times and throwing two interceptions against the Scarlet Knights. He was despondent afterward, but he didn't stay down for long thanks to a pep talk from his always-optimistic roommate, Green. "He joked around and told me that the offense had better do its job against Nebraska because the defense was going to do its job. By Tuesday, I was feeling pretty good about things again," Norley said.

Roughly five minutes into the third quarter, Norley and wide receiver Mike Siano connected on one of the most dramatic passes in SU history—a play that ultimately doomed the mighty Cornhuskers. Although Nebraska defensive end Scott Strasburger was boring in on him like a raging bull, Norley stood his ground and lofted a pass 40 yards downfield toward the end zone. Siano went up over two defenders, caught the ball at the 1-yard line, and fell into the end zone for what would prove to be the winning score.

"I'm sorry I didn't get a chance to see it," Norley joked afterward. "I was lying flat on my back as a result of the hit. But I could hear the crowd. I knew something good had happened."

Norley wrenched his knee on the play and had to be helped off the field. Few in the crowd expected him to return, but he did and though his stats (9-of-18, 106 yards) weren't gaudy, they were good enough. SU iced the win late in the fourth quarter on running back Harold Gayden's 1-yard touchdown run.

In the joyous locker room afterward, Green hugged Norley and bellowed above the din, "This is why I came to Syracuse. I wanted to be able to experience moments like this one." The Orangemen finished 6–5. Three years later, they went 11–0–1 and finished No. 4 in the final Associated Press poll. The upset of Nebraska proved to be a watershed moment for the program. "It showed," Green said, "that we could go toe-to-toe with the big boys."

24 The Manley Zoo

Interestingly, a building that opened in 1962 to enhance the SU football program wound up enhancing the basketball program even more.

Manley Field House, named after benefactor George Manley, was constructed to provide the nationally ranked Orange football team with an indoor facility for bowl preparations in December when the weather became too rainy or snowy to use chewed-up outdoor practice fields. But at the urging of then-Syracuse basketball coach Fred Lewis, and with the blessing of athletic director Lew Andreas, the arena with the dirt floor also became the home of SU hoops. A raised basketball court was purchased, and bleachers that could accommodate crowds up to 8,000 were brought in.

"It wasn't exactly the Taj Mahal," recalled Lewis. "But it wound up being a much more impressive venue than the War Memorial [in downtown Syracuse] or the New York State Fair Grounds or any of the small gyms we had on campus. It made recruiting easier, especially after we got things going and started drawing some decent crowds."

It wasn't long before the building known as "The Zoo" became one of the most intimidating places to play in all of college basketball—a real pit. In 18 seasons there, Syracuse went 190–28, which included a 57-game home-court win streak. From 1971 until that final loss to Georgetown in 1980, when Hoyas coach John Thompson proclaimed the place officially closed, Syracuse lost only five of 126 games.

A zoo, of course, is a place that houses wild animals, and many who attended basketball games at Manley in the 1960s and 1970s behaved as if they belonged in one. They sat so close to the court that they could smell what the player ate during the pregame meal. They were SU's sixth man times several thousand.

"I'd say the Zoo was worth an 8- to 10-point advantage," said Syracuse native and former St. Bonaventure coach Jim Satalin, who took several teams to Manley. "There were teams that were frightened to play there because the fans were so intimidating. Plus, Syracuse always seemed to play with supreme confidence there. It was the toughest place I ever brought a team to."

Although the Carrier Dome has hosted crowds nearly four times the size of Manley's biggest crowd (roughly 9,500), coaches, players, and referees say the smaller venue was vastly more intimidating. "There's no comparison," said Gene Monje, a long-time college basketball official who worked numerous games there. "Manley was 10 times tougher to work than the Dome. At Manley, people were close enough that they could touch you if they wanted to."

Verbal barbs weren't the only things tossed at the opposition. "There was this one game when my assistant, Billy Kalbaugh, got plunked with a softball on the shoulder," Satlin said in an interview with the Rochester (NY) *Democrat & Chronicle* in 2000. "We laugh about it now, but it wasn't so funny then. That could be a tough crowd. They could take your mind off the game."

SU Hoops Homes

Venue	Years
Archbold Gymnasium	1908–47, 1952–55
New York State Fairgrounds	1947–52
Onondaga War Memorial	1951–52, 1955–62
Manley Field House	1962–80
Carrier Dome	1980–present

Roy Danforth, who coached Syracuse in those days, didn't care for any orange-tossing or the occasional vulgarity by the crowd. Before a game against Bucknell in 1974, he asked the student section to keep the obscenities and projectiles in check. "I told them that if we got up by 50, I would lead them in cheers," he said. He never thought he would have to pay up. Late in the game, Syracuse went up by 40 and the students began chanting, "We want Roy!"

"I'm thinking I'm safe because I'm substituting freely, and there is no way our lead is going to get any bigger," he said. But Syracuse's subs were better than Bucknell's starters and, sure enough, the Orangemen increased their lead to 50. The chants became louder. During a timeout, a student walked over and tapped Danforth on the shoulder. "He tells me, 'You made a promise,' and I say, "There's no way I can get up and lead you guys in cheers because that would be rubbing it in,'" Danforth recalled. "He says, 'We students thought you were a man of your word.'" So Danforth reluctantly rose from his seat during the next time out, walked past Bucknell coach Jim Valvano to the student section, and led them in a few cheers. Valvano was incensed. In his autobiography years later, Valvano said the worst defeat he ever suffered was the time he was beaten by Syracuse and the Zoo. "Jimmy laughed about it years later, but I felt badly about it at the time," Danforth said. "I had painted myself into a corner. I had promised my fans."

There were many other strange nights at Manley but perhaps none stranger than the night the priest from Niagara University got the thumb. "The priest was giving me the choke sign, so we had no choice but to eject him," said Monje, who eventually worked NCAA tournament games and several Final Fours. "Frank Layden was coaching Niagara at the time, and he comes storming at me. 'Christ, Gene, you can't throw out the priest.' The sweat is pouring down my face. Layden grabs a chair and sits on the court. We tell him the priest has got to leave or the game will be a forfeit, and Danforth starts yelling, 'You can't forfeit it. We've got 8,000 people here.' We finally worked something out where the priest was able to stay but was nowhere near the bench."

The most painful game for the Manley faithful occurred on February 12, 1980, when Georgetown defeated SU 52–50 to snap the Orangemen's 57-game home-court win streak. That was the night when Thompson made his pronouncement, which launched a rivalry that would become as intense as any in college sports. In reality, though, that game wouldn't be the last played by SU there. A scheduling conflict with the football team resulted in the Orangemen playing a preseason NIT game there on November 16, 1994, which they lost 111–104 in overtime to George Washington University.

Carmelo Anthony

Carmelo "Melo" Anthony had created the type of buzz not felt on the SU campus since the arrival of Pearl Washington in 1983, nearly two decades earlier. Senior guard Kueth Duany was excited, too, but he wanted to see firsthand if the hype was justified. So not long after meeting the highly touted freshman from Baltimore, they headed to Manley Field House for an impromptu pickup game with several other players. Known for his ability to shut down the opposition's top scorer, Duany paired up against Melo. The rookie wound up schooling the veteran. "Let's just say I came away impressed with how developed his game was," Duany said, chuckling at the memory. "I couldn't wait to see our opponents try to stop him."

As it turned out, they would have about as much success as Duany had. The 6'8" forward with the sublime scoring skills and the incandescent Magic Johnson smile, would go on to average a double-double for the season (22 points and 10 rebounds per game) and earn consensus All-American and national Freshman of the Year honors while leading the Orange to their first NCAA basketball title. Anthony stayed for only one season before leaving for the NBA, but that proved long enough to make a memory that would last a lifetime.

Like Duany, Jim Boeheim knew Anthony was going to be a special player the first time he laid eyes on him in 2001. SU assistant Troy Weaver had caught Melo's extraordinary act before other college coaches did and convinced his boss to do something he rarely did—make a long, in-season recruiting trip. Anthony was a junior at Towson (Maryland) Catholic High School at the time, and Boeheim grudgingly agreed to accompany Weaver to see him play.

"Coach told me, 'Troy, this better be worth my time and trouble,'" Weaver recalled. "I assured him it would be as worth-while a recruiting trip as he ever made. After watching Melo for just five minutes, Coach turned to me and said, 'This kid is the best player in the country.'"

From that point on, Syracuse heavily recruited Anthony, and he accepted a scholarship offer shortly after transferring to national high school powerhouse Oak Hill Academy in Mouth of Wilson,

Virginia, before his senior year. "I committed because I didn't want the stress of recruiting to take away from my enjoyment of my senior year," Anthony explained. "I had transferred to Oak Hill to get my academics in order and to play against the best competition possible. Syracuse seemed the perfect place for me. I figured it didn't get much bigger than Syracuse when it comes to college hoops, so why wait?"

Anthony had a monster season for Oak Hill, averaging 21.7 points and 7.4 rebounds per game to earn McDonald's, *Parade*, and *USA Today* All-America honors. For a brief time, after all the accolades had poured in, Anthony considered eschewing SU's scholarship offer to turn pro. But his mother was adamantly opposed to that idea.

"In hindsight, I am so, so glad I listened to her because my time in Syracuse wound up being one of the greatest experiences of my life," he said.

Anthony wasted no time delivering a glimpse of the greatness to come. His first college points came on a rim-rattling dunk early in a nationally televised game against Memphis in Madison Square Garden on November 14, 2002. Although SU would lose 70–63, Anthony established a new school scoring record for freshman with 27 points. His equally precocious freshman teammate, Gerry McNamara, chipped in with 14, so there was a feeling that the unranked Orange might surprise a lot of people. Syracuse won its next 11 games as Anthony averaged 23.2 points. There were times when Boeheim couldn't help but marvel at Melo's man-against-boys performances. "You could be from another planet and not know a thing about basketball and see that he was far and away better than the other nine guys on the court," Boeheim raved. "Some stretches, he was unguardable."

Interestingly, Melo's numbers in the early rounds of the NCAA tournament (17 points, 8.8 rebounds per game) were down slightly from the regular season as opposing teams focused extra

Carmelo Anthony (15) drives past Texas' Brandon Mouton (3) during the Men's NCAA Final Four semifinal on Saturday, April 5, 2003, in New Orleans. Anthony led Syracuse with 33 points to defeat Texas 95–84 to advance to the final against Kansas. (AP Photo/Al Behrman)

attention on him. Despite the drop-off in his production, SU still managed to reach the Final Four. Before the semifinals against third-ranked Texas, Boeheim pulled Anthony aside and told him it was his time to shine and that he needed to assert himself more against the favored Longhorns and carry SU on his shoulders. The All-American forward responded to his coach's charge with a vengeance, scoring 33 points on 12-of-19 shooting from the floor and hauling in 14 rebounds as the Orangemen won 95–84.

Late in the Texas game, Anthony wrenched his back. Treatment before the championship game against Kansas helped alleviate the pain and stiffness, but there was a danger it could flare up again. Based on Anthony's huge performance, Boeheim knew the Jayhawks would be devoting extra attention to him underneath, so he advised Melo to be prepared to kick it back out early to McNamara. The strategy worked to perfection as Melo became a playmaker and McNamara drained six first-half threes. That opened things up for Anthony in the second half. He had an extraordinary game—just missing a triple-double with 20 points, 10 rebounds, and seven assists—as the Orange defeated Kansas 81–78 in the Louisiana Superdome in New Orleans.

What made the performance even more impressive was that Anthony played with a back so tight that, by the second half, he could barely bend over to tie his shoes. Despite the limitations, he gutted it out for 37 minutes. "You spend a lifetime dreaming of playing on a stage like this," he explained afterward. "There was no way I was coming out of that game until the final buzzer sounded."

At a teary-eyed press conference, just 17 days after winning the national championship, Anthony announced that he was leaving school to play in the NBA. "I never for one moment tried to talk him out of it," Boeheim said. "In my mind, it was the right decision. He's ready to go."

During the press conference, Anthony mentioned how he wanted to repay his mom for her years of love and sacrifice, and an NBA contract would help him do just that. He said he was somewhat torn about his decision. "I was still uncertain until about 15 minutes before the press conference started," he said. "I loved Syracuse University, I loved my teammates and Coach Boeheim. But like coach told me, you've accomplished in one year everything a college player could hope to accomplish. But no matter how long I play this game, nothing will ever top the feeling of winning the national championship. That was as good as it can ever get."

Two months later, the Denver Nuggets drafted Anthony third overall, and he would go on to become a perennial All-Star with them and his current team, the New York Knicks. He led the league in scoring during the 2012–13 season and won Olympic gold medals with the United States basketball team in 2008 and 2010.

He returned to campus on September 24, 2009, to participate in the ribbon-cutting ceremonies at the $19 million Carmelo K. Anthony Basketball Center. He got the ball rolling on the project by donating $3 million, the largest single donation ever made by a former SU athlete. "For Carmelo to step up like he has, it just means the world to me personally," Boeheim said. "I told him when we won the national championship that he didn't have to do anything else for me ever again. The reason we have this [state-of-the-art] building is because Carmelo did this."

Myer Prinstein

If Olympic medals are the measure, then Myer Prinstein laps the competition as the greatest track & field athlete in Syracuse history. A superb long and triple jumper, Prinstein won four gold medals and a silver in three Olympiads—the 1900 Games in Paris, the 1904 Games in St. Louis, and the 1906 Games in Athens. He twice established world records in the running broad jump (the forerunner to the long jump) and captured several national Amateur Athletic Union and intercollegiate titles.

Born in Russian-ruled Poland, Prinstein and his family immigrated to New York City in 1883 and moved to Syracuse not long after. He began attending SU in 1897, and though he was small in stature—5'11", 145 lbs.—he had springs for legs. His leaping ability enabled Prinstein to play on some of SU's early basketball teams, but track & field was his first love, running sprints and relays, pole-vaulting, hurdling, high-jumping, long-jumping, and triple-jumping.

After winning the IC4A national title in the spring of 1900, Prinstein set his sights on Paris and the second Olympic Games of the modern era. But he and three of his SU teammates were in danger of not being able to compete because they couldn't afford the transatlantic journey. Fortunately, an oil baron rescued them with an offer to ride on one of his tankers. It worked out well because the big ship afforded plenty of room for training as they crossed the ocean.

Prinstein was shooting for gold in both the broad jump and the hop, step, and jump (now known as the triple jump). And he most likely would have achieved his goal if officials from Methodist-affiliated universities (which included SU at the time) had not restricted their athletes from competing on Sunday, the Christian Sabbath. Prinstein, who was Jewish, was leading the broad-jump competition after the qualifying rounds on Saturday. Grudgingly, he agreed, like most of the American athletes, to comply with the university's rules and sit out the final round on Sunday.

His chief competition, Alvin Kraenzlein from the University of Pennsylvania, took six unchallenged jumps on Sunday, even though he was Christian and reportedly had made an agreement

Orange Olympians

Nearly 40 SU student-athletes have earned spots on Olympic teams. That figure includes seven international students who've competed for teams other than the U.S.

The Orange men and women have done quite well, acquiring gold, silver, and bronze medals through the years. The unofficial medal count through the 2014 Winter Olympics is 12 golds, six silvers, and two bronze.

Track and field standout Myer Prinstein leads the way with four golds. Carmelo Anthony (basketball), Charlie Reidpath (track & field), and Ray Barbuti (track & field) have two golds apiece, while Anna Goodale (rowing) and Al Woodring (track & field) have one gold medal each.

Jim Boeheim was an assistant on the U.S. basketball team that won gold during the 2008 and 2012 Summer Olympics, and he is scheduled to work his third Olympiad in 2016. Tom Coulter, who lettered in boxing, track, and cross country at SU in the 1950s, coached the 1988 U.S. Olympic boxing team to eight medals, including three golds. Former Orange oarsman Drew Harrison coached the Olympic rowing teams of Canada in 1984 and '88 and Japan in 1992 and '96.

Ice hockey player Stefanie Marty is SU's first Winter Olympian. She skated for Switzerland in the 2010 Vancouver Games and 2014 Sochi Games, and she helped the Swiss win a bronze medal in Russia.

with Prinstein that he would not compete. Kraenzlein topped Prinstein's best jump by a quarter of an inch to capture the gold. Angry over the betrayal, Prinstein challenged his rival to a jump-off on Monday, but Kraenzlein refused. Depending on whose account you believe, Prinstein either punched Kraenzlein in the face or was restrained from doing so. The next day, Prinstein won gold in the hop, step, and jump, outdistancing 1896 champion James Connolly to establish a new Olympic record.

Not long after graduating with a law degree in 1902, Prinstein moved to Jamaica, Queens, and continued his track-and-field career by joining the Irish American Athletic Club. He won gold in both the triple and long jumps at the 1904 Olympics and a gold in the long jump at the Summer Games in Athens two years later. He also competed in two sprint events at the St. Louis Games, finishing fifth in both the 60- and 400-yard dashes.

He retired from track after Athens in order to concentrate on his law practice and businesses. In 1925, he died of a heart ailment at age 46. Prinstein was inducted into the International Jewish Sports Hall of Fame in 1982, the USA Track & Field Hall of Fame in 2000, and the Greater Syracuse Sports Hall of Fame in 2008. Though his records have long since been surpassed, his 1904 feat of winning the long and triple jumps at the same Olympics—on the same day, no less—has yet to be equaled.

Gene Mills

He was known as "Mean Gene the Pinning Machine," and the nickname fit because in four varsity wrestling seasons at SU, Gene Mills posted a 144–5–1 record, which included an NCAA career-record 107 pins. The New Jersey native captured two national championships in the 118-pound class and became the first athlete in school history to earn All-American honors four consecutive years.

"I used to think that [two-time heavyweight wrestling champ] Jim Nance was the greatest I had here, then Gene came along," said longtime Syracuse wrestling coach Ed Carlin, who coached 34 All-Americans and seven national champions during his tenure. "[Mills] was pound-for-pound the best wrestler I ever saw, and he may have been the best wrestler anybody ever saw."

Mills was every bit as dominant on the global stage, posting a career record of 1,356–46–1 with 866 victories by fall. He won three world titles, including the 1980 Tbilisi, which was hosted by the former Soviet Union and regarded as the most prestigious wrestling tournament of them all. Soviet officials were so impressed with Mills' dominance that they named him the Outstanding Wrestler.

Yet for all the success Mills experienced, he remains haunted more than three decades later by the one opponent he couldn't defeat—President Jimmy Carter. It was a foregone conclusion

Grappling for Success

Ed Carlin had planned on either joining his family's machinery business or teaching physical education after his scheduled graduation from SU in the spring of 1958. But a gaffe by his academic adviser set him on a different path. The adviser mistakenly left out a core course from his schedule, so Carlin was forced to return for an additional semester. While back on campus, his old SU wrestling coach, Joe Scandura, asked him to help out with the team as a graduate assistant. The experience of coaching at the college level convinced Carlin that this was something he'd like to pursue full-time. After several coaching jobs at local high schools and a stint in the military, Carlin returned to his college alma mater as head varsity wrestling coach in 1964.

He held the position for 36 years, compiling a record of 275–184–7 while coaching 42 Eastern champions, 22 All-Americans, and seven national champions. In his final 15 years of coaching, he led the Orange to national top-three finishes 11 times. Two of his national champions were Jim Nance and Art Baker, each of whom would also distinguish themselves as running backs for the Orange football team. Carlin also coached Mike Rotunda, who achieved worldwide fame on the professional wrestling circuit, along with former Orangeman Dick Beyer. Sadly, the program Carlin built into a national power was disbanded in the late 1990s as the athletic department made adjustments to its lineup in order to comply with Title IX requirements. Carlin received numerous accolades, including a Syracuse LetterWinner of Distinction Award, and he was inducted into the College Wrestling Hall of Fame.

that Mills was going to win a gold medal at the 1980 Olympics in Moscow. But Mills' golden dreams never materialized because Carter decided the United States would boycott the Summer Games to protest Russia's invasion of Afghanistan. Mills and other members of the U.S. Olympic team were devastated that politics had poisoned the world of sports.

"What did it wind up accomplishing?" Mills asked in a 2010 interview. "It was meant to punish the Russians, but the only people it wound up punishing were the athletes who had worked a lifetime to get to this point only to have the rug pulled out from underneath them. I know it's not healthy and I know there are a million things more important, but I think about it almost every day. It's business I'll never be able to finish; it's a goal I'll never realize."

Mills was so invincible in international competition leading up to the Moscow games that the U.S. Olympic Committee honored him with its Athlete of the Year award. But that was little solace. Mills returned to SU for his senior season and took out his anger on his opponents, going 35–0 and literally pinning his way through the NCAA tournament to win his second national title. After graduating with a degree in psychology, Mills continued to rule in national and world tournaments. His new goal was the 1984 Olympics in Los Angeles, but he suffered a shoulder injury just before those Games began. A knee ailment prevented him from competing in the 1988 Olympics in Seoul.

With those dreams dashed, Mills decided to devote his energies to helping other wrestlers realize their goals. He returned to his college alma mater to work on his master's degree in physical education and spent 12 years assisting Carlin. He then landed a teaching job at Phoenix High School, north of Syracuse, and took over the wrestling program. Under his guidance, Phoenix has become a small-school wrestling power, winning more than 200 matches and two state championships in the past decade. He also hosts a popular wrestling camp and is a frequent speaker at wrestling clinics across the country. At many of the camps, he's introduced as a former Olympic champ. Although that technically isn't accurate, there's little doubt in most wrestling experts' minds that he would have pinned down the gold had he been allowed to compete.

Hoya Paranoia

Georgetown was just another team on the schedule, and John Thompson was just another faceless coach. However, that all changed on the night of February 12, 1980, in the Manley Field House finale. That evening, a Hoyas upset that snapped second-ranked Syracuse's 57-game home-court win streak, coupled with six salt-in-the-wound words delivered by Thompson in his post-game press conference, ignited a rivalry that would become one of the most torrid in SU and college sports history. Moments after Georgetown spoiled the Manley farewell party for the 9,251 fans who had packed the place, the hulking 6'10" Thompson smiled broadly into the television cameras and announced in that deep baritone of his, "Manley Field House is officially closed."

Neither the Georgetown rivalry nor the fledgling Big East Conference would ever be the same. Thompson had immediately gone from anonymous coach to public enemy No. 1 in Syracuse. "It was almost like fighting words, like 'Remember the Alamo,' or Pearl Harbor—like casting bad remarks at your mother or something," said long-time Syracuse sports information director Larry Kimball.

No one was more stunned than the SU players, especially senior center Roosevelt Bouie, who had never experienced defeat on his home court before. "They came into town and ruined our party," he recalled. "And then Coach Thompson made that statement. That just got people even more riled up. From that point on, whenever he and his team came to town, the crowds really got on him. He became big bad John, the guy they loved to hate."

During the next three decades, the Hoyas and Orangemen would play some of the most memorable games in Big East annals—often in front of 30,000-plus crowds in the Carrier Dome or packed houses at the Verizon Center in Washington, D.C., or at Madison Square Garden in New York City for the annual conference tournament. There was no shortage of star power in the series as the Hoyas relied on big men like Patrick Ewing, Dikembe Mutombo, Alonzo Mourning, and Otto Porter, while the Orangemen often rode the clutch performances of guards such as Pearl Washington, Sherman Douglas, and Gerry McNamara.

At the focal point of the rivalry were the coaches, who started out as mortal enemies but became good friends. "You had two fairly young coaches that were trying to establish their programs as the best program," Boeheim said in a 2013 *Washington Post* interview. "And you're going to have moments and battles in those games that are going to get heated. We had those in the first years. At the end, it really mellowed. We came together, got to know each other off the court. And we became friends at the end of the rivalry when we were still coaching."

Thompson agreed. "There's a difference between competitive dislike and personal respect," he said. "Regardless of what I felt competitively, Jim Boeheim is a hell of a basketball coach…. I have always respected their program and Jimmy. And I never could have admitted it—never would have admitted it. But you want a good opponent. That's what you measure yourself by." Thompson also loved the passion of the SU fans. He reveled in coming to the Dome and playing the role of the villain. "I always had a love-hate thing with Syracuse because of the atmosphere," he said. "It was competitive dislike, but I respected the fans."

Memorable Moments from the Orange
and Hoyas Hoops Rivalry

Big John's Ejection: On March 4, 1990, at the Carrier Dome, Georgetown coach John Thompson was ejected in the first half after being hit with three technical fouls from three different referees. The Hoyas still almost won the game but foolishly fouled Billy Owens at halfcourt with a second remaining. He hit both free throws to send the game into overtime, and the Orangemen won 89–87.

Manley Field House is Officially Closed: On February 12, 1980, the Hoyas upset the second-ranked Orangemen 52–50, snapping a 57-game win streak in the Zoo's final game. SU blew a 14-point lead by missing several free throws down the stretch, and Thompson incited a rivalry with his incendiary postgame remarks.

Pearl Washington's Game-Winner: On January 28, 1985, Washington sank a 15' jumper with 16 seconds remaining as the Orangemen upset the defending national champs and No. 1–ranked team 65–63 in the Dome. That game will also be remembered for Boeheim reprimanding the crowd after a fan rifled an orange off the backboard as Patrick Ewing released his free throw.

Michael Graham's Punch: On March 10, 1984, during the Big East tournament at Madison Square Garden, tempers reached a boiling point and Georgetown's Graham punched SU center Andre Hawkins after the two battled for a rebound. Referee Dick "Froggy" Paparo tossed Graham out of the game but was overruled by fellow ref Jody Sylvester. The Hoyas won the game 82–71, and Boeheim went ballistic in the postgame press conference, tossing a chair.

Syracuse went 38–36 against their rivals in the Boeheim era, capturing the last meeting between the teams as members of the Big East in the 2013 tournament semifinals at the Garden. In typical SU-Georgetown fashion, the game was closely contested and decided by three points in overtime.

The Orange's decision to leave the Big East for the Atlantic Coast Conference brought at least a temporary end to the rivalry, which will resume with a home-and-home series between the schools in 2015–16. "It's not the same when you're not in the same

McNamara's Garden Party: On March 10, 2006, Gerry McNamara continued his Big East tournament heroics, helping the Orange storm back from a 15-point deficit. G-Mac dished off to Eric Devendorf for the winning basket with 9.3 seconds remaining.

Quarterback Donovan McNabb Hoops It Up: On February 8, 1997, Syracuse's All-American quarterback was forced into action after several Orangemen fouled out. McNabb contributed 10 points in a career-high 19 minutes as SU prevailed 77–74 at the Dome.

Patrick Ewing's Haymaker: On March 8, 1985, in the Big East semifinals at the Garden, Ewing elbowed Pearl Washington in the ribs while running down the court, and Washington retaliated shortly after. Ewing then launched a right-handed punch that barely missed hitting Pearl. Georgetown won the basketbrawl game 74–65.

Smith Beats Sherman: On January 24, 1988, at the Carrier Dome, SU's Sherman Douglas hit what appeared to be a game-winning shot with eight seconds to go. But Georgetown's Charles Smith went coast-to-coast and scored the game winner at the buzzer in a 69–68 victory.

Getting the Last Laugh: On March 15, 2013, in the Big East semifinals, Brandon Triche, James Southerland, and Baye Moussa Keita scored 13 points apiece as SU atoned for two regular season losses with a 58–55 overtime victory in the final meeting between the schools as conference opponents.

Another Hoyas' Streak-Snapper: On February 23, 2013, Otto Porter scored 33 points as Georgetown ended SU's 38-game Dome win streak 57–46 in front of a then-record, on-campus crowd of 35,012.

league," Boeheim said. "It will never be the same. At one time, for a 10- or 15-year period, it was probably the No. 1 rivalry in the country, even bigger than North Carolina and Duke. It will be missed and the Big East will be missed because it's what we knew and what we grew up with and what made us. But it was time to move on. It's just the way college athletics has evolved. The memories of Georgetown-Syracuse will last forever in people's minds. People who attended those games will list them as some of the greatest events they ever witnessed."

Larry Csonka

There was nothing complicated about Larry Csonka's running strategy. In fact, it was pretty straightforward—literally and figuratively. "I just run over people," Syracuse's two-time All-American fullback once told a reporter. "I'm not exciting. There's not much excitement in four yards and a cloud of dust. But that's me."

Actually, there was plenty of excitement each time the 6'3", 240-lb. fullback was handed the football because he was known to send tacklers scattering like bowling pins. Defenders eventually managed to bring down the big farm boy from Stow, Ohio, but they paid a price as the "Stow Steamroller" often hit the tacklers harder than they hit him.

"When we replayed the game films for the team on Sunday afternoons, the boys used to sit and cheer Larry," recalled SU coach Ben Schwartzwalder. "I thought he was every bit as exciting as Big Jim [Brown] and Ernie [Davis] and Floyd [Little]. He just was exciting in a different way."

In three varsity seasons, Csonka bulled his way to a school record 2,934 rushing yards. (That record has since been surpassed by Joe Morris, Walter Reyes, and Delone Carter.) Csonka also spent two years teaming with Little, a three-time All-American, to form one of the greatest inside-outside tandems in football history.

"It was pick your poison with those two," said Giants two-time Super Bowl–winning coach Tom Coughlin, who played in the same backfield with Csonka and Little. "One guy had incredible speed and a million moves, and the other guy could bench-press Archbold Stadium and had the only move he needed—straight ahead."

That Schwartzwalder was able to convince Csonka to play for Syracuse was quite a recruiting coup. The Orangemen caught a break when the Zonk said he wasn't interested in playing for the legendary Woody Hayes at Ohio State because he considered the school way too big for his liking. Clemson appeared to have the inside track until Schwartzwalder paid a visit to Csonka's home. When he discovered that Larry's father was a West Virginia native, too, Schwartzwalder laid on the Mountaineer State charm.

"I came out with the old down-home, country talk that we both grew up with," Schwartzwalder said. "And, by golly, it worked."

Larry Csonka crosses the goal line after scoring the first touchdown for Syracuse in the first half on Saturday, November 4, 1967, at Pittsburgh. The scoring play was a 19-yard pass from quarterback Rick Cassata. (AP Photo)

The legendary SU coach loved Csonka's size and physicality so much that he initially had the lad penciled in at middle linebacker for his first two varsity games as a sophomore in 1965. But Schwartzwalder switched Csonka to fullback after starter Ron Oyer was injured. Csonka gained only 26 yards in his first game at the position, but the following week he rushed for 162 yards. Later that season, he set a school record with 216 yards against West Virginia.

"In hindsight, Old Ben blundered by not recognizing how good a

Syracuse's First-Round NFL Draft Picks

Year	Player	Team	Pick No. (Overall)
1957	Jim Brown	Cleveland Browns	6
1960	Roger Davis	Chicago Bears	7
1961	Art Baker	Philadelphia Eagles	14
1962	Ernie Davis	Washington Redskins	1
1967	Floyd Little	Denver Broncos	6
1968	Larry Csonka	Miami Dolphins	8
1969	Art Thoms	Oakland Raiders	22
1973	Joe Ehrmann	Baltimore Colts	10
1980	Art Monk	Washington Redskins	18
1986	Tim Green	Atlanta Falcons	17
1988	Ted Gregory	Denver Broncos	26
1990	Rob Moore	New York Jets	1*
1996	Marvin Harrison	Indianapolis Colts	19
1998	Tebucky Jones	New England Patriots	22
1998	Donovin Darius	Jacksonville Jaguars	25
1999	Donovan McNabb	Philadelphia Eagles	2
2000	Keith Bulluck	Tennessee Titans	30
2001	Will Allen	New York Giants	22
2002	Dwight Freeney	Indianapolis Colts	11
2012	Chandler Jones	New England Patriots	21
2013	Justin Pugh	New York Giants	19

Supplemental Draft

fullback Larry was," Schwartzwalder said. "He should have been there from the get-go. Fortunately, that mistake only lasted two games."

Csonka finished that season with 795 rushing yards and four touchdowns. In 1966, he rushed for 1,012 yards and seven scores as he and Little both earned All-American honors. Little graduated after that season as did several prominent starters on the offensive line, including All-American tackle Gary Bugenhagen. Csonka would be counted on to carry the load by his lonesome, and he was up to the challenge. He lugged the ball a school record 261 times for 1,127 yards and eight touchdowns as SU won eight of 10 games, including a convincing 32–14 victory against fourth-ranked UCLA in the Los Angeles Coliseum. Csonka was named a consensus All-American and the top player in the East.

The following spring, he was drafted in the first round by the Miami Dolphins and would go on to have a stellar career, rushing for 8,081 yards and 64 touchdowns in 11 seasons. He was selected to the Pro Bowl five times and was voted the most valuable player in Super Bowl VIII after rushing for 145 yards and two touchdowns. Like Brown and Little, Csonka earned induction into both the college and pro football halls of fame and had his number retired by the Miami Dolphins and Syracuse. Interestingly, Csonka was asked if he wanted to wear No. 44 after Little graduated, but he decided to stick with No. 39. It would later be worn with distinction by Reyes, who wound up moving past Csonka into second place on SU's all-time rushing list in 2004.

30 Grab a Slice of Pizza at the Varsity

Neither his sons nor grandsons know how Jerry Dellas ended up in Syracuse shortly after emigrating from Greece in 1923, but he did. And like many immigrants, Dellas arrived in the land of opportunity with not much more than the clothes on his back and a dream.

His dream was to own his own restaurant. And after three years of selling popcorn and candy from a cart near the SU campus, he had saved up enough money to make that dream come true. Dellas purchased a house across the street from where he'd been a vendor and converted it into a restaurant and coffee shop called the Varsity. In time, the popular pizza joint on South Crouse Avenue, three long blocks down the hill from the Carrier Dome, became an integral part of the Orange sports experience. Owned and operated by Jerry Dellas' grandsons, the Varsity remains a must-stop destination on SU football and basketball game days.

It's a place where they serve up slices of pizza—and history. The side walls above the booths are festooned with enormous black-and-white photographs of great moments in SU sports—one of them is even signed by former SU coach Dick MacPherson.

On the back wall, just above the main cafeteria-like serving area, there are rectangular banners of each of SU's football opponents. During the 1959 season, a tradition was started where an Orangeman would show up after a victory, climb a ladder, and turn the banner upside down as the patrons went wild. That year they turned every banner upside down because the Orange went 11–0 to win the national championship. That tradition continues today, and a new tradition recently began where the banners of basketball opponents are turned upside down. Those banners hang from the top of the side walls because there are three times as many hoops

Real Men, Women, Sons, and Daughters Wear Orange

If you're shopping for Syracuse University apparel, Marshall Street is the place to go. The two staples are Manny's, which has been around since 1947, and Shirt World, which is owned by former SU placekicker Dave Jacobs, who still holds the school record for the longest field goal, at 58 yards. Both stores are overflowing with Syracuse-related clothing, including T-shirts, sweatshirts, baseball caps, jackets, sweaters, pants, boxers, socks, ties, belts, baby clothes, etc. The stores also have all sorts of SU ephemera—everything from Otto the Orange stuffed animals to coffee mugs to Nerf footballs to posters to license-plate holders. There are thousands of items from which to choose. Among the most popular sellers are Orange T-shirts with blue lettering proclaiming Real (fill in the blank) Wear Orange.

About a block away from Manny's and Shirt World is the SU Bookstore in the Goldstein Student Center. It's open to the public, and you'll find a huge variety of Syracuse apparel and other items there, as well. There's also a souvenir store and a number of temporary booths in the Carrier Dome, but the variety is much more limited.

games to chronicle. For many years, members of the SU football team worked part-time jobs at the Varsity, baking pizzas, busing tables, and pouring sodas. Among those who played for the varsity and worked at the Varsity was three-time All-American running back Floyd Little.

The restaurant has undergone numerous renovations and menu changes through the past nine decades to keep up with the changing demands of students. But in many respects, the place remains the same. Like the Hall of Languages and Crouse College, it's an enduring symbol of tradition and stability on the Hill.

The Varsity and Cosmos—a small but popular pizza/burger shop a half-block away—are the longest-surviving eateries in a Marshall Street area that has seen considerable turnover. Because SU is a congested, urban campus, parking is at a premium and tailgating is often restricted to small lots on and around the university. M-Street becomes an epicenter on game days (though the quad on campus is also a beehive of activity during football Saturdays.) Faegan's Café & Pub is just a few doors down from the Varsity and offers a greater variety of drink and food than the pizza parlors and other fast-food joints on M-Street. Many people also like to tailgate at the Syracuse Sheraton Inn and Conference Center, which is at the opposite end of M-Street. On football Saturdays, the front drive to the hotel is cordoned off for block parties, featuring live bands and outdoor bars.

31 Michael Owens' Clutch Two-Pointer

Although he wore the legendary No. 44 in football and once rushed for more than 1,000 yards in a season, Michael Owens' SU athletic career was dwarfed by his younger, basketball-playing brother, Billy. But Michael did score one two-pointer that even Billy couldn't match. In fact, it might be the most unforgettable and important two-pointer in Orange sports annals, and it occurred on the football field rather than the basketball court.

With 10 seconds remaining in a game with West Virginia on November 21, 1987, in the Carrier Dome, the elder Owens took a pitchout from quarterback Don McPherson and scampered around the left end into the end zone and into the hearts of SU football fans forever. The conversion gave the Orangemen a heart-pounding, jaw-dropping 32–31 victory and preserved the second unbeaten season in Syracuse football history.

"It's a miracle," bellowed offensive coordinator George DeLeone amid the bedlam that erupted on the floor of the Dome after the final gun sounded. "This is incredible," said McPherson after the Orangemen improved to 11–0. "When I came here, we

The Unbeaten 1987 SU Football Team

Led by consensus All-American quarterback and Heisman Trophy runner-up Don McPherson, the Syracuse football program went 11–0–1 in 1987, the only blemish a disappointing tie vs. Auburn in the Sugar Bowl.

That season would mark the beginning of 15 consecutive winning seasons that would include 12 bowl invitations. One of the highlights would come on October 17, 1987, when they clobbered Penn State 48–21 for their first victory over their Eastern rivals since 1970. SU finished fourth in both the Associated Press and coaches' polls. Here are the scores from that memorable season:

Syracuse 25, Maryland 11
Syracuse 20, Rutgers 3
Syracuse 24, Miami (Ohio) 10
Syracuse 35, Virginia Tech 21
Syracuse 24, Missouri 13
Syracuse 48, Penn State 21
Syracuse 52, Colgate 6
Syracuse 24, Pittsburgh 10
Syracuse 34, Navy 10
Syracuse 45, Boston College 17
Syracuse 32, West Virginia 31
Syracuse 16, Auburn 16

were 2–9. We wouldn't have dreamed we could go 9–2, let alone 11–0. I'm speechless over all of this."

Syracuse had rolled through its first 10 games almost unchallenged, its closest contest a 24–13 victory at Missouri in the first week of October. Before the game with the Mountaineers kicked off, the sixth-ranked Orangemen were aware that officials from the Sugar Bowl were in town, ready to present them with an invitation to their New Year's Day game. But West Virginia could care less about rankings and bowl bids. With precocious freshman quarterback Major Harris leading the way, the Mountaineers were looking to spoil SU's perfect season and its outside shot at a national championship, battling the Orangemen like no other team had during the 1987 season. The 31 points represented one-fifth of the total points Syracuse allowed during the entire regular season, and the Mountaineers gained 267 yards on the ground against a defense that had been allowing barely 100 per game.

For the first time all year, Syracuse found itself trailing heading into the final quarter. Despite the Orangemen twice rallying to tie the game, the Mountaineers responded each time to regain the lead, the last rally coming with 1:32 left to play when Undra Johnson scored on a 10-yard run for a 31–24 advantage. But as SU coach Dick MacPherson would say afterward, it wasn't going to be enough, not against this magnificent Syracuse team. "I think they're still in a state of shock," Coach Mac said of the Mountaineers. "I think they realize they played a team of destiny tonight."

Up until that point, it had not been a particularly good night for McPherson, the All-American quarterback who had thrown a career-high four interceptions after having been picked off just seven times in his previous 10 games. But he would redeem himself during that final drive, which started at the SU 26. McPherson completed a six-yard pass to Owens, then a 23-yard laser to Deval Glover that put the ball on the West Virginia 45 and brought the crowd of 49,866 to its feet with 57 seconds remaining. After an incompletion, Glover came free again and hauled in a twenty-yard pass to the 25. McPherson then hooked up with tight end Pat Kelly for eight yards. After an incompletion in the direction of fullback Daryl Johnston, the clock stopped with 15 ticks to go and Syracuse staring at a third-and-2 from the 17.

"Don looked at me in the huddle and said, 'Shake your man, I'm coming to you,'" said Kelly, who would go on to play several seasons in the NFL. "It's probably the biggest thing anybody has said to me in all my years in athletics." The 6'5" Kelly did as McPherson instructed and made an over-the-shoulder grab for a touchdown that reduced the deficit to one point.

Coach Mac didn't need the sellout crowd to urge him to go for the win instead of the tie. "There was never any doubt we were going for it," he said. "I gathered the offense on the sidelines [after West Virginia went ahead on Johnson's touchdown] and set up what we wanted to do. One of the things I told them was that we were going for two after we scored. We were going for the national championship."

McPherson checked the defense at the line and called a play that had SU running toward the short side of the field. "I wanted the ball, believe me," said Owens, who was only playing because starting tailback, Robert Drummond, had been injured in the third quarter. "I figured Donnie was going in himself in that situation. Then I saw the two guys were going to stop him and I knew I was getting it. I was going to do whatever it took to get that ball into the end zone. I was thinking about 11–0, and when I crossed that goal line I thought, *It's ours.*"

It was indeed theirs. The Orangemen had secured their first unbeaten season since 1959, and Owens had a two-pointer that even his famous little brother couldn't match.

Gerry McNamara

Gerry McNamara was well aware what was at stake when he and his humbled SU teammates arrived in New York City for the 2006 Big East Conference basketball tournament. The Orangemen had stumbled badly down the stretch, losing four straight and nine of their last 13 to finish the regular season at 19–11. G-Mac realized that if they wanted to earn an NCAA tournament bid, they'd probably have to do something that had never been done before—win four games in four days to win the Big East championship. And they'd have to do so with McNamara playing through a stress fracture in his groin that had been hampering him for months.

Not that he needed it, but the 6'1" guard arrived in the Big Apple with a little extra motivation. An anonymous survey of 15 Big East assistant coaches had just been published by the *Syracuse Post-Standard*, and it listed G-Mac as the top vote-getter in the category of the conference's "most overrated player." The balloting caused him to do a slow burn, but he decided to respond to it with actions on the court rather than words off of it.

In the first-round game against Cincinnati, McNamara tallied 17 points, nine assists, and three steals, plus he hit a three-pointer with a half-second remaining to give the Orange a one-point win. However, the dramatic shot was overshadowed by his coach's profanity-laced, impassioned defense of G-Mac in the postgame press conference.

"I have to laugh a little bit when our own paper is calling him [expletive] overrated," Jim Boeheim told the assembled media. "They actually listened to a couple of assistant coaches who I guarantee you will never be head coaches if they think Gerry McNamara is overrated. Without Gerry McNamara, we wouldn't have won 10 [expletive] games this year, okay? Not 10. The other guys just aren't ready. They needed him. Without him there, not 10. We wouldn't be here to even have a chance to play this game. And everybody's talking to me and writing about Gerry McNamara being overrated? That's the most [expletive] thing I've seen in 30 years."

McNamara said he appreciated his coach's defense of him, but G-Mac himself had no comment on the survey, saying he preferred to let his play speak for him. Over the next three days, it would speak volumes. The following day against a Connecticut team ranked No. 1 in the nation, G-Mac hit a three to send the game into overtime and handed out 13 assists as Syracuse upset the

Gerry McNamara (3) drives past Georgetown's Jeff Green (32) during the second half in the semifinal round of the Big East Men's Basketball Championship on March 10, 2006. Syracuse won the game 58–57.
(AP Photo/Frank Franklin II)

Huskies 86–84. In the semifinals against Georgetown, McNamara overcame a poor first half with 15 points after intermission. During the final 52 seconds, he nailed a three to cut the deficit to one point, assisted on Eric Devendorf's go-ahead basket, and forced a turnover with 1.5 seconds remaining to seal a 58–57 win. McNamara completed his Garden party with 14 points and six assists in a 65–61 victory against Pitt in the championship game. As he held aloft the Dave Gavitt Most Outstanding Player Award following that game, thunderous chants of "Gerry! Gerry! Gerry!" rocked the arena.

"What was really great was seeing all the ex-players there," he recalled years later on Syracuse.com. "There were so many in the Garden for that championship game. And every one of them was on the court at the end. To experience that—with those guys who'd gone through the program, who'd built the program—was so special. It was a pretty overwhelming experience. Plus, with that whole "over-rated" thing, a few people ate their words. That's what I told my father when I saw him—that a few people ate their words that week."

Unfortunately, the G-Mac era came to an abrupt end a week later in a 66–58 loss to Texas A&M in the first round of the NCAAs. The four-games-in-four-days ordeal had taken its toll on McNamara's stress fracture. The injury stifled his quickness and he managed just two points in limited action. He had played in 135 games for Syracuse, starting every one, and had endured a spate of injuries that included sprained ankles, torn rotator cuffs, and the groin stress fracture.

His performance in the Garden would be one of many indelible moments from a career that saw the scrappy kid from Scranton, Pennsylvania, become arguably the most popular player in SU basketball history. He'll forever be remembered for the six threes he hit as a freshman during the first half of the 2003 NCAA title game, which created a lead the Orangemen never relinquished, and for the 43-point outburst in the next year's NCAAs that Boeheim called "as good a performance as I've ever seen in college basketball."

McNamara finished his career as the school's fourth all-time leading scorer with 2,099 points. Only Jason Hart had more steals than G-Mac's 258, and only Sherman Douglas had more assists than G-Mac's 648. He is the school's all-time leader in three-point shots made and free throw percentage (89 percent).

"His legacy is pretty clear-cut to anybody who follows the game of basketball," Boeheim said after G-Mac's last game. "He gives you everything he's got from day one. He was an integral part of us winning the national championship. It wasn't just the Kansas game. It was the Oklahoma State game and every other game we played in the tournament, and leading up to the tournament, that got us the national championship. And winning the Big East tournament [in 2005 and 2006] and winning the regular season title [in 2003]—that's a pretty good legacy. He's won 103 games, and every defense we played this year and really most of last year was geared to trying to stop him. He still made first-team All-Conference both years despite that kind of defensive pressure. I don't think there have been too many players that have had a comparable type of career…. He's a special player. He's a one-of-a-kind kid."

After two years of playing overseas and in the NBA Developmental League, which included an invitation to the Utah Jazz's training camp, McNamara returned to his alma mater and was promoted to full-time assistant in November 2011.

John Mackey

John Mackey repeatedly told friend and teammate Ernie Davis that the reason Mackey wore No. 88 was that he was twice the player that No. 44–wearing Davis was. Mackey, of course, was joking.

He knew Davis, who would win the Heisman Trophy in 1961, was better than he was, but Mackey was awfully good, too. And by the time he was through, No. 88 would also stand for something special.

Mackey had came to Syracuse from Hempstead, New York, as a speedy, rugged, running back who reminded some of another Long Island prospect from several years earlier, Jim Brown. A 6'2", 230-lb. back who was quick and light on his feet, Mackey was such a good athlete that Ben Schwartzwalder and his staff decided to convert him to tight end and defensive line so they could make full use of his size, strength, and speed. In those days, tight ends were almost like third tackles. Their primary role was to block and occasionally catch a short pass. But Mackey's wide-receiver-caliber speed helped revolutionize the position, and the roots of that revolution can be traced to his days at SU.

Mackey caught only 27 passes while playing for the run-oriented Orangemen. But he made the most of each opportunity, averaging 17.8 yards per reception and scoring nine touchdowns. "The coaches started utilizing me like they would a wide receiver, or a split end as we called 'em in those days," Mackey said. "Heck, I was faster than any of our ends and most of our backs, so they would send me on deep stuff or they'd dump it off to me and let me punish people." The SU players loved watching game films of Mackey sending linebackers and defensive backs sprawling. "John would just as soon run over you as run by you," said John Brown, one of Mackey's former teammates. "We liked to have the coaches run the film in slow-motion so we could count the number of tackles John broke on a certain play."

During his junior season in 1961, when he averaged a school record 21.4 yards per reception, Mackey hauled in an option pass from Davis and sprinted 74 yards for a touchdown in a 51–8 thumping of Colgate. The following season against George

Washington University, Mackey touched the football 10 times, producing 161 yards.

Although the Baltimore Colts already had two prolific wide receivers in Raymond Berry and Jimmy Orr, they chose Mackey in the second round of the 1963 draft because they believed he would give quarterback Johnny Unitas a potent third target. They would not regret their selection. Mackey averaged 20.7 yards per catch and scored seven touchdowns during his rookie season, earning an invitation to the Pro Bowl in Los Angeles. By his fourth NFL season, Mackey had completely changed the position, catching 50 passes and scoring nine touchdowns, including six of 50 yards or longer. In 10 seasons, he would score 38 touchdowns and catch 331 passes for 5,326 yards, an average of 15.8 yards per catch. That's a full yard better than wide receiver Jerry Rice, widely regarded as the best receiver in football history. All-Pro tight ends such as Kellen Winslow, Tony Gonzalez, and Rob Gronkowski owe a debt of gratitude to Mackey for blazing a trail for them.

Mackey also revolutionized the game after he was through playing, becoming the first head of the players' union following the 1970 merger of the NFL and AFL. Under his leadership, pensions and benefits improved dramatically and players eventually gained free agency. Sadly, the concussive effects of all that football head-banging exacted a heavy toll on Mackey and his peers. During the later years of his life, Mackey suffered from frontaltemporal dementia and required around-the-clock care. Thanks to the courageous efforts of Mackey's wife, Sylvia, whom he met while they were SU students, the NFL and the union adopted the 88 Plan in 2007, which provides $88,000 per year for nursing home care for former players suffering from dementia or Alzheimer's. The name of the plan pays homage to the number worn by Mackey.

In 2007, four years before his death, Mackey returned to the Carrier Dome to have his jersey retired. He was named the 42nd greatest player by the NFL Network in 2010 and is a member of the Pro Football Hall of Fame. Each year, an award named after him is presented to the top tight end in college football.

34 Otto, The Saltine Warrior, and Other Mascots

After dropping the headdress-wearing Saltine Warrior Indian mascot in 1978 because it was insensitive to local Native Americans, Syracuse University struggled to find an acceptable replacement. About four years after the Warrior was retired, Eric Heath, a former SU cheerleader who dropped out of school to join the Ringling Bros. Clown College, said he sent sketches of a fuzzy orange character with a blue baseball cap and blue arms and legs to school officials, and they accepted his idea.

"The Orange's first appearance was at the opening home football game of 1982, SU vs. Temple," Heath said in an interview with the *Syracuse Post-Standard*. "We built a large box, piece by piece, and then the sides fell away, revealing the new mascot." The 29,574 spectators, many of whom were still angry with the university's decision to retire the Saltine Warrior, appeared underwhelmed.

By the mid-1980s, SU fans were still having a difficult time settling on one mascot. The Orange found itself in competition with a parade of other unofficial candidates, including the Dome Ranger, who dressed in an orange cowboy outfit and blue mask; Dome Eddie, who donned an orange wig and gaudy, over-sized Elton John glasses; and the Beast of the East, who looked like a green monster. Slowly but surely the competition dropped by the wayside, and the Orange began to grow on people. During the summer of 1990, the Orange accompanied the SU cheerleaders to a camp in Tennessee, and the students chosen to suit up in the costume narrowed down the mascot's name to two choices—Opie or Otto. They concluded the name Opie would lead to the inevitable rhyme with *dopey*, so they settled on Otto. Later, word got out that the cheerleaders were calling the mascot Otto, and fans and alumni picked up on it.

Otto the Orange gets the crowd going prior to the Syracuse Orange defeating the Pittsburgh Panthers 14–13 in a Big East matchup at the Carrier Dome in Syracuse, New York, on October 5, 2012. (Cal Sport Media via AP Images)

In February 1995, chancellor Buzz Shaw wanted to resolve the issue of an official mascot once and for all. He appointed an 18-member committee of students, faculty, and staff to recommend a logo and mascot. They narrowed the candidates to a wolf, a lion, and the Orange. The lobbying efforts of the students who acted as Otto convinced Shaw to stick with the Orange, and that December it became the school's official mascot. Thanks in large part to comedic appearances on ESPN commercials, Otto has become a beloved figure among students who several years ago renamed their cheering section Otto's Army.

The history of SU mascots goes back more than 100 years. Early 20th-century team photos of SU football teams showed a dog wearing a leather football helmet. In the 1920s, the four-legged theme continued with Vita the Goat. According to Syracuse University archivists, he was "held in leash by freshman guardians" during the games and often showed up wearing signage such as "Beat Colgate."

Vita eventually gave way to the Saltine Warrior, who was born out of a hoax published in the October 1931 issue of the *Syracuse Orange Peel*, a campus magazine. The story claimed that the remains of a 16th-century Onondagan chief were found in the excavations near Steele Hall on campus three years earlier. Though the story was fictitious, it took on a life of its own, and the legend of the Saltine Warrior, also known as Big Chief Bill Orange, was born. In 1951, the senior class commissioned a statue of the Saltine Warrior to be placed near the "discovery" site. Winning sculptor Luise Kaish arranged for a member of the Onondaga Nation to pose for her statue, which depicts a Native American shooting an arrow toward the sky. The bronze statue has been moved several times, and it now resides on the southeast corner of the quad.

In the mid-1950s, the father of a Lambda Chi Alpha fraternity brother designed a Saltine Warrior costume for his son to wear at football games, thus beginning a long tradition of Lambda Chi

Otto's Army

Duke has the Cameron Crazies, Pitt has the Oakland Zoo, Michigan State has the Izzone, and Syracuse University has Otto's Army.

Founded in 2006 by five enterprising students who devised a seat-assignment system for home games, the Army now features more than 5,000 members who form a sea of orange in the first and upper decks behind the basket nearest to the SU bench at the Carrier Dome. The membership of Otto's Army dwarfs most other school's cheer sections. (For example, it boasts four times as many members as Duke's student section.) It's also different in that its members show up for all SU sporting events, not just one sport, and they travel, albeit in much smaller numbers, to away games.

The group was founded in the days leading up to Gerry McNamara's final home game on March 5, 2006, which attracted an on-campus record crowd (since broken) of 33,633 to the Dome. Seats at any given SU home basketball game are first come, first served, which prompts many students to camp out for days outside the Dome's Gate E, an area known as "Boeheimburg." Before the G-Mac finale, student leaders devised a list system to organize the process of students claiming their seats and help keep them safe by preventing the mad dash that usually occurred before most games. The system worked well for that game, and Otto's Army wound up becoming SU's official student section. The group now has a seven-person executive board and even has a philanthropic division, called Otto's Advance, which raises money through T-shirt sales and has made significant contributions to the Relay for Life and the Jim and Juli Boeheim Foundation.

Like its unofficial predecessor, the Manley Zoo, Otto's Army has a number of standard chants, including "Let's Go Orange," as well as the "Who's He? So What? Big Deal! Who Cares? Big Sh#t!" greetings when the opposition's starting five is announced. The signs they generate for each game can be quite creative and occasionally profane. Each student must wear orange, and some enhance their wardrobes with orange wigs, helmets, caps, and face paint. Big Heads of Boeheim and various players are usually prominently displayed. Otto's Army also saves space for SU's longtime pep band, the Sour Citrus Society, which coordinates music with the students. The school's cheerleaders usually set up in front of the Army.

members serving as mascots. In 1976, Native American students at SU and members of the Onondaga Nation, just 10 miles south of campus, began voicing concerns over the Saltine Warrior. Oren Lyons, an Onondaga Chief and former SU All-American lacrosse goalie, said the mascot lacked dignity and authenticity.

"The thing that offended me when I was there was that guy running around like a nut," Lyons said. "That's derogatory." Chancellor Melvin Eggers agreed. In 1977, Eggers decided to remove the Saltine Warrior as SU's official mascot. The announcement was controversial, and debate filled the student and local newspapers for weeks. Many alumni believed the university had overreacted, but Eggers said the decision was the right one and irreversible. Today, SU offers a Native American Studies minor and has established the Haudenosaunee Promise Scholarship Program, which awards scholarships to applicants of Native American descent who qualify academically.

35 The Powell Brothers

As he watched his older brothers embrace on the field at Byrd Stadium on the University of Maryland campus following Syracuse University's 13–7 victory over Princeton in the 2000 NCAA lacrosse championship game, Mike Powell shed a few tears. Ryan Powell had just completed his SU career by tying the school career scoring record set by brother Casey Powell just two years earlier.

Not long after the brothers' embrace, Ryan climbed into the stands, peeled off his No. 22 jersey, and handed it to Mike. "This is yours now," Ryan said, pointing to the most famous number in college lacrosse. Both Ryan and Casey had contributed to No. 22's legendary status, and in 2001, Mike's freshman season, he would be expected to keep the tradition going. "The Powell legacy doesn't end here," Ryan told a reporter after that championship game. "I'm telling you right now—and Casey will back me on this—Mikey is better than both of us."

As hard as that was to fathom, considering the two brothers had combined to win eight All-American awards and one national title apiece, it turned out to be true. The younger Powell scored 307 points to surpass their career scoring record. He also became the first two-time winner of the Tewaaraton Award (lacrosse's answer to the Heisman) and the first four-time, first-team All-American in Syracuse history. Oh, and he also did his brothers one better by winning two national championships to their one. Mike Powell capped his career in grand style by scoring what proved to be the winning goal in a 14–13 victory against Navy in the 2004 NCAA title game in front of 43,898 at Baltimore's M&T Bank Stadium.

"Ever since I was a kid, I'd dreamed of getting the goal that won the championship," Mike said after the game. "And after all this time, it finally came true. Scoring the last goal of the season. Scoring the last goal of my career. Scoring the game-winning goal. There's nothing better than that."

It put an exclamation point on a family lacrosse story that ranks right up there with the ones written by Roy Simmons Sr. and Jr. and the Gait twins, Gary and Paul. The three Powells combined for 445 goals, 881 points, nine first-team All-American selections, four NCAA championships, five NCAA Player of the Year awards, and six Attackman of the Year awards. "The reason I recruited Casey and Ryan is so I could get Mike," Roy Simmons Jr. liked to joke, even though he was retired by that time and John Desko actually closed the deal to bring the third Powell to SU.

The brothers grew up in Carthage, New York, a bucolic village of 4,000 about 85 miles north of Syracuse. The older brothers became fans of the Gait brothers. The opportunity to be part of

SU's run-and-gun offense and wear the No. 22 Gary Gait had first made famous played a big role in convincing Casey Powell to become an Orangeman. He was up to the challenge of following his idol. He won Player of the Year honors twice while surpassing Gait and every other SU player on the scoring list with 287 points on 158 goals and 129 assists.

There was talk that Ryan didn't want to be in Casey's shadow and was considering scholarship offers from schools such as Loyola. But he also wanted to be able to play close to home so his parents would be able to watch. And, like Casey, he thought SU was the best fit for his fast-paced style of play. Like his brother before him, Ryan won an NCAA Player of the Year award and was a four-time All-American. Fittingly, he also finished with 287 points, with his total coming on 137 goals and 150 assists. Mike took five recruiting visits, including one to the Orangemen's arch-rival Johns Hopkins, but he ultimately decided on SU for the same reasons his brother had.

During Mike's senior year at Carthage High, his brothers often called home to reveal their latest accomplishments with the admonition, "No pressure, Mikey." Mike understood there would be enormous expectations at Syracuse, but in a way, he was used to that already because he was forced to deal with his brothers' legends in high school. "They were great high school players, and I face pressure every day," he said in a June 4, 2000, interview with the *Syracuse Post-Standard*. "I think I'm used to it. But I'm going to have to step it up now because I think the pressure is going to be even bigger after last weekend, with Ryan tying the record."

The third son of Sue and Larry Powell not only lived up to the enormous expectations—he exceeded them as the Powells made opponents sigh "Oh, brother!" times three.

Marty Glickman

Long before he was recognized as the man who started the tradition of Syracuse as Sportscaster U, Marty Glickman made his mark as an athlete. Blessed with blazing speed, Glickman was recruited out of Brooklyn's James Madison High School to run track and play football at Syracuse, where he earned All-American honors as a sprinter and was selected to compete on the U.S. Track & Field team at the 1936 Olympics in Berlin.

Glickman and University of Michigan sprinter Sam Stoller were scheduled to run legs on the 4x100 relay team but were

Ben Johnson (left) of Columbia University, who won the 60-yard dash of the annual Intercollegiate Athletic Association Track and Field Championships, is congratulated by Marty Glickman of Syracuse University, who came in second, on March 13, 1937, in New York. (AP Photo)

Syracuse University's Olympians

Year	Olympian	Sport
1900	Myer Prinstein	Track & Field
1904	Myer Prinstein	Track & Field
1906	Myer Prinstein	Track & Field
1908	Marquis Frank "Bill" Horr	Track & Field
1912	Charlie Reidparth	Track & Field
1920	Al Woodring	Track & Field
1924	Chet Bowman	Track & Field
1928	Ray Barbuti	Track & Field
1936	Marty Glickman	Track & Field
	Ed O'Brien	Track & Field
1956	Siegbert Wirth	Soccer
1980	Gene Mills	Wrestling
	Thomas Darling	Rowing
	William Purdy	Rowing
1984	Jose Betancourt	Wrestling
	Thomas Darling	Rowing
1988	Jason Morris	Judo
1992	Jason Morris	Judo
	Anthony Washington	Discus
	Jose Betancourt	Wrestling
1996	Jason Morris	Judo
	Anthony Washington	Discus
	Miroslav Vucetic	Swimming
	Jose Betancourt	Wrestling
	Jose Gonzalez	Swimming
	Orlando Rosa	Wrestling
2000	Jason Morris	Judo
	Anthony Washington	Discus
	Adrian Woodley	Track & Field
	Sam Okantey	Track & Field
	Djordje Filipovic	Swimming
2004	Boldizsar Kiss	Swimming
	Helen Tanger	Rowing
	Froukje Wegman	Rowing

2008	Carmelo Anthony	Basketball
	Anna Goodale	Rowing
	Helen Tanger	Rowing
2010	Stefanie Marty	Ice Hockey
2012	Shannon Taylor	Field Hockey
2012	Carmelo Anthony	Basketball
2012	Natalie Mastracci	Rowing
2012	Mike Gennaro	Rowing
2014	Stefanie Marty	Ice Hockey

scratched at the last minute because they were Jewish and U.S. officials feared their presence would offend German chancellor Adolf Hitler. Glickman's friend, Jesse Owens, protested the move, even though he was named as one of the replacements and would have an opportunity to win a fourth gold medal at the Games. That dashed dream would haunt Glickman for the rest of his life.

In 1986, he returned to Germany as part of a tribute to Owens, and Glickman had difficulty suppressing his anger. "As I walked into the stadium, I began to get so angry," he wrote in his 1996 autobiography, *The Fastest Kid on the Block*. "I began to get so mad. It shocked the hell out of me that this thing of forty-nine years ago could still evoke anger…. I was cursing…. I was really amazed at myself, at this feeling of anger. Not about the German Nazis…that was a given. But the anger at [Olympic officials] Avery Brundage and Dean Cromwell for not allowing an eighteen-year-old kid to compete in the Olympic Games just because he was Jewish. They took my dream away from me."

Demoralized by the anti-Semitic decision in 1936, Glickman returned to Syracuse where he turned his athletic attention to football. His blazing speed served him well on the gridiron. Starting three seasons at running back and end, Glickman helped the Orangemen rebound from a 1–7 record in 1936 to 5–2–1 and 5–3 records in succeeding years. One of his most memorable games occurred in 1937 when he rushed for more than 100 yards as SU handed Eastern powerhouse Cornell its only defeat of the season. In a 1938 victory against Maryland, Glickman broke free on an 80-yard touchdown run—the sixth longest in school history.

Glickman overcame an early-life stuttering problem by taking speech lessons as a child, and he went on to become one of the most recognizable sportscasters in the United States in the 1950s and 1960s. He was recognized as the voice of the New York (football) Giants, Knicks, Rangers, and Jets. The terminology he used to describe basketball games still lives on six decades later. The key, the lane, the top of the circle, the mid-court stripe, and swish— these terms were all coined by Glickman. He would be most closely associated with the Giants, calling their games from 1948 through 1971, and he later would serve as a broadcasting coach for NBC.

In 1998, sixty-two years after the Berlin Games travesty, U.S. Olympic Committee president William J. Hybl honored Glickman and Stoller with plaques "in lieu of the gold medals they didn't win" in Germany. Hybl said that although there was no written proof that anti-Semitism had been at play during the 1936 Olympics, that was clearly the case. "I was a prosecutor," Hybl said. "I'm used to looking at evidence. The evidence was there."

Glickman died at age 83 on January 3, 2001.

37 Jake Crouthamel

To fully appreciate Jake Crouthamel's impact on Syracuse University athletics, one must journey back to his arrival on campus in March 1978.

At that time, the sports landscape on the Hill was desolate by today's standards. The obstacles he faced were the equivalent of fourth-and-long in football. A standout football player and coach at Dartmouth College who played professionally for the Boston Patriots, Crouthamel realized the future success of Orange athletics would depend on his ability to upgrade deteriorating facilities and resuscitate a football program that was on life support.

Archbold Stadium, the concrete bowl that had been home to SU football for nearly seven decades, had become such an eyesore that coaches stopped showing it to recruits visiting campus. The stadium's antiquated locker room, which was occasionally visited by football-sized rats, was also off-limits to potential student-athletes. With the opening of the Carrier Dome on the site of Old Archie in 1980, Crouthamel recognized the building's potential as a catalyst for an athletic renaissance and acted on it. By the time Crouthamel retired in 2005 after 27 years, his imprint could be seen throughout campus—from the Dome and the additions and renovations at Manley Field House to the Lampe Athletics Complex, the softball stadium at Skytop, and the new Hookway Fields just down the road.

"His fingerprints are on just about everything sports-wise here," basketball coach Jim Boeheim said in a 2005 interview with *Syracuse University* magazine. "He has been about as loyal and significant a figure as any athlete or coach in school history. Jake has done a fantastic job putting not only our athletic programs but the entire university on the map." Boeheim's sentiments were echoed by SU alumnus and ESPN sportscaster Mike Tirico: "Jake is one of the 10 most important people ever at Syracuse. I have the utmost respect for his attention to detail, for his care not only of the basketball and football programs but the Olympic sports, as well."

Crouthamel appreciated the praise, but it also made him squirm. The Perkarsie, Pennsylvania, native was never comfortable in the spotlight, and his disdain for it occasionally was mistaken for aloofness. "It's my belief the credit belongs to the student-athletes

SU Athletic Directors

Director	Years
Murray Stedman	1910–15
Walt Smith	1915–21
Cy Thurston	1921–34
Les Bryan	1934–37
Lew Andreas	1937–64
James Decker	1964–73
Les Dye	1973–78
Jake Crouthamel	1978–04
Dr. Daryl Gross	2004–present

and the coaches who guide them," he said at the time of his retirement. "I didn't score the winning goals. I didn't draw up the winning plays." True enough, but he did lay the groundwork for the athletic program to go from being prominent in the East to being prominent nationally. And he had his work cut out for him when he first took the job.

"When I arrived, virtually everything, with the possible exception of Jim Boeheim and the basketball program, needed attention," Crouthamel said. "The facilities on campus were terribly lacking, and the revenues that resulted from a dramatic increase in attendance at the Carrier Dome enabled us to address those issues fairly quickly." It was Crouthamel who convinced Boeheim to move the men's basketball games from Manley to the Dome. The athletic director anticipated a 2,000- to 3,000-per-game bump in attendance. He never envisioned basketball crowds in excess of 30,000.

One of Crouthamel's greatest strengths was recruiting successful coaches. His most significant hire was Dick MacPherson following the 1980 season. Crouthamel stuck with Coach Mac through some difficult seasons early on and was rewarded in 1987 when the Orangemen went 11–0–1 and began a streak of 15 consecutive winning seasons. After MacPherson left to take an NFL job in 1991, Crouthamel hired Paul Pasqualoni and the winning continued for nearly a decade. Crouthamel was also responsible for the hiring of John Desko after Roy Simmons Jr. retired in 1998, and Desko followed up his predecessor's six NCAA lacrosse titles with five of his own. Crouthamel's progressive thinking paid off again when he teamed with Dave Gavitt to form the Big East Conference, which would become an enormous success, especially in basketball. And Crouthamel helped bolster graduation rates of SU's men's and women's teams by beefing up the department's academic support team.

There were also some down times, too, most notably the NCAA investigations of the basketball and lacrosse programs during the early 1990s (which led to probationary sanctions) and the decision later to drop wrestling and men's gymnastics to meet Title IX requirements instituted to create equal opportunities for women athletes.

"Walt Dodge [gymnastics] and Ed Carlin [wrestling] had been loyal, dedicated coaches who had established their programs nationally," Crouthamel said. "To have to call them in and tell them they were no longer part of the family was not an easy thing to do. But we really had no choice. No one contests the purpose of Title IX legislation. But I don't believe the drafters of the legislation considered the unintended results of Title IX. We were dealing with finite resources and had to add several women's sports. That meant we had to rid ourselves of expenses somewhere else, and unfortunately that led to the elimination of gymnastics and wrestling."

38 Wilmeth Sidat-Singh

His No. 19 basketball jersey hangs in the Carrier Dome, along with ones celebrating the marvelous careers of Jim Brown, Ernie Davis, Dave Bing, Derrick Coleman, and Larry Csonka, among others. But chances are that if you polled Syracuse fans about Wilmeth Sidat-Singh, they'd be stumped. And that's too bad because Sidat-Singh was not only a superb basketball and football player but also a pioneer who lived his short, heroic life with dignity and determination at a time when the color line was prevalent in sports and most facets of American life.

As one of the first African Americans to play quarterback, Sidat-Singh engineered one of the most monumental comebacks in Syracuse history on October 15, 1938. And his exploits on the basketball court proved to be just as impressive as he helped lead the Orangemen to a 42–13 record in his three varsity seasons. Although his accomplishments are memorable, Sidat-Singh is remembered as much for what he wasn't allowed to accomplish because of the color of his skin.

Sidat-Singh's parents were African American. But after the death of Wilmeth's father, Elias Webb, who was a pharmacist, his mother married Samuel Sidat-Singh, a medical student from India who adopted Wilmeth, giving him his family name. Because of his surname and the fact he was light-complected, Wilmeth was thought to be Hindu, a term Americans used to describe Indian natives at the time. Sidat-Singh was an exceptional student and athlete, and after leading DeWitt Clinton High School to a hoops championship in 1934, he received a basketball scholarship from Syracuse.

He had no intention of playing football for the Orangemen until assistant football coach Roy Simmons Sr. watched one of Sidat-Singh's intramural football games during his sophomore year. Simmons couldn't help but notice the quick-footed, pinpoint-passing young man playing quarterback for one of the dormitory teams. Although it was just a game of touch, it quickly became apparent to Simmons' trained eye that Sidat-Singh was as adept with an oblong ball as he was with a round one. After watching the kid deliver one tight spiral after another, Simmons decided to do a little pitching of his own.

"I went over there and stopped the game," Simmons recalled during an interview in the mid-1970s. "I said, 'Singh, you don't belong here. You belong down on that other field [Archbold Stadium] with the varsity. With your ability, you could make the football team, and you could make it with ease." Sidat-Singh, who had played football in high school, was intrigued by what Simmons had to say. The following season he took the coach up on his offer. Neither he nor Simmons would be disappointed.

The greatness that caught Simmons' eye during that touch football game was there for the college football world to see during the final nine minutes of a 1938 clash with upstate rival Cornell at Archbold. With 35,000 spectators looking on during an unusually hot October day, Sidat-Singh led Syracuse to a 19–17 victory by completing six passes for 150 yards and three touchdowns in a six-minute stretch in the fourth quarter.

Grantland Rice, perhaps the most famous sportswriter of all time, was at the game and couldn't help but gush, calling it the most exciting college football contest he had ever covered. Employing the flowery prose of the times, Rice wrote, "A new for-ward-pass hero slipped in front of the great white spotlight of fame at Syracuse today. The phenomenon of the rifle-shot event went beyond Sid Luckman and Sammy Baugh. His name is Wilmeth

Sidat-Singh." Rice's syndicated account of the game was carried in virtually every newspaper in the country. Headline writers had a field day. "Singh's Slings Sink Cornell," read one. "It Don't Mean a Thing If It Ain't Got That Singh," read another. It wasn't merely that SU had upset the top football team in the East, but rather the spectacular manner in which the victory was accomplished that made it such a huge sports story.

That game would be the highlight of his football career and should have opened the door to a career as a professional quarterback. But racist policies did what few opponents on the football field had been able to do—stop Sidat-Singh cold. From 1934 to 1946, the NFL bylaws included a clause banning black players.

Sidat-Singh had become painfully familiar with racial injustice during his college football and basketball careers. A year before Sidat-Singh's heroics against Cornell, Sam Lacy, a prominent African American newspaper reporter, broke the story that the young man was black, not Hindu as his surname suggested. Lacy's blockbuster ran a week before Syracuse was scheduled to play the University of Maryland. Like many schools south of the Mason-Dixon Line, Maryland had a policy of not playing any home games against teams with African American players on their roster. Sadly, SU officials kowtowed to Maryland's demands and played the game without Sidat-Singh.

"My sister and my husband went up there that day," Sidat-Singh's aunt, Adelaide Webb Henley, recalled in a 2001 interview with the *New York Daily News*. "Wilmeth was just sitting there, with his head down, so embarrassed and humiliated." None of Sidat-Singh's teammates were more torn than SU receiver Marty Glickman, who the year before was denied an opportunity to compete for a gold medal at the 1936 Olympics in Berlin because he was Jewish and U.S. officials didn't want to "offend" German chancellor Adolf Hitler. Glickman contemplated sitting out the Maryland game in a show of support for his friend and teammate but eventually chose not to. It was a decision Glickman would regret for the rest of his life.

Syracuse lost that game 13–0. The next year at Archbold Stadium, with Sidat-Singh in the lineup, the Orangemen clobbered the Terrapins 53–0. During his senior basketball season, Sidat-Singh was forced to deal with racial injustice once more. Naval Academy officials said their team would not play any squad that included African Americans. Once again, SU's administrators caved in to the discriminatory demands, and Sidat-Singh was forced to sit out the game.

Rice's comparisons of the SU star to NFL all-time greats Luckman and Baugh indicate that Sidat-Singh had the potential to become a great quarterback more than a half-century before modern-day African American quarterbacks Donovan McNabb, Cam Newton, Colin Kaepernick, and Russell Wilson put an end once and for all to racist arguments that blacks aren't qualified to be signal-callers.

With the door to the NFL closed, Sidat-Singh began carving his professional sports niche in basketball. Playing for the Harlem-based New York Rens, he teamed with several men who would become black pioneers when the NBA began play in the late 1940s. Sidat-Singh certainly would have joined them had his life not been cut tragically short at age 23. After the attack on Pearl Harbor, he signed up for the Tuskegee Airmen, an all-black fighter squadron whose success in shooting down Nazi planes during World War II would lead to the integration of the Armed Forces. An aspiring doctor, Sidat-Singh earned his wings quickly and was ready to head off to the European theater. But during a training mission over Lake Huron, the engines on his P-40 pursuit plane began to malfunction, and he was forced to parachute. When he hit the frigid waters, he became entangled in the ropes of his parachute and drowned.

For the longest time, Sidat-Singh's legacy at Syracuse was forgotten. But on February 26, 2005, during halftime of the

Providence-Syracuse game, Singh's basketball jersey was officially retired. And during SU's November 9, 2013, football game at Maryland, school officials there officially apologized for what had transpired 76 autumns earlier. During halftime of the game at Byrd Stadium, they showed a four-minute tribute video of Sidat-Singh and presented a Wounded Warriors jersey to relatives of the late SU star. The Orange football players honored Sidat-Singh that day by wearing No. 19 decals on the backs of their helmets.

39 Kathrine Switzer

Kathrine Switzer prepped for one of the most famous moments in sports history by training with the Syracuse University men's cross country team in late 1966 and early 1967. A 19-year-old sophomore journalism student at the time, Switzer gladly would have trained with the women's team, but there was just one problem— there wasn't one there, or at any other college for that matter.

While running with the Orangemen, Switzer befriended Arnie Briggs, a chatty 50-year-old who served as the team's assistant coach. Briggs loved to regale Switzer with tales about the 15 Boston Marathons he had run. One night, Switzer told him that she intended to run Boston herself. At first, Briggs scoffed. He barked that the distance was too long for "fragile" women to run. This angered Switzer, who pointed out that women had run the marathon before, just unofficially. After jawing back and forth a bit, Briggs agreed to take her under his wing and help her prepare for the race that would change her life and the lives of women throughout the world.

On April 19, 1967, flanked by Briggs, ex-boyfriend and SU football player Tom Miller, and Orange cross country runner John Leonard, Switzer became the first woman to officially complete the 26.2-mile Boston Marathon course.

Two miles into the race, she briefly considered quitting—not because she was gassed but because she was assaulted. That's when race organizer Jock Semple attempted to rip off the No. 261 pinned to her Syracuse sweatshirt because he didn't want any women competing in "his" race. Semple had a handful of her shirt until Miller, the ex-football player and Olympic-caliber hammer thrower, sent the race director sprawling to the ground.

All of this was captured on film as news photographers clicked away. Briggs told the dazed and confused Switzer to run like hell, and she followed orders. "Now, [Semple's] hurt, we're in trouble and we're going to get arrested," she wrote in her 2006 autobiography, *Marathon Woman: Running the Race to Revolutionize Women's Sports.* "That was how scared I felt, as well as deeply humiliated, and for just a tiny moment, I wondered if I should step off the course. I did not want to mess up this prestigious race. But the thought was only a flicker. I knew if I quit everybody would say it was a publicity stunt. If I quit, Jock Semple and all those like him would win. My fear and humiliation turned to anger."

So she kept running, even after Semple showed up again several minutes later, riding in a bus and screaming at Switzer in a Scottish brogue, "You all ere in beeeeeeggg trouble!"

Despite bloody, blistered feet, Switzer crossed the finish line in four hours and twenty minutes. The photos of Semple accosting her were splashed in newspapers and magazines around the world. They sparked a furor and were eventually included in *Life Magazine*'s "100 Photographs that Changed the World."

Switzer immediately became a hero to women everywhere. And her work in creating opportunities and equal status for women

Runner and Syracuse alumnus Katherine Switzer jogs in White Plains, New York, on April 8, 1975, while training for the Boston Marathon. In 1967, she was the first woman to run the fabled race. (AP Photo/Ron Frehm)

in sports would not stop there. Women, initially banned by the AAU from competing with men, were officially welcomed into the Boston Marathon in 1972. Switzer ran and finished third. Two years later, she was the first woman across the finish line at the New York City Marathon. She would go on to run 39 marathons and form an international running program for Avon, organizing more than 400 races in 27 countries for more than a million women. She also successfully led the drive to make the women's marathon an official Olympic event, just as it had always been for men.

Switzer, who received undergraduate and graduate degrees from SU, was feted for her life's work in 2011 when she was inducted into the National Women's Hall of Fame in Seneca Falls, New York. Despite not being able to compete in cross country during her college days, she still became one of the most influential athletes ever to attend Syracuse University.

40 The Louie and Bouie Show

There have been several dynamic duos in Syracuse sports history— Little and Csonka, the Gait Brothers, Bing and Boeheim, Simmons Sr. and Jr.—but none with such a catchy nickname as the one dreamed up for basketball teammates Roosevelt Bouie and Louis Orr. During the 1978–79 season, some enterprising editors and graphic artists at the student newspaper, *The Daily Orange*, came up with the concept of "The Louie and Bouie Show" to celebrate the crown jewels of Jim Boeheim's first recruiting class.

"They took this photo of us running up the court together and drew a caricature of us with top hats and canes in our hands, like we were the leads in some old vaudeville dance routine," Bouie recalled. "It was pretty creative, and the students really took to it. But Louis didn't like it at first because he didn't like being called Louie. He wanted to know why it couldn't be 'The Louis and Roosevelt Show,' even though he understood that it just didn't have the same ring to it."

For four seasons, this two-man act was a box-office smash. It was critically acclaimed, especially by Boeheim, who can thank Louie and Bouie for leading him to 100 wins and four NCAA tournament appearances in his first four years as head coach. "They were the two that got the ball rolling for us in the late 1970s," Boeheim said. "As far as my head-coaching career, it all goes back to them. They helped me get off to a great beginning."

That they did. The two young men provided an interesting contrast. Bouie was a sinewy, menacing, 6'11" center from a rural one-traffic-light town on the shores of Lake Ontario in upstate New York. Orr was a pencil-thin 6'8" forward from a big high school in Cincinnati. Though they hailed from disparate backgrounds and featured disparate basketball skill sets and physiques, they became a lethal one-two punch and the best of friends. They combined to average roughly 26 points and 16 rebounds per game during their SU careers, but those numbers are deceiving because they spent so much time on the bench during second halves of blowout victories.

Bouie had been the New York State Scholastic Player of the Year at Kendall High School in 1976 and was the first big-time recruit Boeheim landed. "We were in a dogfight with St. Bonaventure for Rosie, and I'm so glad we got him because he gave us instant credibility," Boeheim said. "He was a big, intimidating, shot-blocking center. He made everybody better, particularly on defense, because he was quite a presence in the middle. If you got past one of our defenders, you'd still have to face Roosevelt and that was like driving against a brick wall."

No one would have described Orr as a brick wall, but his skinny build belied superb skills as a scorer and rebounder. "I think his body actually worked to his advantage," Boeheim said. "People looked at him and thought they were going to have an easy night. They quickly discovered that appearances can be deceiving."

How Orr wound up at SU is the stuff of legend. At Boeheim's urging, SU assistant Rick Pitino delayed his honeymoon and went to Cincinnati to stake out Orr. Pitino, who would win a total of three national championships with Kentucky and Louisville, eventually convinced Orr that Syracuse was the place for him.

By the time their careers on the Hill were over, Louie and Bouie were two of SU's all-time greats. Bouie still ranks second all-time in blocks, third in field goal percentage, and seventh in rebounds. Orr ranks 25th in scoring.

Orr was chosen five slots ahead of Bouie in the second round of the 1980 draft and spent eight productive years in the NBA with the New York Knicks and Indiana Pacers. Bouie decided to forgo the NBA for a more lucrative basketball contract in Italy. He spent a decade there, becoming one of the first big American stars of European basketball. His success there helped grow the sport of basketball throughout the continent and opened the door for numerous other Americans to play professionally overseas.

Sherman Douglas

He had shown his mettle in his daily practices against Pearl Washington and had been a solid contributor off the bench as a freshman, averaging 5.4 points and 2.1 assists in 11 minutes per game. But skeptics remained in the media and even among his teammates and coaches. They couldn't help but wonder whether the lightly recruited Sherman Douglas would be up to the challenge of succeeding the Pearl at point guard in 1986.

Jim Boeheim was among those who had some reservations. Yes, he loved Douglas' fire and work ethic and basketball smarts, but he was concerned about the pressure the young man would face following in the sneaker steps of the most publicized athlete in school history. "The situation Sherman walked into reminded me of what it must be like to play center field for the New York Yankees," the coach said. "Every guy who plays that position is automatically

SCOTT PITONIAK

expected to be Joe DiMaggio or Mickey Mantle. I was worried that everyone would expect Sherman to be the next Pearl Washington. I didn't know how he would handle it."

The incredibly motivated and talented Douglas handled it better than anyone could have imagined, and by the time he graduated he had a career that may have been even better than the Pearl's. In his three years as a starter, the Orangemen went 87–24, including a 9–3 record in the NCAA tournament, and came within a Keith Smart jumper of winning the national championship. Along the way the player nicknamed "The General" established himself as the school's all-time leader in points (2,060) and the NCAA's all-time leader in assists (960). Though he no longer holds the top spot in either category, his legacy remains indelible. On March 9, 2003, his No. 20 jersey was retired by Syracuse.

"He had an amazing career," Boeheim said. "Dave Bing was a one-of-a-kind player because he could do so much. Sherman's like that, too. He plays both ends of the court. He's inside and outside. He's the greatest passer I've ever seen."

Not bad for a guy who had been overlooked by just about every major college basketball program, including Syracuse, while coming out of high school in Washington, D.C., a basketball hot bed. A product of Spingarn High, the same school that produced Bing and Los Angeles Lakers superstar Elgin Baylor, Douglas' dream had been to stay in the D.C. area and play for Georgetown. But Hoyas coach John Thompson didn't show much interest in the small shooting guard with the slightly awkward-looking outside shot because Georgetown already had an abundance of talented guards on its roster and more on the way.

"I was especially disappointed when they didn't recruit me because they played my type of basketball—full-court pressure and lots of running," said Douglas, who averaged 18.2 points and 8.1 assists per game his senior season. "Georgetown was kind of like home, and I wanted to stay home. But they didn't want me."

Point guard Sherman Douglas (20) holds his Most Valuable Player trophy in New York's Madison Square Garden on March 13, 1988. Douglas won the trophy for averaging 20 points in the Orangemen's three Big East Conference Tournament victories. (AP Photo/Mark Lennihan)

The Hoyas weren't alone in that sentiment. Until Syracuse became interested in Douglas, most major college programs shied away from the 6', 175-lb. player because they believed he wouldn't hold up against the rigors of a Big East or Atlantic Coast Conference schedule.

Boeheim became interested in Douglas only after highly touted New York City point guard Greg "Boo" Harvey failed to meet SU's admission standards in 1985. Assistant SU coach Wayne Morgan stumbled upon Douglas while visiting D.C. to check out another prospect. Morgan returned to campus, raving to Boeheim about Douglas' incredibly quick first step and his tenacity. The scintillating review was enough to convince SU's head coach to offer a scholarship. Douglas, who only had scholarship offers from Old Dominion and Rutgers, grudgingly accepted. "Don't get me wrong," he said. "I wanted to play in the Big East and Syracuse was a great program, but I was concerned about playing time. I knew with Pearl already there that my opportunities were going to be limited because he was a durable guy who would be out there 95 percent of the time."

Despite a sensational senior season, which resulted in him being named the District of Columbia's player of the year, Douglas began questioning whether he had what it took to play at college basketball's highest level. "I had self-doubts coming out of high school," he said. "I had confidence I would make a good point guard, but after not being recruited, I began thinking that maybe I wasn't as good a player as I thought."

It didn't take long for Douglas to brush aside those doubts. In his first practice in October 1985, he didn't give an inch to Pearl. "Dwayne had a considerable size and strength advantage on Sherman, and I remember him knocking Sherman on his butt about four or five times that day," Boeheim recalled. "Each time, Sherman got right back up and played tenacious defense against Dwayne. Heck, he even went after [6'10" center] Rony Seikaly. Sherman had no fear."

The unknown became intent on establishing himself on a team of well-knowns. "I wasn't one of the top players in the country, and Syracuse had plenty of them," Douglas said. "I didn't want them to think I was a pushover." Few were more impressed or appreciative of Douglas' intrepid play and work ethic than Washington. "He made me work more than most of the guards I faced in games that year," Pearl said. "He got after it from the start of practice until the end. Going against Sherman was like going against Georgetown on a daily basis. He was relentless."

When Washington announced after that season that he was skipping his senior year to turn pro, the door appeared open for Douglas. But the opportunity didn't come until star recruit Earl Duncan failed to qualify for enrollment in 1986. Douglas showed immediately he was up for the challenge, guiding the Orange to the NCAA title game in his first season as the starting point guard. After SU defeated second-ranked North Carolina in the 1987 East Region finals, legendary Tar Heels coach Dean Smith paid homage to Douglas. "They lost Pearl," he said, "but in many ways they may be better than if Pearl had stayed."

One of the highlights of Douglas' extraordinary career occurred on January 28, 1989, when he set an NCAA single-game record by dishing out 22 assists in a 100–96 win vs. Providence. Six of the baskets came on his signature pass—the alley-oop. In a game two months earlier, Douglas dazzled a sold-out crowd at Madison Square Garden when he grabbed a loose ball and hiked it, football-style, through his legs to a streaking Stephen Thompson for a basket in a 102–78 victory against Indiana.

Douglas was selected by the Miami Heat in the second round of the 1989 NBA draft and defied the odds again. He made the All-Rookie team that season and played 12 seasons, with five different teams, averaging a respectable 11 points and 5.9 assists per game. And just like the man he succeeded at Syracuse, Douglas eventually had his jersey retired by the school.

42 The Hoodoo and the Colgate Rivalry

Harry Truman occupied the White House the last time Colgate University beat Syracuse in football. The date was November 18, 1950. John F. Kennedy was president the last time the Orangemen lost to the Raiders on the basketball court. That date was February 24, 1962.

So given the fact that through the spring of 2014, the Orangemen had won 15 consecutive football games and 48 straight basketball games in the series, it's easy to forget that there was a half-century stretch when this was one of the most fiercely contested rivalries in all of college sports. In fact, the Orangemen's football series with the Raiders from nearby Hamilton, New York, was arguably more intense and wacky than SU's modern-day basketball rivalry with Georgetown.

Long before the Hoyas, there was the "Hoodoo," a bastardization of the word *voodoo*. The Hoodoo purportedly was a hex on SU that resulted in Colgate's football team going 31–15–5 against the Orange during the first half-century of the rivalry. The Raiders dominance was never greater than from 1925 through 1937 when legendary Colgate coach Andy Kerr's teams went 11–0–2.

Just how the myth originated isn't clear, but the most creative theory claims that a student buried a Colgate letterman's sweater into the concrete during the construction of Archbold Stadium and that "a wraith-like spectre of the Hoodoo slipped out of its resting place and joined 11 Colgate men on the football field," helping the Raiders win 6–0 in the first game between the schools at the new arena in 1908. SU indeed seemed cursed that day, failing to score despite moving the ball inside the Raiders 10-yard line eight times. Not long after that, a tradition began where the Colgate student section would begin chanting "Hoodoo! Hoodoo!" before and during games. Eventually, the SU student section began chanting "We do! We do!" in response.

It was all just part of the craziness that over time helped Colgate Weekend became *the* sporting and social event of the year in central New York. Each game from 1908 through 1961 was played at Archbold because it was the only place big enough to accommodate the large crowds, which for many years were the largest to witness football games at any level, college or pro, in New York state.

"You hear about Ohio State–Michigan and Texas-Oklahoma. Well, those Syracuse-Colgate games were every bit as intense," Roy Simmons Sr. said in a 1981 interview with the *Utica Observer-Dispatch*. "Today's rivalries are just as great on the field, but I don't think they could match the Syracuse-Colgate rivalries for the amount of enthusiasm and spirit on the part of the alumni and student bodies."

The close proximity of the schools clearly added to the fervor. "Most of the big rivalries today are separated by hundreds of miles," Simmons said. "We were separated by 30, 40 miles. Alumni and followers from both schools are spread throughout central New York. So when you lost, you heard about it for an entire year. People would really rub it in."

The passion and creativity of the fans seemed to know no bounds. Yes, the requisite bonfires, pep rallies, and parades were staged, but the high jinks ratcheted the rivalry up several notches. Intercampus painting raids become an annual event, though not without risk. Captured students were often "scalped" and held hostage until game day. (No, they didn't lop off anyone's head, but they did trim the perpetrator's hair so that an "S" or a "C" was visible on the back of one's noggin.)

The night before one of the games, three Syracuse students rented a plane and flew over the Colgate campus, dropping pamphlets forecasting an SU victory and pouring bags of Orange dye into Taylor Lake. At virtually the same time, a group of Colgate students scaled the gate at Archbold and, using gasoline, burned a huge "C" near the middle of the field. After completing that task, the infiltrators sneaked around the SU campus, painting "Colgate" in large maroon letters on several buildings.

The rivalry began with a 22–16 Raiders victory in 1891. After being blown out by Colgate by a combined score of 90–8 in their next two meetings, SU finally garnered its first win against its neighbors with a hard-fought 4–0 victory in 1895. The following year, the teams were deadlocked 6–6 when a Syracuse ball carrier broke free for what appeared to be the winning touchdown. But a newspaper reporter (we're not making this up) came off the Colgate sideline and tackled the runner. No penalty was called, and the game ended in a tie. The incident created such ill will that the series was suspended for four years.

The 1915 game featured a matchup of two teams in contention for the national championship. Colgate came to town with a 5–0 record and had out-scored their opponents 223–0. The Orangemen were 6–1 and had allowed just 10 points. The Hoodoo must have taken the day off because Frank O'Neill's SU squad throttled the Raiders 38–0 en route to a 9–1–2 season that would result in a Rose Bowl bid they turned down.

One of the most memorable games in the rivalry occurred on November 5, 1938, when Phil Allen scored on an end-around play in the fourth quarter and the Syracuse defense held tough as the Orangemen won 7–0 to snap Colgate's 13-game unbeaten streak in the Syracuse-Colgate series. When the final gun sounded, fans swarmed the field and tore down the goal posts. Chimes from SU's Crouse College could be heard from miles around as thousands of delirious people formed a human train and danced their way down the hill to the downtown bars.

The raids and campus vandalism reached a head by 1947, prompting administrators from both schools to threaten cancelation of the series if the students didn't get things under control. Student leaders from the schools gathered in Cazenovia—the halfway point between the campuses—and signed the Cazenovia Pact, which put limits on the tomfoolery.

Following a 19–14 Colgate victory in 1950, the Orangemen slowly pulled away from the Raiders. In 1956, Jim Brown scored a then-NCAA record 43 points as SU pummeled its rival 61–7. Three years later, during their national championship season, the Orangemen annihilated Colgate 71–0. After 46–6 and 51–8 Syracuse romps the next two years, the schools agreed it was senseless to continue. Twenty years later, in 1981, the series was briefly revived, but SU's dominance continued. A scheduling quirk resulted in another game in 2010, and the Orangemen rolled again with a 42–7 win. The schools are scheduled to play again in 2016.

As of now, the Raiders hold a 31–30–5 lead. The basketball series, though, remains active and lopsided. Through the 2013–14 season, SU leads 121–45. It's the most victories by the Orange against any opponent in any sport.

Joe Morris

Every recruiter who watched the films believed the kid was too small to play big-time college football—every recruiter except one.

Joe Morris stood only 5'7" and weighed just 175 pounds, and he played at a small high school in Ayer, Massachusetts, just south of Boston. But Syracuse University assistant coach Dave Zuccarelli saw something in Morris that others didn't...something not easy to quantify. So when he returned to campus, Zuccarelli made an impassioned plea to Orange head coach Frank Maloney to take a chance on the little running back with the lion's heart.

"I credit Dave for doing a heck of a sales job," said Maloney, who coached the Orange from 1974 to 1980. "No Division I school—not even Boston College, which was in Joe's backyard—thought he could do it, so that led to some skepticism on my part. I'm thinking, if he's that good, why isn't BC all over this kid? But sometimes in life you have to take a chance on a person. So we decided to gamble a scholarship on Joe, and it paid off for us big-time."

Did it ever.

During his four seasons at Syracuse, Morris left tacklers and everyone who ever carried a football for SU in his wake, establishing the school's career rushing standard with 4,299 yards. Not bad for a guy who initially battled his own doubts about whether he

Road Warriors

The 1979 season proved to be one of the most unusual and challenging in SU football history as the Orangemen were forced to play all of their games on the road while the Carrier Dome was being constructed. Syracuse tried to mitigate matters by playing one home-away-from-home game at Cornell University's Schoellkopf Field, an hour south of campus, and two games each at Buffalo's Rich Stadium (three hours to the west) and Giants Stadium in East Rutherford, New Jersey (four hours southeast). The Orange beat West Virginia (24–14) and lost to Penn State (35–7) at Giants Stadium; beat Washington State (52–25) and Miami, Florida (25–15) at Rich Stadium; and lost to Boston College (27–10) at Cornell. An interesting side note is that the Miami quarterback they beat was Jim Kelly, who would later call Rich Stadium home during his Pro Football Hall of Fame career with the Bills.

Led by future NFL stars Art Monk and Joe Morris and All-ECAC quarterback Bill Hurley, SU finished 6–5 that season and earned a berth in the Independence Bowl in Shreveport, Louisiana, where they clobbered McNeese St. 31–7. "I can't tell you how proud I was of that team," said Frank Maloney, SU's coach at the time. "To have a winning record when you've played every game on the road is pretty remarkable. Those kids showed tremendous perseverance."

would be up for the challenge of playing powerhouses such as Penn State, Pitt, and Ohio State. "My expectations were pretty modest," Morris recalled. "I set a goal of gaining a 1,000 yards total over four years." After rushing for 1,001 yards his freshman season (1978), Morris was forced to set some new goals. "I remember Coach [Maloney] bringing me into his office and saying, 'Joe, you have the potential to play in the NFL,'" he recalled. "And I thought he was crazy. I said, 'Thanks Coach, but I'm just going to focus on having the best college career I can.'"

Three decades after graduating from SU with a degree in family studies, Morris remains king of the hill. However, his historical impact on the program is occasionally overlooked because the Orange experienced only one winning season in his four years with the varsity. The truth is that Morris—along with future NFL players Art Monk, Bill Hurley, Craig Wofley, Jim Collins, Craig Bingham, and Ray Preston—helped SU football make the transition from Old Archie to the Carrier Dome.

"Joe was always the focal point of those teams because he had such a profound effect on the outcome of the game," said former SU athletics director Jake Crouthamel. "His presence…was a great way to open the Carrier Dome [in 1980]. I'm not sure we all appreciated just how good Joe was."

Morris' humility may have contributed to that lack of appreciation. He was never one to blow his own horn. He's still deflecting praise to his teammates and his coaches all these years later. "I played with some great players," Morris said. "Guys like Art Monk, who reached the top of our profession and is in the Pro Football Hall of Fame. And I had coaches who believed in me when others didn't. I was blessed to have Dave Zuccarelli and Frank Maloney think I deserved a scholarship to play Division I football. And I was fortunate to have Tom Coughlin as my position coach. He was such a stickler for detail. He drove people nuts at times, but he also taught me how the game should be played."

The numbers Morris put up at SU have stood the test of time. In addition to the career rushing mark, he holds school records for most yards in a season (1,372 in 1979) and a game (252 in a 1979 game vs. Kansas). He also leads SU with 22 career 100-yard games and a career per-game average of 113.1 yards. One of his most memorable games occurred on September 20, 1980, when he helped christen the Dome by gaining 300 all-purpose yards and scoring four touchdowns in a 36–24 victory against Miami of Ohio in front of 50,564.

When the Giants selected Morris in the second round of the 1982 draft, the skeptics resurfaced. One New York writer called Morris the worst second-round pick in the history of the NFL. Morris filed away that assessment for future motivation. He wound up rushing for more than 1,000 yards in a season three times, and he finished his eight-year stint with the Giants as the franchise's all-time leading rusher with 5,296 yards. (His record was later broken by Tiki Barber.) He also earned two Pro Bowl invitations and a Super Bowl ring.

"I think that guy who said I was the worst was wrong," Morris said, chuckling. "And thank God for Dave Zuccarelli and Frank Maloney. They took a chance on me and never stopped believing in me. The Syracuse experience molded me, gave me a game plan for life."

Morris and his teammates helped the football program begin to reestablish itself following the departure of legendary coach Ben Schwartzwalder and talks by school officials about de-emphasizing the program. "Looking back, I think we laid the foundation for the success they had later in the 1980s and throughout the 1990s," Morris said. "Coach Maloney told us, 'You guys should always feel proud of your college football days because you helped keep Syracuse University football afloat.'"

44 Down the Field

It's not in the same league as "Three Cheers for ol' Notre Dame," or "On Wisconsin," or "Fight on USC," or Michigan's "Hail to the Victors." But Syracuse's "Down the Field" is still a pretty catchy, foot-stomping, hand-clapping fight song. It's great to hum but not so great to sing because the words, quite frankly, don't exactly mesh well with the music. The rousing tune was composed by SU student C. Harold Lewis in 1915. A year later another student, Ralph Murphy, penned the following words to accompany the music:

Out upon the gridiron stands old Syracuse,
Warriors clad in orange and in blue,
Fighting for the fame of Alma Mater.
Soon those Crouse chimes will be ringing,
Soon you'll hear those fellows singing.
Onondaga's braves are out to win today,
The sons of Syracuse are ready for the fray,
The line holds like a wall and now the Orange has the ball,
So ready for that old long yell. Rah! Rah! Rah!

Chorus:
Down, down the field goes old Syracuse,
Just see those backs hit the line and go through.
Down, down the field they go marching,
Fighting for the Orange staunch and true.
Rah! Rah! Rah!
Vict'ry's in sight for old Syr-a-cuse,
Each loyal son knows she ne'er more will lose,
For we'll fight, yes, we'll fight, and with all our might
For the glory of old Syracuse.

We're obviously not talking about a Lennon and McCartney or Rodgers and Hammerstein collaboration here, but Murphy does deserve some credit for being a clairvoyant with the line about the backs hitting the line and going through. He clearly must have gazed into a crystal ball and saw the likes of Brown, Davis, and Little running for daylight in the decades to come.

"Down the Field" was actually the third fight song in Syracuse history. The first, "Bill Orange: A Syracuse Football Song," was written by Harry Sheridan Lee from the class of 1899.

Bill Orange is upon the sidelines
With a megaphone and flag in hand.
He leads the crowd to cheer like demons,
All up and down the old grandstand;
And as the ball is moving goal-ward
Each yard that's gained he's marking well
It's worthwhile to play for Old Bill Orange
For win or lose you'll always hear him yell:

Chorus:
Get in the game to win, boys,
Ev'ry blessed mother's son of you;
Stand firm along the line, boys,
Watch the ball, this time it's going through.
Last night the sun set orange,
Omen ever sure and true,
Get in the game and win, boys,
Old Syracuse, she calls to you!

This song was written in the 1890s before Archbold Stadium was built and all the cheerleaders were men because it was thought that their voices would be louder than women's voices. Bill Orange was just a made-up character that played off the school's primary color. The other fight song, titled "The Saltine Warrior," was a collaboration between composer David R. Walsh (class of 1912) and lyricist Samuel E. Darby Jr. (1913).

In the days of old, when knights were bold
Every city had its warrior man.
In the days of new, when fights are few
You will view them from a big grandstand.
In our college town one has great renown
If the game of football he should play.
With his pigskin ball he is cheered by all,
He's the Saltine Warrior of today.

Chorus:
The Saltine Warrior is a bold, bad man,
And his weapon is a pigskin ball,
When on the field he takes a good, firm stand,
He's the hero of large and small.
He will rush toward the goal with might and main
His opponents all fight, but they fight in vain,
Because the Saltine Warrior is a bold, bad man,
And victorious over all.

According to SU archivists, this song was originally written to be part of a student musical program, but the show never saw the light of day. This song did, though, and it became quite popular among students. Interestingly, this Saltine Warrior, unlike the school mascot that followed, is based on a medieval knight rather than a Native American. This song continued to be played on Syracuse football highlight reels into the 1960s, but it faded away in the late 1970s after the university stopped using the Saltine Warrior as its mascot and official logo.

The other song of note is the Syracuse alma mater, which is played at home football and basketball games. It was written by Junius W. Stevens, class of 1895. The next-to-last line in the original alma mater was changed in the spring of 1986 from "May thy sons be leal and loyal" to "Loyal be thy sons and daughters" to reflect the fact SU has always been co-educational.

Interestingly, when Doug Marrone took over as football coach in 2009, he began a tradition of having his team sing the alma mater after games in the end zone where the band was seated. His successor, Scott Shafer, has continued that tradition, win or lose, at home games.

Where the vale of Onondaga
Meets the eastern sky
Proudly stands our Alma Mater
On her hilltop high.
Flag we love! Orange! Float for aye,
Old Syracuse, o'er thee,
Loyal be thy sons and daughters
To thy memory.

Tim Green

Tim Green always had a nose for the football and his nose in a book. So it didn't come as a shock to those who knew him well that Green would eventually accomplish his boyhood dreams of becoming an NFL player and a best-selling author. Nor was it surprising that before sacking quarterbacks for the Atlanta Falcons and churning out 29 books, this renaissance man would accept the enormous challenge of leading a football renaissance at Syracuse University.

Green could have gone anywhere to play college football. That's how highly regarded he was back in the fall of 1981. But the erudite young man with the superb athletic skills ultimately decided not to travel far at all—from suburban Liverpool just a few miles south on Interstate 81 to the SU campus. Coach Dick MacPherson had sold Green on the idea of becoming the cornerstone recruit in Syracuse's gridiron resurrection, the coveted magnetic player whose very presence would lure other high school standouts to join him in making the Orangemen an Eastern football power once more.

"I was intrigued with the idea of being on the ground floor of something really special," recalled Green, who became a two-time All-American defensive end and a Rhodes Scholar candidate at SU. "It was an enormous challenge because the program certainly was down at the time. However, I saw it as an opportunity to make some history. My teammates and I had a chance to write a memorable chapter."

Green signed on the dotted line in February 1982 and that fall began work on the rough draft of a chapter that remains special all these years later—a chapter that would include the most improbable victory in Syracuse history, the 17–9 upset of Nebraska in 1984. Green would earn college football's Player of the Week honors from *Sports Illustrated* after his 12-tackle, two-sack effort vs. the Cornhuskers.

Three times he led the Orangemen in sacks, recording 14.5 as a sophomore, 15 as a junior, and 13.5 as a senior. His career total of 45.5 remains a school record, as do his 341 tackles as a down lineman. After going 2–9 his freshman season, SU improved to 6–5, 6–5, and 7–5 in ensuing years, earning the school's first bowl bid in six seasons when they were invited to the Cherry Bowl in 1985.

"Fans here had distant memories of greatness, and we brought them back to the edge of it," Green said in Michael Mullins' book, *Syracuse University Football: A Centennial Celebration.* "But we weren't all the way back." That wouldn't occur until two years after Green graduated when the Orangemen went 11–0–1. Still,

Green and his teammates had helped lay the foundation. "It all started turning in the right direction for us when we got Timmy Green to stay home," MacPherson said. "That was crucial. A lot of guys don't want to stay in their hometowns…too much pressure. But Tim handled the pressure just fine. He epitomized what the student-athlete should be. That darn kid always had his nose in a book."

Green was indeed a voracious reader, and he found the differences between his two passions somewhat amusing. "It's kind of like *The Strange Case of Dr. Jekyll and Mr. Hyde*," he once explained. "On the football field, aggressiveness and violence aren't merely tolerated, they're celebrated. You can do combative things out there that would land you in jail if you behaved that way in normal society. Away from the field, I'm a totally different personality. I love the solitary moments of getting lost in a good book and seeing where an author is going to take me."

After graduating Phi Beta Kappa and as the co-valedictorian of his class, Green's journey took him to the NFL. He was drafted in the first round, 17th overall, by the Falcons in 1986 and had a solid career, recording 24 sacks and recovering nine fumbles before retiring after the 1993 season. Green then earned his law degree from SU and became a practicing attorney. Around this time, he also began to write novels, many based on his football experiences. Some of these novels delved into the dark, seamy side of the game. They became hits with readers, and several of them shot up the *New York Times* best-seller lists. Around this time, the articulate Green also began cultivating a lucrative broadcasting career that saw him work as a football analyst for FOX Sports, co-host the news show, *A Current Affair*, and become a regular contributor to National Public Radio and ABC's *Evening News*. In 2001, he was inducted into the College Football Hall of Fame, and 10 years later he received a prestigious Silver Anniversary Award from the NCAA.

About the only thing that didn't turn to gold for Green was his short stint as a high school football coach, which resulted in the team not being eligible for postseason play amid charges of illegal recruiting of players from other school districts. In recent years, Green has shifted to writing children's books, and they have also become best-sellers. In an effort to promote reading among young people, Green travels the country to speak to students. One of his themes focuses on reading being "weight-lifting for the brain." Green clearly used both his brains and his brawn at SU. The result was a football renaissance spearheaded by a true renaissance man.

46 1975: SU Basketball's First Final Four

The Orangemen's first extended foray into March was engineered by an unlikely cast of characters. They included Earnie Seibert, a pudgy center who looked as if he had been recruited out of a tavern; Jim "The Bug" Williams, a small but super-quick point guard who constantly wore sunglasses in a city where the sun doesn't shine eight months of the year; Chris Sease, a small forward known as "Rocket Man" for his astounding leaping ability; Jimmy Lee, a floppy-haired shooting guard who looked like one of the Beach Boys; and Rudy Hackett, who developed into an All-American forward after having been cut from his high school basketball team.

The 1974–75 Syracuse squad was coached by the glib Roy Danforth, who became a media darling at that year's Final Four with lines like this one: "I don't know if I'm for a 30-second shot clock because I don't know if Earnie can make it up and down the court in that length of time."

Four decades later, it's still difficult to comprehend how this motley crew managed to dribble and shoot their way to the school's first basketball Final Four, but they did. And in the process, they helped Syracuse begin the transition from regional to national program. "There had been a rich tradition with Dave Bing and all, but we like to think our team gave the school national recognition in basketball that it didn't have before," said Bob Parker, who was a reserve center and forward on that team, which went 23–9. "After the exposure we received for making the Final Four, Syracuse began landing blue-chippers, players like Roosevelt Bouie and Pearl Washington and Billy Owens. We like to think that we helped set the wheels in motion."

That SU team, which featured Jim Boeheim as an assistant, peaked at just the right time, winning its final four regular season games, two more to claim the ECAC title, and three more in the NCAA tournament to punch their ticket to the Final Four in San Diego, where the clock finally struck 12 on their Cinderella journey. Two of their NCAA victories were achieved in overtime, and the other was decided by just two points. "Sometimes," said Parker, "you get on a roll, and before you know it, you've reached the Promised Land."

After knocking off Niagara and St. Bonaventure in Buffalo to cop the ECAC crown, the NCAA tournament selection committee didn't do the Orangemen any favors, pitting them against Philadelphia-based LaSalle University at the Palestra, smack-dab in the middle of the City of Brotherly Love. But the SU players didn't seem bothered by the prospect of playing what amounted to a LaSalle home game. Co-captains Lee and Hackett combined for 50 points as the Orange defeated the Explorers 87–83 in overtime. SU did catch a break at the end of regulation when La Salle's Joe "Jelly Bean" Bryant had a 6' jumper roll off the rim. "That gave us a second life," said Boeheim, who would go on to coach Jelly Bean's son, Kobe Bryant, at the Olympics. "It also gave us confidence in the next two games we played, which also went down to the wire."

Next up was sixth-ranked North Carolina at the East Regionals in Providence, Rhode Island. Few in the media gave SU any chance against a Tar Heels lineup featuring future NBA players Phil Ford, Walter Davis, Mitch Kupchak, and Tommy LaGarde. But North Carolina's Hall of Fame coach Dean Smith was concerned, telling reporters, "I think Roy has done a great job coaching the team, especially the way he's got them running the fast break. I think it's going to be a hell of a game." He thought right.

SU trailed by just a point at the half—impressive considering the foul-plagued Hackett hadn't scored a single point. Nursing a one-point lead with 30 seconds left in the game, Ford threw the ball away on the inbounds. SU worked it inside to Hackett, and when four defenders converged on him, he quickly zipped the ball out to Lee, who was positioned just beyond the foul line, about 18' from the basket. The sweet-shooter let fly and his nothing-but-net jumper put the Orangemen up by one with five seconds remaining. Smith then called a timeout to draw up a final play. Boeheim instructed Parker, who would be guarding the player inbounding the ball, to just stand there and jump up and down with his arms extended. Kupchak, the inbounder, began running down the end line in hopes that Parker would move with him and bowl over stationary Tar Heel guard John Kuester and be called for a foul. And that's what happened, except no foul was called. Kupchak's pass bounced off a teammate, and Jimmy Williams was then fouled and sank a free throw to give SU a 78–76 win. "If they had called me for a foul, I think Coach Boeheim would have shot me," Parker recalled, chuckling.

Two days later, in the East Region finals, Syracuse defeated Kansas State 95–87 in overtime. With five seconds remaining in regulation and SU trailing by two, Williams took the inbounds, dribbled the length of the floor, and flipped the ball to Hackett, who bobbled it for an instant before throwing up a 5' shot that went through the cylinder as the buzzer sounded. The Orange then dominated in overtime to secure their first trip to the Final Four.

Their magic ran out at that Final Four, which was historically significant because it marked the 10th and final time legendary UCLA coach John Wooden would win an NCAA title. The Orangemen lost to second-ranked Kentucky 95–79 in the semifinals. In those days, there was a consolation game, which SU lost to fourth-ranked Louisville 96–88 in overtime. Lee wound up leading all scorers at the Final Four and was named to the All-Tournament team.

Although the Orangemen didn't win it all, they did, as Parker said, help set the wheels in motion. "It may have seemed like a strange mix, but we really gelled near the end of the season," he said. "I think it all started to come together when we found out the Final Four was going to be in San Diego. We were all sick of the Syracuse winter."

Billy Owens

One writer said Billy Owens was Carmelo before Carmelo. It seems an apt description because, like Carmelo Anthony, Owens did just about everything imaginable on the basketball court during his three seasons with the Orangemen—everything except deliver a national championship.

"I think people sometimes forget just how great an all-around player Billy Owens was," Jim Boeheim said. "He was just spectacular his junior season. He did virtually everything that Carmelo did during his freshman season, and he did so with a weaker supporting cast." Indeed the 1990–91 campaign turned in by Owens remains one of the greatest in SU history. That season, the 6'8" point-forward from Carlisle, Pennsylvania, converted nearly 51 percent of his shots and became the first player in the Boeheim era to average more than 20 points per game (23.3). But he was much more than just a scorer, as evidenced by his 11.6 rebounds and 3.5 assists per contest. He also made his presence felt on defense with a combined 115 blocks and steals.

Owens turned in 19 double-doubles for an Orange team that went 26–6 and ascended as high as No. 3 in the polls. Although that team received solid contributions from center LeRon Ellis, guards Michael Edwards and Adrian Autry, and forward David Johnson, it was clearly Billy Owens' team. In fact, after a 13–0 start to the season, the Orangemen became known as "Billy and the Beaters." The numbers he put up game after game were astounding. Owens had 36 points and 14 rebounds vs. Boston College; 33 and 16 vs. Pitt; 31 and 10 vs. Notre Dame; 30 and 12 in his second meeting with BC; 28 and 14 vs. St. John's; 28 and 13 vs. Indiana; 25 and 16 vs. Providence; 24 and 13 vs. Seton Hall; and 21 and 12 vs. North Carolina State.

"Watching Billy Owens play basketball and coaching him is a privilege that only one coach gets to do," Boeheim said in the midst of that campaign. "I get satisfaction in life from my daughter and from watching guys approach perfection playing basketball. So someday down the road, I'll look back on this season and say, 'That was the year I had Billy Owens. He reached toward perfection in basketball.'"

Unfortunately, when the subject of the 1990–91 season is broached, Owens' consensus All-American and Big East Conference Player of the Year honors aren't the first thing that come to mind. His brilliance was overshadowed by the way that season crashed to a halt as the Orangemen became the first No. 2 seed to lose to a

No. 15 seed when they were upset by the Richmond Spiders in the first round of the NCAA tournament. Not long after that shocking defeat, Owens announced he was skipping his senior year to play in the NBA and was chosen No. 3 overall in that June's draft. "It's asinine for people to associate that last loss with Billy," Boeheim said. "We don't even make the tournament without Billy. That's what makes his junior season even more spectacular. It's not merely the individual numbers he put up; it's the way he consistently carried that team."

Boeheim had an inkling that Owens was going to be spectacular when he watched the 17-year-old put up 63 points in a summer league game in July 1987. "He had eight three-pointers in a 15 mph wind!" Boeheim said. "It was just a pleasure to watch. I don't want to sound corny, but to watch him play was like seeing a work of art. I walked away from there shaking my head. I kept saying to myself, 'I've got to get this kid.'" Boeheim was able to beat out Owens' other top suitors—North Carolina and Villanova—and he can thank SU football coach Dick MacPherson for his good fortune. You see, Coach Mac had recruited Billy's older brother and best friend, Michael, a few years earlier to play running back for the Orange. Both of Billy's parents, Bill and Marisha, wanted Billy to join Michael at SU, and the younger brother happily complied.

Although Billy Owens' arrival on campus didn't generate the tsunami of interest that Pearl Washington's had several years earlier, it was still a huge achievement and another indication of just what a national program SU had become. Before he stepped on the court for his first game at SU, Owens achieved a milestone by becoming the first basketball player in school history to appear on the cover of *Sports Illustrated*. Actually, he was supposed to share cover honors with the nation's other top-rated incoming freshman, Georgetown's Alonzo Mourning, but Hoyas coach John Thompson wouldn't give Mourning permission to

Billy Owens (right) blocks an attempted stuff by Tom Greis of Villanova in first half Big East tournament action at Madison Square Garden on Saturday, March 10, 1990, in New York. (AP Photo/Ron Frehm)

be featured, so Owens flew solo. The magazine raved about the new Orangeman, writing that he was "the most gifted of the new arrivals, with an all-around game that has a touch of Magic," as in Magic Johnson.

Owens was intrepid in his early practices, going toe-to-toe with junior forward Derrick Coleman and not backing down. Despite deferring to the upperclassmen, which included Coleman and guard Sherman Douglas, Owens still put up excellent numbers for a freshman, averaging 13 points, 6.9 rebounds, and 3.1 assists per game.

The highlight of his career would come against hated rival Georgetown toward the end of a sophomore campaign that saw him average 18.2 points, 8.4 rebounds, and 4.6 assists per game. On March 4, 1990, in front of a national television audience and a then-record Carrier Dome crowd of 33,015—a crowd that included filmmaker Spike Lee and Chicago Cubs legend Ernie Banks—Owens calmly sank two free throws with one second remaining to send the game into overtime. The Orangemen ended up winning 89–87. It marked the first time they swept a season-series from Georgetown, prompting Owens to make motions with an imaginary broom at center court after the final buzzer sounded. With the graduation of Coleman and Stephen Thompson, Owens was called upon by Boeheim to carry a much bigger role, and Owens responded with his scintillating season in 1990–91.

After the disappointing loss to Richmond at the end of that season, Owens opted to forgo his senior year. The NCAA's investigation into the program and the possible sanctions that might include banishment from the following year's tournament was a factor in his decision. But Owens also realized that he had a good shot to be drafted in the top three. If he waited until after his senior year, he wasn't projected to go any higher because that class included Shaquille O'Neal and Mourning.

Owens was drafted by the Sacramento Kings but was traded to the Golden State Warriors after he held out. He made the NBA's All-Rookie team in 1992 and averaged 15 points and nearly eight rebounds during his first three seasons. He spent 10 years in the NBA with six different teams. Although he put up respectable career numbers—11.7 points and 6.7 rebounds—he never lived up to his dreams of becoming the next Magic. He later worked as an assistant coach at the college level and as an NBA scout. On March 8, 2008, Syracuse retired his No. 30 jersey during a game at the Dome.

48 Don McPherson

As a youngster growing up on Long Island, Don McPherson dreamed about becoming a Nittany Lion instead of an Orangeman. He fantasized about playing for Syracuse's arch-rival, Penn State, and its legendary coach, Joe Paterno. But when McPherson, a highly coveted recruit from West Hempstead High School, didn't get the answers he was looking for from a Penn State assistant in the spring of 1983, McPherson called an audible that brought him to the Carrier Dome rather than Happy Valley. And by so doing, he changed the course of SU football history.

McPherson, an African American, asked the same pointed questions of each of the approximately 70 schools that were recruiting him nationwide: "Has your school ever had a black quarterback? And what would you think about having one now?" What's necessary to understand is that the early 1980s were vastly different times in America. Stereotypes persisted that African Americans weren't "qualified" to quarterback or coach football teams—or run companies or countries, for that matter. This was still a quarter-century before a black man would be elected president of the United States and nearly three decades before a wave of young black quarterbacks—including Russell Wilson, Colin Kaepernick, and Robert Griffin III—would take the NFL by storm.

"There were only a handful of black quarterbacks in Division I and even fewer in pro football at the time," McPherson said. "So there were still racist doubts about whether an African American was intelligent enough to handle the position. And I needed those questions answered because I had no intention of playing any other position."

When he broached the questions with Syracuse head coach Dick MacPherson, he immediately received the answers he had hoped to hear. "Coach Mac never flinched," McPherson recalled. "He told me, point blank, that he didn't care what my skin color was. He said, 'All I care about is if you can play and help us win football games. And if you can play and help us win football games, you're gonna play. Period.' That gave me the confidence that this was the right place for me."

So McPherson came to Syracuse and proved that he could indeed play, helping revive an Orange football program that had been wallowing in mediocrity. McPherson eventually led SU to an 11–0–1 record in 1987, the school's first unbeaten season since the national championship campaign 28 years earlier. Along the way, he established 22 school records, led the nation in passing efficiency, was named a consensus first-team All-American, and finished runner-up in the Heisman Trophy voting. He also received the Maxwell Award as the nation's top player and the Johnny Unitas and Davey O'Brien awards as college football's best quarterback.

"Donnie McPherson helped make Syracuse football relevant again," Coach Mac said. "He put Syracuse University football back on the map."

Quarterback Don McPherson (9) heads up field during late action in the Sugar Bowl in New Orleans on Friday, January 1, 1988. McPherson was named the MVP for his efforts. Auburn and Syracuse tied 16–16, the first in Sugar Bowl history. (AP Photo/Tannen Maury)

In 2009, McPherson was enshrined in the College Football Hall of Fame, and at halftime of the 2013 game against Clemson in the Dome, his alma mater retired the No. 9 jersey he wore during his football glory days. "Football is the ultimate team game, so I feel somewhat funny about being signaled out," McPherson said before the ceremony. "When that jersey goes up there to the rafters, I'm going to think about all my teammates and how there is not one thing I did that's not owed to those guys."

Football is indeed a team game, but there is no position in the sport more important than quarterback. While it's true that McPherson had plenty of help from his mates, he was the guy who led the way. "Don's a real humble guy, but the reality is that he was the undisputed leader and we wouldn't have come close to enjoying the success we did without him," said Daryl Johnston, the bruising fullback on that '87 squad who would contribute mightily to three Dallas Cowboy Super Bowl victories. "He was the heart and soul of our team."

One of the things that resonated with Johnston and his teammates was McPherson's perseverance. Each of his first two seasons was cut short by injuries. In 1985, as a red-shirt sophomore, he was finally healthy enough to realize his enormous potential, throwing for 12 touchdown passes and running for seven more as SU earned a berth in the Cherry Bowl.

There were great expectations for the 1986 season, but after a 0–4 start, many Syracuse fans were calling for Coach Mac to be fired. "It was a very disappointing season because we knew we were so much better than we showed," McPherson recalled. "Fortunately, we rallied down the stretch. [The team won 5-of-7 to finish 5–6.]

"I remember before our last game, Coach Mac [told] me that we were going to really open things up the following season. I think our success in 1987 was born out of our frustrations of '86."

McPherson recalls a large number of players spending the summer of '87 in Syracuse so they could participate in strength and conditioning coach Mike Woicik's off-season program. The extra work paid immediate dividends as SU opened with wins against Maryland, Rutgers, and Miami of Ohio. In the fourth game at Virginia Tech, the Orange trailed at halftime but stormed back to beat the Hokies 35–21. A win at Missouri improved their record to 5–0 and set up a nationally televised game against Joe

Paterno's Nittany Lions, a team to which SU had lost 16 consecutive times. McPherson was at his absolute best against the football program he rooted for as a kid, passing for three touchdowns and running for two more in a resounding 48–21 rout in the Carrier Dome.

Syracuse would run the table to go 11–0. Its most memorable victory came in the final game of the regular season—a last-second 32–31 victory against West Virginia that was decided by a 17-yard touchdown pass to Pat Kelly and a two-point conversion pitch to Michael Owens. Although the campaign ended with a deflating 16–16 tie against Auburn in the Sugar Bowl, a statement had been made. Orange football was back, and McPherson was one heck of a quarterback. Not only had he thrown 22 touchdown passes, he also rushed for five and even had a scoring reception on a gimmick play. "He brought a skill set," Johnston told reporters, "that was virtually impossible to defend on the college level."

After a brief career in the NFL and several more years in the Canadian Football League, McPherson joined Northeastern University's Center for the Study of Sports in Society and began a remarkable career as a social activist. A riveting, in-demand speaker, McPherson presented lectures at more than 200 college campuses, often focusing on domestic violence issues and the concept of masculinity. The husband and father of two appeared on Oprah Winfrey's show, twice testified in front of Congress, and became one of just three male members on the board of directors of the Ms. Foundation for Women. He also remained close to the game of football through the years, serving as a television analyst for ESPN, BET, NBC, and SportsNet New York.

Coach P

Paul Pasqualoni joined Dick MacPherson's Syracuse staff as a linebackers coach in 1987. And when Coach Mac announced after the 1990 season that he was leaving to become the head coach of the New England Patriots, Pasqualoni expected to follow him to Foxboro, Massachusetts, as an assistant. But Syracuse athletic director Jake Crouthamel changed those plans when he offered Pasqualoni the Orangemen's head coaching job. "Jake caught me totally off-guard," Pasqualoni said. "I never expected to be offered the job. I was stunned."

Stunned—and ready. A walk-on linebacker at Penn State, Pasqualoni went on to become a successful small-college head coach at Western Connecticut State, where he guided the Colonials to a 34–17 record and an NCAA Division III playoff appearance in five seasons. He had done a stellar job as the SU linebackers coach, and Crouthamel was amazed at Pasqualoni's work ethic and devotion to the job. The son of a first-generation Italian-American farmer, Coach P spent his youthful days in the fields picking tomatoes, corn, and cabbage from sunrise to sunset every summer. "People think I put in a lot of hours coaching football," Pasqualoni said. "You should have seen the hours we racked up in the fields and in the greenhouses."

In retrospect, he believed farming was perfect preparation for coaching football. It taught him that in order to reap the fruits of your labor, you had to put in long days and be meticulously organized. It also taught him that no matter how hard you work, circumstances beyond your control could turn a bumper crop into a bummer crop. Uncooperative weather, pesky insects, and rocky soil were the farmer's equivalent of fumbles, penalties, and injuries.

Bottoming Out

Greg Robinson was hired in 2005 to replace Paul Pasqualoni and snap SU football out of its lethargy. Instead, the man with the two Super Bowl rings, a sparkling recommendation from Pete Carroll, and no head coaching experience, led the Orangemen into the basement. Robinson's first team went 1–10, marking the first time in program history that Syracuse had lost that many games in a season. After a slight rebound to 4–8, the Orangemen sank to 2–10. A 3–9 record the next year put an end to the Robinson error at SU.

Coach P inherited a bumper crop of talented players from MacPherson and was able to cultivate 10 victories in each of his first two seasons. After so-so campaigns in 1993 and '94, when the Orangemen went a combined 13–8–1, some fans began questioning Pasqualoni's ability to recruit. He quickly allayed those concerns by luring future NFL stars such as quarterback Donovan McNabb and wide receiver Marvin Harrison to campus. The influx of talent helped elevate the program back to its lofty position as the Orangemen went 35–14, including a 2–2 mark in bowl games, from 1995 to1998.

In Pasqualoni's 14 seasons, Syracuse posted a 107–59–1 record that included a 6–3 mark in the postseason. Only Ben Schwartzwalder won more football games at SU. But Pasqualoni's stellar accomplishments always seemed unappreciated by Orange fans, many of whom remember him more for the way his SU career ended—with a 16–20 record in his final three seasons, including an embarrassing 51–14 loss to Georgia Tech in the 2004 Champs Sports Bowl in Coach P's last game. Part of it had to do with the public's perception of Pasqualoni. Many believed that, despite the impressive success, his teams somehow underachieved by losing games they should not have lost, costing the Orange an opportunity to compete for a national championship.

The shy, robotic, cliché-ridden Pasqualoni also suffered in comparison to his glib, charismatic, life-of-the-party predecessor.

Coach Mac loved the limelight and loved interacting with the public, and he was beloved by Syracuse fans. He was clearly a tough act to follow. "I think there is something to that," said George DeLeone, Pasqualoni's long-time coaching colleague, in a December 2002 interview. "Because he's not super quotable doesn't mean Coach P is any less of a football coach. I can't think of any coach in America who does a better job of graduating his kids and winning games than Coach P."

That was the case until his final years, when SU began losing recruits and football games to emerging programs at Rutgers and UConn. Pasqualoni would go on to successful stints as an NFL assistant with the Dallas Cowboys and Miami Dolphins before returning to the college ranks as the head coach at Connecticut. He lasted just four games into his third season before being fired and hooking on as an assistant with the Chicago Bears in 2014. His greatest work, though, was done at Syracuse, where he won 10 games three times and went to nine bowl games before the program plunged into the worst era in school history under his successor, Greg Robinson.

50 Conference Calls: ECAC, Big East, ACC

For much of its sports history, Syracuse University operated as an independent that basically played schools in the Northeast and Midwest. The football team occasionally ventured to the West Coast for games, but for the most part the Orangemen competed against schools within reasonable travel distance—upstate New York colleges such as Colgate, Cornell, Army, Niagara, and St. Bonaventure, as well as schools in New York City and nearby states.

The Ivy League, which competed in a conference originally known as the Eastern Intercollegiate League, was athletic royalty in the late 19th and early 20th century, dominating in most sports but particularly football and basketball. By the turn of the century, SU began holding its own against the Ivy League—to the point where in 1908 the school applied for membership. Nothing came of it so another attempt was made four years later, again to no avail. Some sports historians believe that Cornell may have thwarted Syracuse's efforts. Bad blood had developed between the schools as the result of several brawls that broke out between the Orangemen and Big Red during a 1900 football game. The fights resulted in a suspension of the schools' football series, and the two universities did not play each other in football again until 1933.

Just before the onset of World War II, SU began an affiliation with the newly formed Eastern Collegiate Athletic Conference, better known as the ECAC. At its peak, the conference had more than 100 schools at the Division I, II, and III levels. Although SU abided by the ECAC's rules and participated in many of its tournaments, the ECAC was too large and unwieldy to be thought of as a league. In the 1950s, '60s, and '70s, the Orangemen were part of an unofficial league known as the East Indies. This was a collection of Eastern independent programs that included Penn State, Pitt, West Virginia, Boston College, Army, and Navy. Each of the schools had a gentlemen's agreement that they would play one another regularly, which helped alleviate the burden of scheduling.

The league affiliation that everyone associates most with Syracuse is the Big East Conference. SU was a charter member in 1979, along with Georgetown, St. John's, Providence College, Connecticut, Boston College, and Seton Hall. The brainchild of Providence basketball coach and athletic director Dave Gavitt, the Big East was formed as a basketball conference that would later expand to include several more schools and all men's and women's sports. The league was born out of fear after the NCAA announced

Huge Hoops Achievement in the Big East

Syracuse University's basketball team finished its 34-year run in the Big East Conference atop the all-time standings with a 366–192 regular season record and a .656 winning percentage, 28 games ahead of runner-up Georgetown. During that time, the Orange won 10 regular-season titles and five conference titles. Jim Boeheim was the only coach to work all 34 seasons of the conference, setting records for wins (416, which includes 50 in the tournament) and games coached (637). SU also led the way with a league-record 101 Big East selections, including 35 first-team picks.

in 1977 that you would have to be part of a conference in order to get a bid to the Big Dance. While others panicked, Gavitt saw a golden opportunity. He figured that if the Big East focused on big markets such as New York, Philadelphia, Boston, and Washington, D.C., they'd be able to land a huge television contract. At first, the schools he approached balked because they couldn't see his vision. But Gavitt was a persuasive, trustworthy guy who was seen as a peer rather than a bureaucrat by coaches and athletic directors. "We trusted Dave," said SU coach Jim Boeheim. "And I'm glad we did because his vision wound up exceeding everyone's expectation, maybe even his own."

Thanks to a perfect storm of circumstances, the Big East clearly lived up to its name. It hooked on with a fledgling cable network called ESPN, and both the conference and the network experienced dramatic growth together. You had colorful coaches in Boeheim, John Thompson, Rollie Massimino, and Lou Carnesecca. There was star power on the court, beginning with Pearl Washington, Patrick Ewing, and Chris Mullin. You had intense rivalries, especially Syracuse-Georgetown. The spectacle of Carrier Dome crowds in excess of 30,000 also played a role. So did Gavitt's brilliant idea of planting the Big East tournament in Madison Square Garden, where it quickly became the most compelling postseason event this side of the NCAAs.

The Big East eventually had to expand to accommodate the demands of football, adding schools such as Pitt, West Virginia, Virginia Tech, and Miami, as well as allowing Notre Dame to become a member in everything but football. As the landscape of major college sports changed, schools began realigning based on their football programs, and that led to the demise of the Big East as we knew it. First Miami, Virginia Tech, and Boston College departed for the Atlantic Coast Conference, and in 2014, Syracuse and Pitt followed suit. The downside, of course, was the end of old rivalries, particularly SU's basketball wars with Georgetown and UConn. The upside was the start of new rivalries with Duke and North Carolina plus the move to a stronger football league that featured powerhouses such as 2013 national champion Florida State.

"I was as saddened as anyone to see us leave, but we weren't leaving the Big East we had known," Boeheim said. "It had changed dramatically in recent years, and we had to make a move to better secure our future as an athletic program. I think Syracuse fans have embraced the move, but it's going to take time before we feel a total part of it. And I don't know if it will ever be like it was with the Big East. That was something truly special and probably impossible to duplicate."

51 Jim Nance

By the seventh grade, Jim Nance had sprouted to 6'1" and 220 pounds. He was the biggest kid in his school, but he had yet to discover organized sports. "I was very shy," he explained. "I remember walking down the hall one day when the school's football coach,

Dick Fairburgh—we called him Fireball—started yelling in my direction. I was praying he wasn't talking to me. But he was. He said, 'Hey, why aren't you out for football? You're big enough to eat hay.'" Nance tried out that fall and quickly displayed a knack for knocking people on their keisters. He also took up wrestling, which became his passion. "In football, you can depend on other people," he said. "In wrestling, you have no one but yourself."

During his junior and senior years in the small coal-mining town of Indiana, Pennsylvania, Nance won back-to-back heavyweight state wrestling championships. But it was his football prowess that earned him a scholarship to Syracuse University in 1961. He would eventually make a huge impression—on the gridiron and the wrestling mat. "Syracuse was an unbelievably great experience for me," Nance said. "You have to understand that I was a poor black kid from a small town. Syracuse seemed so big to me. You could fit two or three of my hometowns in Archbold Stadium. I got a tingle up my spine just walking around campus."

People who attempted to tackle Nance or get in the way of his pulverizing blocks experienced a tingling sensation of a different sort. "Some guys described it like trying to tackle a freight train," said long-time Syracuse assistant coach Joe Szombathy. "He wasn't just a big lug, either. The wrestling had made him extremely quick on his feet."

Nance ran for 1,605 yards during his three years at Syracuse, and he led the Orangemen in rushing with 951 yards and 13 touchdowns during his senior season in 1964. That year, he and halfback Floyd Little led SU to a 7–3 record and a berth in the Sugar Bowl, which Louisiana State won 13–10.

Big Jim was even more impressive as a wrestler, winning 92-of-93 varsity matches and two NCAA heavyweight titles. "I'll never forget this one match against this big oaf from Penn State," said Alan Brickman, a Syracuse attorney who negotiated Nance's professional football contracts. "Jim used to psyche himself into a frenzy. Before this particular match, Jim stomped around and snarled at his opponent. The guy decided to forfeit instead of going out onto the mat against Jim."

Nance was drafted in the fourth round by the Chicago Bears of the NFL but opted instead to sign with the AFL's Boston Patriots, who had selected him in the 19th round (151st overall). After a mediocre rookie season in 1965, Nance came into his own his second year in the league, rumbling for 1,458 yards and 11 touchdowns in 14 games to capture the AFL rushing title and league MVP honors. The next year he led the league in rushing again with 1,216 yards. The Patriots traded him to the Philadelphia Eagles in 1972, but the Eagles released him and he finished his career with the New York Jets the following year. In eight pro seasons, Nance rushed for 5,401 yards and scored 45 touchdowns. He also caught 133 passes for 870 yards and one score.

Sadly, Nance had problems controlling his weight once he stopped playing football, and he ballooned to more than 300 pounds. In 1984, he suffered a debilitating stroke. Eight years later he died at age 49.

Lawrence Moten

As high school teammates at Archbishop Carroll in Washington, D.C., Marvin Graves saw firsthand just how good Lawrence Moten was at football. As a ball-hawking safety during his senior season in 1990, Moten intercepted 13 passes to earn District of Columbia Defensive Player of the Year honors. So it's not surprising that after Graves accepted a scholarship to play quarterback for SU, he tried to convince Moten to play football as well as basketball for the Orangemen.

"I considered it, but it was going to be too tough academically, and basketball was my first love," Moten said. "Plus, you don't see too many 6'5", 175-lb. safeties out there. I think I made the right choice." That he did. While Graves was breaking many of the school passing records established by predecessor Don McPherson, Moten was scoring more points (2,334) than anyone in Syracuse and Big East Conference basketball history.

Not bad for a guy who was considered an afterthought in SU's 1991 blue-chip recruiting class, which included Luke Jackson, Anthony Harris, Glenn Sekunda, Lazarus Sims, and J.B. Reafsnyder. It didn't take long for Moten to establish himself as the class of that class. He wasn't expected to see a great deal of playing time his freshman season, but when veteran guard Adrian Autry went down with a severely sprained ankle, Boeheim decided to replace Autry with the unheralded Moten. It was a risky move because Syracuse was going to play a powerful Florida State team that boasted future NBA players Sam Cassell and Doug Edwards. Moten proved equal to the task, scoring 18 points to lead SU to an 89–71 upset. The superlative performance was a harbinger event as Moten averaged 18.2 points per game that season to earn national Freshman of the Year honors.

During his next three seasons, his silky smooth and almost effortless style of play would become known to Orange fans as "Poetry in Moten." Despite being limited athletically, the player who wore his socks up to his knees had an uncanny knack for finding different ways to score. His career numbers, though impressive, tell only part of his story. In addition to being a prolific scorer, Moten will be remembered for helping the Syracuse program weather its NCAA probation and remain a basketball powerhouse.

Georgetown's Alonzo Mourning (33) goes up for two, but is stopped by Syracuse's Lawrence Moten (21) as Dave Johnson (4) looks on during their Big East Championship matchup at New York's Madison Square Garden on Sunday, March 16, 1992. The Orangemen defeated the Hoyas 56–54.
(AP Photo/Ron Frehm)

All-Time SU Basketball Scoring Leaders

Player	Years	Total Points
Lawrence Moten	1991–95	2,334
Derrick Coleman	1986–90	2,143
John Wallace	1992–96	2,119
Gerry McNamara	2002–06	2,099
Hakim Warrick	2001–05	2,073

"He wouldn't win any race, he wasn't able to jump out of the building, and his outside shot didn't have a great deal of trajectory, but Lawrence definitely had a nose for the basket and knew how to score," Boeheim said. "He was what I'd call an old-school player. He was also a quiet assassin. You might not think he did much out there because he didn't look like he was expending a lot of energy. But then you'd look at the box score and see 25 points next to his name. He's another one of those guys who people tend to overlook when they talk about great Syracuse players. And that's a shame. I think it might be because he played during that period when we were coming off the probation."

During his sophomore year, Moten averaged 17.9 points per game as a shooting guard and small forward. His heroics that season included a 10' jumper with 24 seconds to go to beat Providence; a 16-point second half to knock off Connecticut; 21 points in an upset of ninth-ranked Seton Hall; and a 26-point effort in a Big East tournament semifinal victory vs. St. John's.

He continued to elevate his game during his junior year, averaging a career-high 21.5 points. His scoring average dipped a bit to 19.6 his senior year as the Orangemen stumbled down the stretch and were one-and-done in the Big East tournament for the second consecutive year. After beating a pesky Southern Illinois squad in the opening round of the NCAAs, Syracuse faced defending national champion Arkansas. Moten scored 27 points against the Razorbacks' "forty minutes of hell" full-court pressure defense.

Sadly, though, a play near the end of regulation would overshadow Moten's impressive performance and bring a premature and ignominious end to SU's season and his career. Rallying from a 12-point second-half deficit, the Orange took an 82–81 lead with just 4.3 seconds left. The Razorbacks attempted an inbounds, and Jackson dived onto the floor to steal the pass. As an Arkansas player tried to wrest the ball from Jackson, Moten instinctively did what players do in those situations. He called a timeout so that SU would maintain possession. Unfortunately for him and his teammates, Syracuse didn't have any timeouts left, resulting in a technical foul. Arkansas converted 1-of-2 to send the game into overtime, nipping the Orangemen 96–94. It was the third time in four years that Moten's season ended with an overtime loss in the NCAAs. His faux pas conjured memories of the championship game two years earlier when Michigan's Chris Webber called a timeout he didn't have.

Boeheim came to Moten's defense in the postgame press conference, reminding reporters that the senior captain had smartly used timeouts in those situations several times that year. "I think in the heat of the moment like that, your instincts take over," the coach said. "You forget the situation and just react. The other thing people forget is that we aren't anywhere close to being in a position to win that game without Lawrence going off on the Razorbacks the way he did. Without Lawrence scoring like he did against that tenacious defense, we get run out of the gym."

That June, Moten was drafted by the Vancouver Grizzlies in the second round and played parts of three seasons in the NBA—two with the Grizzlies and one with the Washington Wizards. One of his highlights came when he scored 10 points against the legendary Michael Jordan. After being released following the 1997–98 season, he played several years of minor-league basketball in the U.S., Spain, and Venezuela. After retiring from playing in 2006, he worked as president of player development for the Maryland

Nighthawks and coach of the Rochester (New York) RazorSharks in the Premier Basketball League.

53 Check Out Ernie Davis' Heisman, Statues, and Grave Site

Of all the athletes to come through Syracuse University, none has been more revered than Ernie Davis. There are two life-sized statues of him—one on campus and the other in front of Ernie Davis Middle School in his hometown of Elmira, New York, about 90 minutes south of Syracuse. There is a recently constructed dormitory named in his honor on the SU campus. The words "Ernie Davis Legends Field" are painted onto the turf at the Carrier Dome. And, of course, there's the historic Heisman Trophy Davis won in 1961 when he became the first African American to receive the award.

The statue on campus depicts Davis in a Syracuse football uniform, holding his helmet in his left arm. It's located on the quad, which is not far from the steps of Hendricks Chapel, where pregame pep rallies are held before football games. The statue stands on a pedestal with the nearby Dome prominent in the background. With several of Davis' relatives, Floyd Little, actor Dennis Quaid, and the SU Marching Band looking on, the statue was unveiled during a ceremony on September 13, 2008. On that day several people—including Little, who came to Syracuse because of Davis—gave moving speeches about what Davis meant to them.

A few days later, the source-of-pride statue became a source of embarrassment as members of the media reported that the icon lacked historical accuracy because it showed Davis holding

Other Tributes to SU's Athletic Stars

In the same wing of the Iocolano-Petty complex, you'll find trophies from the bowl games that SU participated in, along with plenty of photos, cards, etc., of the great teams and personalities in Orange football history. In addition, there are sculpted busts of Jim Brown and Ben Schwartzwalder.

At the entrance to Manley Field House, there's a bust of legendary SU athlete and lacrosse coach Roy Simmons Sr. beneath a picture of him with his son, Roy Jr., who succeeded him. Inside Manley's lobby are display cases of men's and women's sports, current and discontinued, as well as trophies from the more than 20 national championships won by SU squads through the years. Nearby, on the back wall, is a marvelous timeline collage tracing the rich history of Orange lacrosse, replete with photos, stories, and quotations. To the left of the lobby is a hallway leading to the Carmelo Anthony Center, with two long display cases devoted to the special players, teams, and moments in Syracuse basketball history.

The Carrier Dome is a great place to catch up on SU's athletic history. Retired basketball and football jerseys hang from the rafters, along with photo banners of championship teams and All-American players. The corridors are festooned with action photos of SU athletes from a wide variety of sports, as well as pictures of entertainers who have performed in the Dome, including such acts as Bruce Springsteen, Billy Joel, Frank Sinatra, and the Rolling Stones. There is also a special display case that features the trophy from the Orangemen's 2003 NCAA basketball championship.

a modern-day helmet and wearing cleats with a Nike swoosh. The stories were picked up nationwide, and the university hired renowned Italian sculptor Bruno Lucchesi to repair the errors of the original sculptor. Roughly a year later, this time without an unveiling ceremony, the revised statue was placed back on its pedestal.

Lucchesi was the perfect choice to do the repairs because he sculpted the first statue of Davis that stands in front of the middle school that used to be the high school Ernie attended—Elmira Free Academy. That statue, unveiled on June 19, 1988, shows Davis wearing a letterman's sweater with a football in one hand, and books in the other. At its base is a plaque that reads:

Ernie Davis

1939–1963

1961 Heisman Trophy Winner

A football player...a student...a friend...a hero.

He lived with integrity and died with courage.

This statue given by his admirers as an inspiration to the youth of tomorrow.

In memory of a life full of determination and honor.

The bronze likeness is located a few miles from Woodlawn Cemetery, where Davis is buried. It's worth a trip to his grave site. Prominent signs at the cemetery direct you to his final resting place. While there, you can also view the grave of great American novelist Mark Twain.

Davis' Heisman, presented to the university by his mom following his death in May 1963, can be viewed in the Iocolano-Petty Football Complex, which is adjacent to Manley Field House on south campus. One of Davis' game-worn jerseys is also on display, along with pictures of him in action.

Interestingly, Davis' Heisman was located in a case in the Manley Field House corridor for years. But someone stole it on St. Patrick's Day in 1976. The trophy went missing for 14 days before an anonymous person dropped it off at the newsroom of the *Syracuse Post-Standard.*

54 Laurie Cox

Canadian-born and Harvard-educated Laurie Davidson Cox had already made a name for himself as a leading American landscape architect by the time he arrived at Syracuse University as an associate professor at the College of Forestry in 1915. He would spend 32 years there as a faculty member and department chair and would have a lasting impact on parks and trails in New York City, Los Angeles, and Vermont.

The arborist would plant more than trees during his time at SU—Cox would also change the landscape of college athletics by starting Syracuse's lacrosse program in 1916. An outstanding player during his undergraduate days at Harvard, Cox believed the sport had great potential on the collegiate level. In 1920, he led the Orangemen to a share of the United States Intercollegiate Lacrosse Association championship, the equivalent of an NCAA title today. From 1922 through 1925, his teams would go 53–4–3 and win three more crowns.

Over time, Cox would become regarded not only as the father of Syracuse lacrosse but as the father of college lacrosse in America. In 1922, he arranged for a combined squad from Oxford and Cambridge to journey to the U.S. to play several colleges, including Syracuse. The month-long excursion proved to be an enormous success. It received widespread coverage in the press, and sizable crowds attended each game. More than 5,000 people showed up for the Syracuse match, which saw the Orangemen eke out a 4–3 victory. The tour boosted support for existing lacrosse programs and prompted more than a dozen American colleges to add the sport to their athletic lineup. In 1923, Cox's Orangemen reciprocated by participating in a lacrosse tour in England. These international tours would continue for the next 14 years.

Cox immersed himself in all aspects of the sport, from strengthening participation in the USILA to arranging matches against teams from the nearby Onondaga Nation. He believed much could be learned by playing against the originators of the game, particularly in regard to improving his players' stick-handling skills. Cox was among the first college coaches to recruit Native Americans to coach and play for his team. He hired Ike Lyons from the reservation as an assistant coach in 1919 and recruited Victor Ross to play for him. Ross became a two-time All-American and a star on SU's 16–0 national champion team in 1922. Roy Simmons Sr., a star quarterback for the SU football team, played on Cox's 1924 and 1925 national champion teams, earning All-American honors as a junior. When Cox stepped down as coach following an uncharacteristic 3–8 finish in 1930, Simmie took over and held the post for the next 40 years.

In Cox's fourteen seasons (play was suspended in 1917 because of World War I), the Orangemen went 116–40–15, a .722 winning percentage, and they won four national titles. Cox, who died at age 85 in 1968, was a charter member of the National Lacrosse Hall of Fame. A prominent youth camp and tournament named in his honor is held each summer in New England.

The 2–3 Zone

Mention the words "2–3 zone" to a basketball coach and it's a slam dunk the conversation will quickly get around to its patron saint, Jim Boeheim. Arguably no coach in hoops history—maybe even sports history, for that matter—has been more closely identified with a tactical operation than Boeheim has been with the defense his Syracuse teams have used with smothering success for nearly two decades. Every SU basketball broadcast, be it national or local, at some point invariably includes a discussion about the zone's web-like ability to entangle opponents and induce turnovers, shot-clock violations, and missed shots.

Boeheim was first exposed to the defense while playing for innovative Lyons High School coach Dick Blackwell in the 1950s. Lyons, which was a Rochester-area scholastic basketball power-house, employed both the 2–3 and 2–1–2 zones about 30 percent of the time as an effective change of pace to the tenacious man-to-man defense Blackwell liked to employ. While playing at Syracuse in the 1960s, Boeheim played it some more, although coach Fred Lewis was a bigger proponent of full-court pressure. As an assistant coach under Roy Danforth, Boeheim's study and execution of the zone continued. And when he became head coach at SU in 1976, he began using it more than his predecessors had.

Still, it wasn't really until SU's 1996 NCAA tournament run that Boeheim utilized the 2–3 zone virtually 100 percent of the time. "Finally it dawned on me, after about 27 or 28 years, that if we played zone all the time and didn't waste time playing man-to-man and put some wrinkles in the zone, [then] our defense would be better," he said.

That team, which lost to Kentucky in the title game, boasted a lineup of long-armed, lanky players. The backcourt featured 6'5" guard Lazarus Sims and 6'6" guard Jason Cipolla, while the front court was led by 6'8" John Wallace. "Having guards that tall really made it difficult for other teams to toss the ball inside," Boeheim said. "And our front court guys, especially John, had big wing-spans." Since that time, he has recruited players with the zone in mind.

"We've had plenty of guys whose wing span was actually greater than their height," said longtime SU assistant Mike Hopkins. "Long arms result in a lot of tipped passes in the lanes and a lot of turnovers for easy baskets. Plus, it makes the trapping we do within the framework of the zone much more effective." The other advantage of the zone is that few teams play it, so there's an element of unfamiliarity that opponents have to deal with. In this case, unfamiliarity breeds contempt. "The thing about their zone is that you can try to prepare for it in practice, but there's no way your second team is going to be able to replicate the athleticism and length of the players Jim has playing it," said ESPN analyst Jay Bilas.

Through the years, Boeheim has tinkered with his zone and will even make adjustments to it during the course of a game. ESPN basketball analyst Fran Fraschilla coached against it several times during his tenure as head coach at St. John's. The aggressiveness of Boeheim's zone sets it apart from its passive ancestors. "The fascination for most people is it's got a reputation as a summer-league defense," Fraschilla told the *Syracuse Post-Standard* in a March 2010 interview. "For most people, it's a defensive defense. Most teams use a zone in reaction to keeping a big guy from hurting you or keeping a guard from driving in the lane. But for Jim, it's a weapon that Syracuse opponents have to react to. Because of the length and athleticism of his players through the years, it's become a weapon as opposed to something you do as a reaction to a good team."

Although the offensive dynamism of Carmelo Anthony and Gerry McNamara attracted the headlines during SU's drive to the national championship in 2003, it was actually the Orangemen's defense that secured the title. Their zone totally discombobulated Oklahoma in the East Region title game, and the clinching play of the NCAA championship matchup with Kansas occurred when forward Hakim Warrick streaked to the corner in the final seconds and swatted away Michael Lee's three-point attempt.

In recent years, the 2–3 continued to be Syracuse's bread and butter. The Orangemen have annually ranked among the nation's leaders in steals, turnovers forced, blocked shots, field goal percentage defense, and points allowed. "Jim's zone," Fraschilla said, "is the Mariano Rivera cutter—nearly impossible to hit."

56 SU's National Champs

Syracuse University has fielded 28 national championship teams through the years, including 15 in lacrosse, six in crew, three in basketball, and two in cross country. The Orangemen have also captured titles in football and boxing. Twenty-two individuals have won national championships, including eight in boxing, seven in wrestling, six in gymnastics, and one in track & field. Four athletes have won multiple titles: wrestler Gene Mills (1979 and 1981), wrestler Jim Nance (1963 and 1965), gymnast Leo Minotti (1950 and 1951), and boxer John Granger (1954 and 1955). According to the University's website, boxer Al Wertheimer was the first individual to win a national championship (1932), while the 1904 men's rowers were the first SU team to take national honors.

Not all of the titles are recognized by the NCAA, since sports such as boxing and crew are not sponsored by the major governing body of college sports. The boxing, wrestling, and gymnastics programs have since been dropped by the school. Through the 2014 spring season, no SU female athlete or team has won a national title, although the Orange women have reached either Final Fours or championship games in field hockey, ice hockey, and lacrosse.

Here's a look at SU's team and individual national champions:

Team

Sport	Years
Men's crew	1904, 1908, 1913, 1916, 1920, 1978
Men's lacrosse	1920, 1922, 1924, 1925, 1983, 1988, 1989, 1990, 1993, 1995, 2000, 2002, 2004, 2008, 2009
Men's basketball	1917–18, 1925–26, 2003
Men's cross country	1949, 1951
Football	1959
Boxing	1936

Individual

Boxing

Year	Boxer	Weight Class
1932	Al Wertheimer	126 lbs.
1936	Ord Fink	155 lbs.
1936	Ray Jeffries	165 lbs.
1942	Salvatore Mirabito	Heavyweight
1947	Jerry Auclair	125 lbs.
1949	Marty Crandell	Heavyweight
1954	John Granger	139 lbs.
1955	John Granger	139 lbs.

Wrestling

Year	Wrestler	Weight Class
1959	Art Baker	191 lbs.
1963	Jim Nance	Heavyweight
1965	Jim Nance	Heavyweight
1967	Tom Schlendorf	191 lbs.
1979	Gene Mills	118 lbs.
1980	Gene Mills	118 lbs.
1992	Mark Kerr	190 lbs.

Gymnastics

Year	Gymnast	Apparatus
1950	Leo Minotti	rope climb
1950	Gene Rabbitt	side horse
1951	Leo Minotti	rope climb
1953	James "Corky" Sebbo	tumbling
1964	Sydney Oglesby	long horse
1992	Jason Hebert	vault

Track & Field

Year	Runner	Specialty
2012	Jerret Eaton	60m hurdles

Rony Seikaly

Jim Boeheim didn't have to recruit Rony Seikaly. Seikaly recruited him.

A native of Lebanon who was raised in Greece, the 6'11" Seikaly had a brother attending nearby Colgate, a small liberal arts school about an hour southeast of SU in the middle of nowhere. The family bought Seikaly's older brother an apartment in Syracuse for him to use when he grew bored with life at Colgate. The Seikaly brothers also had a sister who briefly attended SU.

One day during the summer of 1983, Rony showed up to watch some games at the basketball camp run by Boeheim and his staff. The young man had only played basketball for a brief time, but he had fallen in love with the game. He decided to pay Boeheim a visit one day. "I had no idea who he was, but when a

6'11" kid knocks on your door, you listen because you can't teach height," Boeheim joked.

Boeheim and assistant Bernie Fine watched Seikaly play in some pickup games and realized immediately that the young man was a diamond in the rough. "It was obvious from the way he ran the floor and leaped that he was a very gifted athlete," Boeheim said. "But it was also apparent that he was way, way behind most kids his age as far as basketball instincts. We knew he was going to be a project, and it was going to take a lot of work on his part to try to play catch-up. It was going to depend on him and how hard he wanted to work." Boeheim turned over Seikaly to Fine, SU's designated teacher of big men.

The basketball education of Seikaly did not always go smoothly. He had been raised in an affluent family and in a different culture. He wasn't used to being yelled at, and he often reacted poorly when Boeheim began pushing him. "I think Rony definitely was a little spoiled," the coach said. "We certainly had our moments where we would be exasperated with him and he would be exasperated with us. But, to his credit, he responded. And looking back, he became one of the best players in the history of our program."

Seikaly admitted that it was quite a culture shock at first. He had been used to finesse basketball while playing at the American School in Athens, Greece. But he quickly discovered that wouldn't be the style of play he would encounter in the rugged world of the Big East, where bodies often crashed beneath the basket. "When I first got to Syracuse, I didn't know a two-shot foul from a one-and-one," Seikaly said. "All I did was run around out there, dunking and blocking shots. Other than that, I had no idea what I was doing."

In time, he would learn—and his progression from season to season would be steady and dramatic. After red-shirting a year, he averaged 8.1 points and 6.4 rebounds per game during the 1984–85 campaign. He improved to 10.1 and 7.8 the next season but was

Rony Seikaly scores two of his 33 points over Florida's Dwayne Schintzius during their NCAA Eastern Regional game at the Meadowlands Arena in East Rutherford, New Jersey, on March 20, 1987. (AP Photo/Ron Frehm)

constantly in foul trouble, fouling out of eight games. During his junior year, he made a quantum leap, averaging 15.1 points and 8.2 rebounds. He turned in a dominating performance in the 1987 NCAA tournament, propelling the Orangemen to within a basket of a national championship.

Seikaly scored 22 points in a first-round 79–73 victory against Georgia Southern that year, then he had 23 points in an easy second-round victory vs. Western Kentucky. Many believed Seikaly would be overmatched in the Sweet 16 against Florida's Dwayne Schintzus, a cocky 7'2" center regarded as the best big man in America. A few days before the game, Schintzus told reporters he wasn't impressed with SU's center. Derrick Coleman and walk-on Joel Katz made sure the newspaper clipping found its way into Seikaly's locker. The motivational ploy worked as Seikaly schooled his more-hyped rival, scoring 33 points and hauling in nine rebounds as the Orangemen knocked off Florida 87–81. Seikaly out-scored Schintzus 23–4 in the first half, and the flummoxed Gators' center fouled out in the second half.

Two days later, Seikaly continued his remarkable roll with 26 points and 11 rebounds in his matchup with North Carolina All-American J.R. Reid as Syracuse shocked the No. 2–ranked Tar Heels 79–75 to advance to the Final Four. The Orangemen easily disposed of Providence, but their charmed run ended with the painful loss to Indiana on Keith Smart's jumper in the title game. Seikaly played well against the Hoosiers, finishing with 18 points and 10 boards.

After briefly contemplating a jump to the NBA, Seikaly returned for his senior season at SU and earned All-American honors after averaging 16.3 points and 9.6 rebounds per game. Selected ninth overall in the 1988 draft by the expansion Miami Heat, Seikaly went on to have one of the better NBA careers by a former Orangeman, averaging 14.7 points and 9.5 rebounds per game during his 11 seasons. He set the Heat record for most rebounds in a season (934 in 1991–92) and had 20 games of at least 20 points and 20 rebounds in the same game.

Seikaly returned to the Carrier Dome on January 13, 2007, to have his No. 4 jersey retired. Known during his NBA career as "The Spin Doctor" for moves in the lane, Seikaly has become one of the world's most successful music producers and DJs.

Jim Konstanty

Nicknamed "Big Jim," Casmir James Konstanty was one of the most versatile athletes in SU history, lettering in baseball, basketball, boxing, and soccer before graduating with a degree in physical education in 1939. Eleven years later, after a circuitous journey through professional baseball, Konstanty shocked himself and the sports world by winning the National League Most Valuable Player Award and being named the professional Athlete of the Year by the Associated Press. His MVP was a milestone moment in baseball history because it marked the first time a relief pitcher had received the award. Only three relievers since—Rollie Fingers (1981), Willie Hernandez (1984), and Dennis Eckersley (1992)—have accomplished the feat.

The 6'2" bespectacled Konstanty never envisioned reaching such lofty heights. In fact, despite experiencing some success with the Orange, he figured his baseball-playing days were pretty much over after college. The game plan, upon graduation, was to teach and coach. And that's what he did, immediately landing a job as a physical education teacher at St. Regis Falls (New York) High

Philadelphia Phillies relief pitcher Jim Konstanty in action on September 26, 1950. (AP Photo)

School. But two years later, a scout convinced him to give professional baseball a shot, and Konstanty signed a contract with the Eastern League team in Springfield, Massachusetts.

His rookie season was a disaster as he went 4–19. He was ready to kiss baseball goodbye, but he decided to stick with it. In 1944, with major-league rosters depleted because of World War II, Konstanty was called up to the Cincinnati Reds and went 6–4 with a respectable 2.80 earned run average (ERA). Following a year in the navy, Konstanty was traded from the Reds to the Boston Braves. After 10 appearances the Braves sold him to Toronto of the International League. It was there, in Triple A, that Konstanty developed a slider and palm ball that would baffle hitters and lead to big-league fame. In 1949, he pitched in 53 games for the Phillies, all in relief, and posted a 9–5 record with seven saves and a 3.25 ERA.

Despite the decent season, no one—not even Konstanty—had an inkling of what was about to unfold. In 1950, the 33-year-old right-hander experienced a career year while leading the "Whiz Kids" to the Phillies' first pennant in 35 years. Konstanty appeared in 74 games (then a major-league record), winning 16 and saving 22 others. One of just a handful of college graduates in baseball at the time, Konstanty had a positive, calming influence on the Phillies young roster, which featured several players in their early twenties. His scintillating season also resulted in an invitation to the All-Star Game, where he pitched a scoreless inning. In a surprise move, he was chosen by Phillies manager Eddie Sawyer to start Game One of the 1950 World Series against the New York Yankees. Konstanty took the loss but acquitted himself well, allowing just four hits and one run.

Four years later, Konstanty was waived by the Phillies and picked up by the New York Yankees and is credited with fueling their 1955 pennant drive with a 7–2 record and 11 saves. His work

Lew Carr and the SU Baseball Program

Trivia question: who played shortstop for the Pittsburgh Pirates before baseball Hall of Famer Honus Wagner?

Answer: Lew Carr.

An injury to Carr opened the door for Wagner to move over from third base, and the rest, as they say, is history. But Carr would go on to become a baseball legend and a Hall of Famer, too—as a college coach.

After his professional career ended, Carr enrolled in Syracuse Law School, where he earned his degree and became the school's head baseball coach in 1910. He spent 34 years on the job—the fourth-longest coaching tenure in SU history—and led the Orange to 275 wins in 543 games. Carr became known as "Mr. Baseball" on campus, and in 1952 the baseball field behind Manley Field House was re-named in his honor. He would later be inducted into the College Baseball Hall of Fame.

The Orangemen fielded a baseball team, off and on, from 1870 through 1972 when it was disbanded because of budgetary cuts. During baseball's 102-year history at SU, the university produced 23 major-league players, including relievers Jim Konstanty, the 1950 National League MVP, and Dave Giusti, who compiled a 100–93 record with 145 saves in 16 seasons. Syracuse baseball's high-water mark occurred in 1961 when the Orange went 18–5, including a 2–2 mark in the College World Series. That club was paced by Giusti and fellow pitcher Billy Connors, who has been the vice president for player personnel for the New York Yankees from 1996 to 2012.

both for and against the Bronx Bombers impressed Yankees Hall of Fame skipper Casey Stengel, who said, "Konstanty is one of the greatest I've ever seen in the clutch."

In 11 seasons, Konstanty pitched in 433 games, posting a 66–48 won-lost record with 74 saves and a respectable 3.46 ERA. After hanging up his spikes, Konstanty scouted for the Yankees and worked as a minor league pitching instructor for the Cardinals. He also opened up a sporting goods store in Oneonta and spent four years as the athletic director at Hartwick College before passing away at age 59 in 1976. In 2008 he was inducted into the National Polish-American Sports Hall of Fame, and in 2014 he was nominated for the Phillies Hall of Fame.

59 Leo Rautins' Tip-In

The 1980–81 season had not been an especially fruitful one for the Syracuse basketball team. Having lost stars Roosevelt Bouie and Louis Orr to graduation, SU stumbled to a 10–6 start. And no Orangeman struggled more than Leo Rautins, the much-ballyhooed sophomore transfer who had yet to live up to the hype of being one of the greatest high school players to ever come out of Canada.

On the bus ride home from Olean, New York, after a putrid performance in a loss to St. Bonaventure, Rautins was summoned by Jim Boeheim to the front of the bus. "[Coach] said, 'I have to bench you,' and I told him, 'I understand. I'd bench me, too,'" Rautins recalled. "The only thing I asked was that I'd like a chance to get my job back, and he said that would happen if my play came around."

The benching of Rautins failed to change SU's fortunes as the Orangemen dropped five of their last nine to finish the regular season at 15–11, a far cry from their 24–2 regular season mark the year before. The only saving grace was that the Big East Tournament was being held in the Carrier Dome. (It wouldn't establish permanent residency in Madison Square Garden until 1983.) Boeheim and his players believed they might be able to turn things around in the postseason. And they did, thanks to Rautins, who had regained his confidence in practices and games down the stretch, despite the losses. "It's funny—we probably had no right to think this way—but with all those games on our home court, we felt going in that the tournament was ours," Rautins said.

SU dispatched St. John's in the first round, but Rautins suffered a knee injury when Wayne McKoy of the Redmen barreled into him and was called for a charge. Rautins spent the night in the infirmary. Before the next day's game against Georgetown (a 67–53 win) and the championship game against Villanova, SU trainer Don Lowe had to spend several hours getting Rautins physically ready to play.

The title game, played in front of 15,213 fans, was a nail-biter, with Alex Bradley hitting a jumper with twenty seconds to go to send it into overtime. Interestingly, were it not for a lane violation by Rautins during teammate Eddie Moss' second free throw with 1:04 to go, SU would have won in regulation. Before you knew it, the game was into its third overtime and players from both teams were dragging. These were the days before the shot clock, so Boeheim decided to play stall ball after center Danny Schayes won the opening tap in the third OT. After three minutes of dribbling and passing the ball by the Orangemen, the Wildcats fouled Schayes. He made both free throws only to see Stewart Granger knot the game at 80. Syracuse held the ball on its next possession and, with eight seconds remaining, Boeheim called a timeout to draw up a final play. It called for Rautins to take the final shot. He did, but not the way the play was designed.

Rautins was supposed to inbound the ball to Erich Santifer who was supposed to drive a bit then dish off to Rautins. Instead, Santifer kept driving to the basket and tried to lay it in. Rautins sensed that Santifer might do that, so he immediately headed to the basket after he passed the ball in. When Santifer's shot fell off the rim, Rautins was there to put it back in. The instant the ball went through the hoop, Villanova coach Rollie Massimino called a timeout. The problem was that the Wildcats were out of timeouts, so the Orangemen were awarded a technical, which Schayes converted to close out the 83–80 win. Rautins received the tournament's Most Outstanding Player Award and was serenaded with chants of "Leo! Leo! Leo!" by the crowd.

Today, the winner of the conference tournament receives an automatic bid to the NCAAs. However, that wasn't the case in 1981, and the 18–11 Orangemen were snubbed by the selection committee and wound up in the NIT, where they won three games before losing to Tulsa in overtime in the title game.

Rautins, the Toronto kid who chose high-top sneakers and hoops over skates and hockey, had an excellent three years at SU, averaging 12.1 points per game during his career and leading the team in rebounding and assists his senior year. He recorded the first triple-double in Big East history in 1983 and was the first-round selection of the Philadelphia 76ers. Unfortunately, Rautins' NBA career was cut short by a knee injury. Two decades later, he would make another big contribution to the program when his son, Andy Rautins, helped shoot the Orangemen to a Big East regular season title and two NCAA appearances. Interestingly, Andy would play in a six-overtime game at the Big East Tournament.

Oren Lyons

Roy Simmons Sr. was seething. His undefeated Syracuse University lacrosse team had never beaten Army before, and it appeared that trend was going to continue on that mid-May afternoon in 1957. As the Orangemen jogged to the locker room at halftime, they trailed the Cadets by three goals.

During intermission, the fiery Simmons lit into his players, sparing no one, including his usually dependable goalie, Oren

Lyons. "He rarely spoke to me directly, but this time he did," Lyons recalled in a 1993 interview with the *Syracuse Post Standard.* "I said, 'Don't worry, Coach, we'll get them in the second half.' Coach Simmons looked at me and said, 'You'd better.' Well, we weren't on the field for more than 30 seconds and they come down and scored on me again. I was thinking, *Wow. What's happening here?*"

Lyons settled down after that and blanked Army the rest of the way. Led by the incomparable Jim Brown, the offense scored six goals, and SU won 8–6 to finish the year 10–0. "Oren was on his knees at one point, and he stopped three straight shots within a matter of seconds," Simmons said. "You could see how frustrated [the Cadets] were. I knew we would be okay then. He would stop shots no one else would even think of stopping."

What made Lyons' performance even more impressive was that it was achieved even though he was playing with torn knee ligaments. "You always knew Oren would be out there when it counted, no matter what," Simmons said. "There were times you could see that he was in pain. He would always look to the bench to signal that he was all right. He was a tough competitor."

Lyons earned All-American honors that season and the next, and he was awarded the Orange Key, which is presented annually to the school's top scholar-athlete. Thirty-four years later, he became just the second Native American inducted into the Lacrosse Hall of Fame. A faithkeeper and chief of the Onondaga, one of the six nations of the Iroquois Confederacy, Lyons was honored as "a player who had made a truly great contribution to society."

During his acceptance speech, Lyons advocated for the addition of more Native Americans to the Hall. "It's not just another award," Lyons said at the time. "It's an important landmark in my life. But really, this is an important day for all Indians. You see, I have to keep this in perspective. I'm only going to be one of two Indians in the Hall of Fame. And I can tell you without a doubt that there have been many Indians who were much better players than I ever was. I accept this award on behalf of them.

"I think you have to broaden your perspectives and horizons. You should consider other aspects of lacrosse that aren't involved in academia. There are great players in club lacrosse leagues all over, but they are rarely considered." Lyons also encouraged college coaches and others "to look closer at Indians who play on territories as opposed to high schools and consider extending to them a scholarship. We have a lot to offer."

Lyons was living proof of that. He had dropped out of high school to "save" himself, since he believed that Indians were programmed for failure in white schools. He joined the Army Airborne, received his high school equivalency diploma, and continued to hone his skills as an illustrator before returning to the Onondaga territory, just a few miles south of the SU campus. Simmons had wanted to recruit Lyons for years and finally convinced the admissions committee that this skilled artist deserved a chance. Lyons was accepted and would earn his degree in fine arts in 1959. After graduating, he worked as the planning director for Norcross Greeting Cards in New York City, began exhibiting his own paintings, and established himself as a successful commercial artist. But his heart yearned for his people, and when he was named sub-chief of the Turtle Clan, he moved his family back to the Onondaga Nation.

In the years following his return, Lyons devoted his life to advocacy on behalf of indigenous people and the environment. He helped found a national council that brought together respected Indian leaders from tribes throughout North America. The group enabled various nations to exchange cultural ideas and unite to encourage political change. In 1982 he established the Working Group on Indigenous Populations at the United Nations, and he began traveling the globe, giving voices to groups that had been overlooked. He received numerous honors along the way, including the Ellis Island Congressional Medal of Honor, the Elder and Wider Award from the Rosa Parks Institute, and Sweden's Friends of the Children Award, which he shared with his friend, Nelson Mandela.

Lyons wrote and illustrated several books, including *Exiled in the Land of the Free*, co-authored with John Mohawk. He was the subject of a PBS documentary by Bill Moyers, and he appeared in *The 11th Hour*, a documentary film produced by Leonardo DiCaprio and released in 2007. In 1993, Syracuse presented Lyons with an honorary law degree.

He achieved success in the beloved sport of his ancestors by stopping shots, but his victories in life came from taking shots on behalf of others. When he reflects on his extraordinary life, he can't help but think how Roy Simmons advocated for him to have an opportunity to attend SU. It wound up being a life-changing experience. "It's clear he was much more than a coach…he was a father figure," Lyons said of Simmons after learning of the coach's death in 1994. "He was an excellent person who had a genuine concern for the people he was involved with. He gave people a chance. He understood what the quality of a person was, rather than the color of a person…. In order to do that, he had to challenge the administration."

And by doing so, he opened a door for Lyons and provided a role model for others to emulate.

# John Wallace

With all-time leading scorer Lawrence Moten and two other starters graduating in 1995, John Wallace figured that maybe the timing was right for him to leave, too.

The 6'8" forward from Rochester was coming off a sensational junior season in which he impressed a number of NBA scouts by averaging 16.8 points and 8.2 rebounds per game, so he decided to do some research into the upcoming draft. However, after learning that he was projected as a late first- or early second-round pick, he decided another year of college seasoning would be beneficial. No one, of course, was more pleased with his decision than Jim Boeheim, who might very well have faced the first losing record of his storied career had Wallace not returned.

By staying put, Wallace was able to go places he had only dreamed about. Not only did he greatly enhance his draft stock, he almost shot, passed, and rebounded the Orangemen to a national championship. Along the way, he turned in two of the most indelible plays in SU hoops history while becoming the school's third all-time leading scorer (2,119 points) and rebounder (1,065). He, along with Moten, are credited with helping SU weather its probationary period following NCAA sanctions.

Wallace had guided his Greece Athena High School team to a New York State championship during a senior season that saw him named to the McDonald's, *Parade* magazine, and Converse All-American teams. Growing up roughly 90 miles west of Syracuse, he followed the Orangemen, particularly his idol, Derrick Coleman, closely.

"I loved everything about the program," he said. "The fast-paced offense, the humongous crowds in the Carrier Dome, and the intensity of Big East play. When my high school coach [Don Brown] told me in the 10th grade that he had received a recruiting letter from Coach Boeheim, I was ecstatic."

Still, there was some question if the NCAA investigation of the program and the threat of sanctions might test Wallace's loyalty. Kansas and Providence were among several schools that kept inquiring to see if he was still committed to the Orangemen after he accepted SU's scholarship offer in 1992. But their efforts to get Wallace to change his mind were in vain. "I talked to Coach [Boeheim] about the possible penalties, and he was straight with me," Wallace recalled. "He told me that they probably were going to get hit with a one-year ban from the NCAA tournament, and I was fine with that because I was making a four-year decision, not a one-year decision."

Despite not having the carrot of a postseason tournament appearance to dangle in front of his players, Boeheim's 1992–93 squad cobbled together a solid season, going 20–9 and making it all the way to the Big East Championship game, where it was clobbered by Seton Hall by 33 points. Wallace had a solid freshman season, averaging 11.1 points and a team-leading 7.6 rebounds per game. Wearing the same No. 44 jersey worn by Coleman, Wallace elevated his play his sophomore year, averaging 15 points and nine rebounds per game as SU improved to 23–7 and returned to the NCAAs, where it reached the Sweet 16 before running out of gas in overtime against a very good Missouri team. The Orangemen slipped a bit to a 20–10 record during Wallace's junior year, and they lost a heart-breaker in overtime to sixth-ranked Arkansas in the second round of the NCAAs.

Wallace blossomed into a superstar during his senior year. Joining a lineup that included his friend and long-time AAU teammate Lazarus Sims at point guard, senior Otis Hill at center, promising sophomore Todd Burgan at small forward, and junior college transfer Jason Cipolla at shooting guard, the Orangemen were talented enough to prove the naysayers wrong. "That may not have been the most talented team in my four years there, but it was the team where the pieces fit together best," Wallace said. "Most of the guys stayed in Syracuse that summer, and we played a lot of pickup basketball in our free time. I think that really helped us a lot. We developed a pretty tight bond."

SU began the season unranked but forced the pollsters to take notice when it opened with 11 consecutive victories, including a

79–70 upset of third-ranked Arizona on the road. Wallace had a monster game with 26 points and nine rebounds. The Orangemen finished the regular season at 22–7 and ranked 13th, but few expected much from them in the postseason. They wound up reaching the Big East tournament title game, where they lost decisively to third-ranked Connecticut.

After easy wins vs. Montana State and Drexel in the opening round of the West Region, they defeated Georgia 83–81 in overtime in a game that cemented Wallace's reputation as one of SU's all-time greats. Trailing by two with 2.1 seconds remaining in regulation, Boeheim, in a strategic move that went against conventional coaching wisdom, instructed Wallace, his best player, to inbound the ball from near half-court. The young man who grew up playing football and dreaming of becoming the next Randall Cunningham had the best arm on the team (other than SU's starting quarterback Donovan McNabb, who was a basketball reserve). When Sims was double-covered, Wallace went to his second option and rifled a pass to Cipolla, who drilled a 12' shot to send the game into overtime. The instant the ball swished through the net, the Syracuse players began whooping it up wildly in front of their bench, but Wallace quickly restored order and reminded them that they still had a five-minute overtime to play. The team's senior leader also reminded them that SU had lost in OT in each of their previous two NCAA tournaments.

With about 10 seconds remaining in OT and Georgia up by one, Wallace took the inbounds and began dribbling furiously up court. "I called for the ball right away, but I would have had an easier time getting a piece of meat from a hungry wolf," Sims said, chuckling. "John [Wallace] absolutely hated to lose, and he was determined that no one was going to stop him from making sure our season and our college careers didn't end there." Wallace pulled up at the top of the key and let fly with a shot that found nothing but net to earn SU the victory and a berth in the Elite Eight.

"I just felt unstoppable on that play," Wallace said after finishing with 30 points and 15 rebounds. "It was like, 'Give me the ball and get out of my way.'" In a nationally televised postgame on-court interview, commentator Al McGuire encouraged Wallace and his teammates to sing a catchy rap song they had created during their NCAA run. "When the 'Cuse is in the House, oh, my god, oh, my god," they sang as McGuire danced along with them.

Two days later, not only were they in the House, they were in the Final Four as they defeated fourth-ranked Kansas 60–57. Then they knocked off Mississippi State in the semis to earn the school's second trip to the NCAA title game. The Orangemen turned in a gritty performance before losing 76–67 to a Kentucky team that featured a lineup full of NBA players, including Antoine Walker, Ron Mercer, Walter McCarty, and Tony Delk. Wallace had been brilliant in defeat, scoring 29 points and hauling in 10 rebounds before fouling out while scrapping for a loose ball with about two minutes left and SU trailing by three. "I still believe," Wallace said resolutely in an interview years later, "that we would have found a way to win that game if I hadn't fouled out."

Wallace couldn't have been happier with his decision to return for his senior year. He had averaged 22 points and nearly nine rebounds per game to earn All-America honors. The New York Knicks drafted him in the first round that June and he spent seven seasons in the NBA, averaging 7.6 points and 2.8 rebounds.

62 Joseph Alexander

How good a football player was Joseph Alexander? He was so good that Walter Camp, the father of American football, described

Alexander as "one of the greatest defensive guards ever seen on the gridiron." Alexander the Great was so good he became the first athlete from Syracuse University to win All-American honors three times. In 1937—nearly two decades after his final college football game—he was named to the *New York World Telegram*'s All-Time All-America team.

"There was no greater lineman… there is only one and there never will be another… either in ability as a defensive player, charm of manner, aplomb and ability to make and hold friends," wrote Dr. Harry March in his book, *Pro Football: Its Ups and Downs*. While at Syracuse from 1916 to 1920, Alexander developed a unique defensive style where he occasionally dropped off the line and roved like a modern-day linebacker. It enabled him to better diagnose plays and utilize his great speed and agility to make tackles. Before long, players on other teams began copying Alexander, and the position of linebacker was born.

The son of Russian-Jewish immigrants, Alexander learned the game of football on the sandlots of Syracuse. He went to SU and played five varsity seasons while earning undergraduate and medical degrees. (You were given an extra year of eligibility in those days if you were in graduate, law, or medical school.) Before Alexander began a successful career as a doctor in New York City, the rugged 5'11", 200-lb. player became known for breaking bones rather than healing them. The Orangemen went 32–11–2 during his career. That included an 8–3 record by the 1919 squad, which both legendary coach Pop Warner and renowned sportswriter Grantland Rice believed was the best in the land.

Warner had an opportunity that season to witness firsthand the dominance of Alexander and his mates when the Orangemen pummeled his Pittsburgh team 24–3 at Archbold Stadium. It was the first time in four seasons that Warner's Panthers had lost a game. "I have a wonderful eleven," the coach said after the beatdown. "But they can't beat Syracuse. I have never seen a team that could. [SU Coach] Buck O'Neill's eleven is the best and fastest of all time."

Alexander's exploits became legendary. He was a punishing blocker and tackler, and when he got his hands on the ball, he could quickly change the course of the game. During a 21–0 victory against Rutgers in 1918, he intercepted two passes and returned an attempted kick 75 yards for a touchdown. A year later he blocked a kick that led to a touchdown and recovered a fumble to secure a 13–7 victory against arch-rival Colgate. In 1920, after switching from guard to center, he led the Orangemen to a 6–2–1 record that included a 10–0 win at Dartmouth College, which hadn't lost a home game in 16 years. In the final game that season, Alexander made an astonishing 11 tackles in a row as Syracuse blanked Colgate 14–0. During a memorable goal-line stand in that game, Alexander made the touchdown-stopping tackle on the first three plays, then intercepted a pass on fourth-and-goal to preserve SU's fifth shutout of the season. Alexander was also known for his remarkable endurance, often playing the full 60 minutes each game.

After receiving his medical degree from SU in 1921, Alexander began playing for the Rochester Jeffersons in the American Professional Football Association, which became the National Football League the following year. He was an All-NFL selection in 1922 and three years later became the first player to sign with a new franchise called the New York Giants. In 1926, he became the team's head coach, but that arrangement lasted just one season because Alexander needed to devote more time to his medical duties. He returned to being a player only and helped lead the Giants to their first championship in 1927. After that season, he retired as a player, but in 1934 he became involved in football again as an assistant coach at City College of New York under Benny Friedman, spending eight seasons in that position before taking over as head coach.

Alexander was inducted into the College Football Hall of Fame in 1954. Fourteen years later he received a LetterWinner of Distinction Award and was named to Syracuse University's All-Century team in 1999. Each year, the SU football team awards the Joe Alexander Award for excellence in football, scholarship, and citizenship. He is also a member of the International Jewish Sports Hall of Fame.

63 1983: Birth of a Lacrosse Dynasty

The sun as well as the torrid Johns Hopkins lacrosse team had burned the Orangemen pretty badly that late May afternoon in 1983, and when the first half of the NCAA lacrosse title game mercifully came to an end, with Syracuse trailing 8–4, the Orangemen couldn't wait to escape to the air-conditioned locker room at Rutgers Stadium. But as they began jogging toward the tunnel, Coach Roy Simmons Jr. summoned them back to the bench.

"Here's the crowd, and here's the scoreboard," he told them in a firm voice. "There is no sanctuary." So they sat in silence in the searing sun for the next 20 minutes. Simmons, who always seemed to know what psychological buttons to push, realized a chalk talk wasn't going to do any good at this point. He knew this close-knit team of his was embarrassed by what had transpired those first thirty minutes. He believed that by keeping them there and letting them stew a little bit, they'd respond with a spirited effort in the second half.

Brad Kotz, a sophomore midfielder who would one day end up in the Lacrosse Hall of Fame, thought it was a stroke of coaching genius. "I think everybody came out in the second half saying,

'Hey, if we keep playing hard, keep fighting like we've been fighting all season, we can claw our way back into this,'" he said. And that's what they did, although they would suffer a few more setbacks before staging one of the most stirring comebacks in lacrosse and Syracuse sports history.

After Randy Lundblad scored early in the third quarter, the top-ranked Blue Jays responded with four more goals to go up 12–5. It seemed like an insurmountable lead, but then defenseman Darren Lawlor shocked Johns Hopkins with an unassisted goal, and the tide started turning. Before the third period was over, the 'Cuse had scored three more times and trailed 13–9.

"I felt like we were controlling the tempo of the game, and in the third quarter we started to control the ball more," Kotz said. Hopkins, comfortably ahead and feeling confident, seemed to lose interest. "The worst thing that could have happened to Hopkins was getting that big lead," Simmons said. "They had lost their intensity. They couldn't measure the intensity of our team. They thought the fire was out." Added Syracuse All-American attackman Tim Nelson, "When they got up by all those goals, they just started throwing the ball out of bounds. You could see it in their eyes. They didn't think this game was such a big deal. It just didn't seem like they cared anymore."

The Orangemen, meanwhile, appeared to be growing stronger. They ripped off six consecutive goals—three by Kotz and one each by Nelson, Dave Desko, and Tom Korrie—against their listless opponents to take a 15–13 lead. "That was characteristic of our team that season," Kotz said. "Once we got into a groove, we could carry that groove for half a period or a period, and I think we got there in the third and fourth. There definitely was some added focus in the second half."

The Blue Jays finally regrouped down the stretch, scoring two goals against Travis Solomon to knot the game at 15. But Kotz scored his fifth goal with two minutes and 36 seconds left, then

Nelson recorded his sixth assist of the game, feeding Lundblad on the crease for what would prove to be the decisive goal with 1:09 remaining. Del Dressel threw a scare into SU with a goal to cut it to 17–16 with nineteen seconds remaining, but the Orangemen controlled

The Greatest Lacrosse Team of All Time

The NCAA vacated Syracuse's 1990 lacrosse championship because star Gary Gait was ruled ineligible after an investigation claimed the wife of coach Roy Simmons Jr. co-signed a car loan for the player. SU, however, continues to recognize that squad as national champs in its media guide and on its website.

Most lacrosse historians will tell you that the '90 Orangemen were the best college team of all time—and the most entertaining. In fact, that fast-breaking, high-scoring outfit is credited for igniting the explosion in popularity that has seen lacrosse become the fastest growing sport in the U.S. during the past decade. Those Orangemen clearly played a style that players loved to play and spectators loved to watch. An April game against Hobart in the Carrier Dome attracted a regular season record crowd of 18,458. SU averaged 11,640 fans per game that spring, which is still a school and NCAA attendance record.

Boasting five first-team All-Americans—Gary and Paul Gait, Greg Burns, Tom Marachek, and Pat McCabe—that SU team pummeled opponents by an average score of 21–9. The Orangemen's closest game in that 13–0 season was a 15–12 victory against Pennsylvania. Gary Gait led the scoring barrage with 46 goals and 72 points, while his twin, Paul, had a team-leading 34 assists. They were virtually unstoppable during the NCAA tournament, clobbering Brown 20–12 in the quarterfinals, North Carolina 21–10 in the semifinals, and Loyola 21–9 in the championship game. Gary Gait scored a tournament record 15 goals in those three games, Marachek had 10 assists, and Matt Palumb was outstanding in goal. Gary won the Lt. Raymond J. Enners Award as the nation's top player, McCabe was named the nation's top defenseman, and Burns was named the top attackman.

That squad had one other distinction—it was the first SU team invited to the White House, where it was feted and photographed with the first President George Bush.

the ensuing faceoff and ran out the clock to win their first NCAA lacrosse championship and their first national crown since 1925.

Interestingly, Roy Simmons Sr. had been an All-American defenseman on that last championship team, and he was at Rutgers Stadium to witness his son capture his first. When the Orangemen were finally allowed to go indoors and escape the heat, they found Simmons Sr. in the locker room waiting to congratulate them. "To come back like that was magnificent," said the patriarch of SU lacrosse. "I have never seen a comeback like that against such a great team." And then his son did something he'd always dreamed of doing. He took the national championship trophy and handed it to his father. "The only time I ever saw him cry," Roy Jr. said. "And he said, 'Thank God He let me live long enough to see you be a champion.'"

On that day—May 28, 1983—a lacrosse dynasty was born that would see Simmons Jr. win six NCAA titles before passing the torch to John Desko, who has guided the Orange to five more. Syracuse would return to the Final Four in 21 consecutive seasons, establishing a record for lacrosse excellence that likely will never be matched. Kotz was named the outstanding player of the 1983 tournament, and he and Nelson became three-time All-Americans for a team that finished 14–1, its only loss coming to Army midway through the season. Kotz and Nelson were named, along with SU legends Gary and Paul Gait, to the NCAA's Silver Anniversary lacrosse team in 1997.

Of all the great teams Simmons Jr. coached in his 28 seasons at the helm, he still calls that squad his favorite. "Heck, we were down seven goals and people were leaving the stadium, saying we didn't have a chance," he said. "And we came roaring back to beat Johns Hopkins, the No. 1 team in the nation. It was very surprising, the come-from-behind finish, an upset—and it was my first."

64 Joe Pa and the Penn State Rivalry

The man with the Coke-bottle glasses and rolled-up khakis had become a villain in central New York. That was understandable because for 16 consecutive years, Joe Paterno's Penn State teams had not merely beaten the Orange, they had beaten them to a pulp, winning these mismatches by an average of three touchdowns. As a result, a once-storied Eastern rivalry had been reduced to college football's version of the Globetrotters vs. the Washington Generals.

So it's not surprising that when SU All-American quarterback Don McPherson and his teammates put a resounding end to the ignominious streak with a 48–21 victory over Penn State inside the Carrier Dome on October 17, 1987, they earned a permanent spot in Orange sporting lore. And neither is it surprising that nearly three decades after that game, the Heisman Trophy runner-up continued to receive huzzahs for tossing that Nittany Lion from SU's collective back.

"It was clearly a statement win for a lot of reasons," recalled McPherson, who finished that glorious day with 15 completions in 20 attempts for 336 yards and three touchdowns, including a stunning 80-yard flea-flicker scoring heave to Rob Moore on the game's opening play from scrimmage. "[The win] said that we had arrived as a legitimate Eastern and national football power, and it kept alive our dreams for an unbeaten season. But I think the thing that Syracuse fans enjoyed most was that it came against Paterno. Joe Pa had become a generational nemesis to Orange followers. He had been a thorn in their sides seemingly forever."

Indeed he had. From Ernie Davis to Antwon Bailey, from Ben Schwartzwalder to Doug Marrone, from Archbold Stadium to the Dome, Paterno was a common thread, a sports icon both despised and respected in these parts. He was the John Thompson of the gridiron, if you will—only with three times the longevity of the Georgetown hoops legend.

So it wasn't surprising that Paterno's passing in January 2013 at age 85 would stir such complicated emotions among the citizens of Orange Nation. In central New York, he was certainly remembered, first and foremost, for his dominance against SU, beating the Orange 23-of-27 times during a Hall of Fame coaching career that saw him win a Division I record 409 games before NCAA sanctions stripped 111 of those victories. But he was also remembered for playing hardball with Syracuse, thereby altering the landscape of Eastern football and contributing to the game of musical chairs played by the college sports super conferences. And, of course, parallels were drawn by many between the child sexual abuse scandal involving his longtime assistant Jerry Sandusky that led to Paterno's dismissal and the subsequent child sexual abuse allegations against venerable SU basketball assistant Bernie Fine, although Fine was never charged.

"Any way you cut it, Paterno definitely had a major influence on Syracuse sports," McPherson said in a 2013 interview with *Central New York Sports* magazine. "In many respects, he set a standard for excellence. And looking back, I believe he drove us to become better, to take the next step as a program. We didn't necessarily aspire to be Penn State. But we sure did aspire to beat Penn State."

McPherson believed that Paterno's decision to turn his back on Eastern rivals SU, Pittsburgh, West Virginia, and Boston College and join the Big Ten in the early 1990s set in motion the events that eventually prompted Syracuse and Pitt to bolt the Big East for the Atlantic Coast Conference and for West Virginia to depart for the Big 12.

"I think the quandary the Big East [found] itself in can be traced to that decision," said McPherson, who was recruited by the

Nittany Lions. "Penn State was the core of Eastern football. The Big East initially attempted to stop the bleeding by adding Miami and Virginia Tech, and that worked for awhile, but they were never accepted as true eastern schools and they eventually left the conference. I was saddened to see the rivalry with SU end. It would have been better if something could have been worked out, but for whatever reason, it didn't happen."

Paterno and former SU athletic director Jake Crouthamel were at the center of the acrimonious split that played out publicly in the late 1980s and early 1990s. Paterno claimed the Big East, with its roots as a basketball conference, only wanted to accept Penn State's football program. And he intimated that Crouthamel sabotaged the acceptance of the Nittany Lions' entire sports program. "My problem is with the Syracuse athletic director," Paterno told reporters on several occasions, refusing to use Crouthamel's name. Crouthamel countered by saying he had lobbied for Penn State's total inclusion but was voted down. In the late 1980s, Penn State asked Syracuse to play six games in a 10-year span in Happy Valley. SU, not wanting to give up a home game that would sell out the Dome, countered with a four-and-four deal and two off years in which Penn State could schedule someone else. Penn State's athletic director, Jim Tarman, refused and the annual series, which began with a 0–0 tie in 1922, was terminated following the 1990 game, which saw Penn State win 27–21 at home.

In a *Syracuse Herald-Journal* interview before the final game, Crouthamel called Paterno vindictive and a liar. "He's saying I'm responsible for the fact that nothing was put together in the East, and it's a lie," Crouthamel said. "He's saying I'm responsible for the cessation of the series; it's a lie. I did everything I could possibly do with the Big East Conference over a 10-year period to get something done, specifically for Penn State, and couldn't get it done. And I have documentation to prove that." Crouthamel added that the shifting of blame was typical of Paterno. "He represents Joe

Paterno and everything he does is for Joe Paterno. He took the situation as a personal affront—that Joe Paterno was not able to get this done. It was a slap in the face of Joe Paterno. So it becomes a personal matter with him, not an institutional matter or a regional matter. And so, yes, he is vindictive."

The series, which Penn State leads 41–23–5, was briefly revived with games played in 2008, 2009, and 2013—and at least two more scheduled for the 2020 and 2021 seasons. Legendary running back Floyd Little served as the honorary Orange captain at the '08 game in the Dome. He was quick to remind people that he went 3–0 vs. the Nittany Lions during his All-American career at Syracuse. But his magic didn't work four decades later as Penn State clobbered the Orange 55–13—one of nine defeats SU would suffer during coach Greg Robinson's final season.

That game would mark Paterno's final visit to Syracuse.

"I remember him joking that the mere sight of me caused him nightmares because of all the success I had against him when he was an assistant and a head coach at Penn State," Little said. "I always respected the way Joe built Penn State into a national powerhouse. He was a great leader and a good rival for Syracuse for many years. It's sad the way it ended for him. Very sad."

65 John Desko

John Desko was well aware of what he was getting into because he had played a role in making Syracuse University into the most storied program in college lacrosse. As an All-American defenseman his senior year, he helped the 1979 Orangemen go 10–5 and earn their first NCAA tournament bid. A year later, he was hired by

Syracuse Orange head coach John Desko reacts during the second half of an NCAA Men's Lacrosse game between the Syracuse Orange and the Hobart Statesmen at Boswell Field in Geneva, New York, on April 19, 2014. Syracuse won the game 15–9. (Rich Barnes/CSM / Cal Sport Media via AP Images)

Roy Simmons Jr. as the first paid assistant lacrosse coach in school history.

Over the next 19 years, Desko would play a vital role as a recruiter and teacher, helping SU make 17 trips to the NCAA Final Four and win six national championships. Along the way, Desko received several enticing offers to become a head coach elsewhere, but each time he was courted, Simmons would remind Desko that if he stayed put, eventually he'd be "inheriting something pretty special." So Desko eschewed the other offers and, after Simmons retired following the 1998 season, Desko became just the fourth head lacrosse coach in program history.

A Rally for the Ages

Cody Jamieson had spent most of the 2009 lacrosse season in academic limbo. Finally, with two games remaining in the regular season, the talented Syracuse attackman was cleared to play. Better late than never. Jamieson scored the winning goal in overtime of the NCAA championship game as the Orange nipped Cornell 10–9 in front of more than 41,000 fans at Gillette Stadium in Foxboro, Massachusetts. "He'd been through so many highs and lows all season with the various appeals," said coach John Desko after the win in which SU successfully defended its title. "We were finally able to insert him our last couple of games, and he came up huge."

So did the defense, which forced several turnovers, enabling the Orange to wipe out a three-goal deficit in the final five minutes of regulation. With 28 seconds left, SU's Kenny Nims checked the ball away from a Cornell defenseman. Orange teammate Stephen Keogh retrieved it and passed to Matt Abbott, who passed to Nims, who scored with four seconds remaining to send the game into overtime.

After losing the faceoff at the start of OT, SU's Sid Smith stripped a Cornell attackman and the Orange worked the ball down the field. Dan Hardy found Jamieson just off the crease, and he rifled a low shot past Cornell goalie Jake Myers to complete the comeback. Nims was named Most Outstanding Player of the Final Four, and Jamieson was one of five Orange players to make the All-Tournament team as SU finished 16–2.

"If it had been any other place but Syracuse, I probably wouldn't have hung around for as long as I did," he said. "But Coach Simmons was right. To me, this is the most prestigious job in college lacrosse." And the most pressure-packed. "I think Syracuse is different from most places because the expectation every year is a national championship," he said. "That might seem unrealistic, giving the growth and increased parity of the sport, but that's kind of the monster we've created. The bar has been set very high."

Despite the immense pressure, Desko has managed to maintain the standards he played a role in establishing. In his first 15 years as head coach, he won 76 percent of his games, a higher percentage than his three predecessors—Laurie Cox, Roy Simmons Sr., and Simmons Jr.—and he made eight trips to the NCAA title game, winning five of them. During his first six seasons, he extended SU's Final Four streak to 22 consecutive years. He had a couple of rough campaigns along the way. In 2007, the Orangemen went 5–8, their first losing season in 32 years. But Desko quickly righted the ship. Led by Tewaaraton Award winner Mike Leveille, SU went 16–2 the next season and won the national championship. The improvement of 8.5 games from the previous season tied the NCAA record for best one-year turnaround and earned Desko national Coach of the Year honors. The Orangemen posted the exact same record in 2009 as they successfully defended their title.

Desko's 31–10 record in NCAA tournament play is the best among active Division I coaches. "There was no doubt in my mind that John would keep things moving in the right direction," Simmons Jr. said. "He grew up in the program and contributed mightily to us elevating it a few notches. I was comfortable with turning the keys over to him. I felt it would be in very good hands, and it has been."

Desko has clearly lived up to the legacy.

66 Edmund Dollard and First Golden Era of Orange Hoops

The Syracuse University basketball program operated without a full-time paid coach for its first 11 seasons, but after a disastrous 3–11 campaign in 1909–10, the school's athletic governing board decided that a coach needed to be hired if the sport was going to be retained.

Edmund Dollard's name came up and before the start of the 1911 season, the former Orange basketball player was hired at a salary of $75. According to the book, *Syracuse Basketball: 1900–1975*, Dollard "was re-engaged at $87.50 the following year, with the promise of $12.50 more, provided the season that followed was reasonably successful." It was, and so were the next 10. The money turned out to be well spent as Dollard began a trend of former Orangemen leading the program to great success. (Lew Andreas and Jim Boeheim would later follow his lead.)

During his 12 seasons at the helm, Dollard's teams went 151–59 for a .719 winning percentage. Two of his squads would stand above the rest—the 1913–14 club that finished 12–0, which is the only unbeaten season in program history; and the 1917–18 team, which won SU's first national basketball championship. Dollard would also coach SU's first three All-Americans in basketball: Lew Castle (1912 and 1914), Joseph Schwarzer (1918), and Leon Marcus (1919). Dollard endeared himself to Orange fans by winning 14-of-20 games against neighboring Colgate and established himself as one of the nation's most respected coaches by taking 23-of-31 games against powerhouses Penn, Princeton, Yale, Dartmouth, and Columbia from the Ivy League, which at the time was known as the Eastern Intercollegiate League.

Dollard's undefeated squad was led by Castle, one of the greatest basketball players and athletes in Syracuse annals. At 6' tall and weighing 190 pounds, Castle was considered big for his time, and he played center for Dollard's five. Lew Ryan, one of Castle's teammates, remembered the center as "the greatest dribbler of his time. He dribbled with either hand and was a powerful fellow. He was a terrific all-around athlete." In addition to hoops, Castle was a star halfback on the football team and helped stroke the varsity crew to a national championship at the Intercollegiate Rowing Association regatta on the Hudson near Poughkeepsie in 1913. Castle also served as president of the student body his senior year and was a highly popular ragtime piano player. Castle, senior forward Walter Notman, and senior guard Richard Seymour helped the 1913–14 hoopsters pummel opponents by an average score of 31 to 18. The only close game that year was a 29–28 squeaker at Colgate.

Next year's team was nearly as successful, losing only to Army in an 11-game schedule. After 9–3 and 13–3 finishes the next two seasons, the Orangemen were ready to make another run at a national title. World War I had just ended in the spring of 1917, and patriotic fervor and school spirit were running high on campus. That fall, Schwarzer helped the SU football squad to an 8–1–1 record that included a season-ending victory vs. Nebraska that earned the Orangemen a Rose Bowl bid, which the chancellor turned down. Schwarzer immediately made the transition from the gridiron to the hardwood. After a 5–0 start, the Orangemen traveled to Philadelphia to play powerful Penn. SU prevailed 27–24, with Schwarzer assisting on the go-ahead basket, then icing the win with a swish from halfcourt.

The Philadelphia sportswriters heaped praise on the Orangemen, particularly Schwarzer. One scribe wrote, "The Orange leader will rank in basketball annals with the greatest collegiate players of all-time. He was the coolest man on the court, much calmer than the majority of the spectators. He outplayed the Penn center from whistle to whistle; was the mainstay of the team on defense; and on the attack scored eleven points."

SU would go to win its first 16 games before dropping a 17–16 heartbreaker to Penn in the season finale. Despite the loss, many scribes who wrote about college basketball at the time anointed the Orangemen as the nation's top team, an accolade the Helms Foundation would reaffirm nearly 20 years later when it named national champions retroactively.

233

Dollard's teams would go 56–23 over the next four seasons before suffering losing records in 1922–23 and 1923–24. He would be replaced by Andreas, who would hold the job for the next 25 seasons. Andreas would win the school's second Helms title in 1925–26 and go 358–135 for a .726 winning percentage during his career. He also served as SU's athletic director from 1937–64.

67 Women Hoopsters Slay Mighty UConn

The second-ranked Connecticut women's basketball team strutted into Manley Field House on January 2, 1996, expecting a cakewalk. Their cockiness was understandable. Not only were the defending national champions riding a 40-game Big East Conference win streak, but they were also facing a so-so Syracuse team that just two days earlier had been annihilated by Duke by 44 points. Connecticut coach Geno Auriemma tried to convince his players not to take the Orangewomen lightly because anything could happen on any given night. But they weren't buying what he was selling. They were already looking ahead to that weekend's showdown with top-ranked Tennessee. In their minds, an easy victory over SU was a foregone conclusion. All they had to do was show up.

Despite a crushing defeat to Duke, Syracuse coach Marianna Freeman was feeling good about this game. She surmised that UConn wouldn't be taking her team seriously and that they would probably be preoccupied with thoughts of Tennessee. She believed this could definitely be a trap game and that her team might be ready to spring it. And that's what happened.

In one of the biggest upsets in SU's sports history—by men or women—the Orangewomen won 62–59 to snap Connecticut's streak and give them their first victory ever against a ranked opponent. "I guess you could say this is the biggest victory in the history of SU's women's basketball," Freeman said afterward. "The Huskies seemed to play not to lose, and that gave us more encouragement and we built on it."

At the Big Four ACC Classic two nights earlier in Greensboro, North Carolina, a Duke team that used its bench liberally dismantled Syracuse 84–40. It was so bad that one Syracuse player sat sobbing outside the locker room. The night before, SU played a much better game while losing to North Carolina State 79–70. Fortunately for Freeman, the team that had played against the Wolfpack and not the Blue Devils showed up to play the Huskies.

Perhaps no one was more surprised to learn the result of the SU–UConn game than Duke coach Gail Goestenkors. "If there's ever been a game that I was shocked to see the result of, that was it," she said. "I saw it on the [Headline News] ticker, and I had to watch about four times to make sure I saw it right. Syracuse is a good team when they attack, and we took them out of their style. When you have a big loss like that, it's gut-check time." It also helped that SU had guard Kristyn Cook back after she sat out the Duke game due to injury. She made two free throws for the winning points vs. UConn.

The Huskies' last Big East loss had come almost two full years earlier—on January 5, 1994—against Seton Hall. The loss to SU would be the only one they suffered in 18 conference games during the 1995–96 season. It would be two more years before they would lose another Big East game.

68 Stopping the Great Jim Thorpe

Although they had just edged defending national champion Harvard 18–15 to improve to 9–0, and they boasted the best player in America in Jim Thorpe, Carlisle Indians Coach Glenn "Pop" Warner continued to fear the worst.

As his team prepared for its game against Syracuse at Archbold Stadium on November 18, 1911, Warner predicted to reporters that this would be the week his team turned in a sub-standard performance and lost. The sportswriters scoffed at what they considered "boy-cries-wolf" yammering. It was the same gloom-and-doom forecast Warner had spewed before each of the previous four contests. The scribes expected the Indians to continue their roll toward a national championship by thumping a Syracuse team that had gone 3–3–1 in its first seven games. "About all that is left for [Warner] to fear is that the train that carries the squad to the Salt City may be wrecked and that all his players may lose their eyes, arms, and legs before the game with the Onondaga pale faces," wrote one.

This time, however, the worrywart coach was spot-on. His prophecy came true as the Orangemen edged Carlisle 12–11. Weather certainly played a factor as heavy rains turned Archbold into a quagmire, negating some of Thorpe's speed advantage. And the wet conditions coupled with a fierce, chilly wind made passing risky.

The Indians scored first on a run by Thorpe, but he failed to convert the extra point, and Carlisle led 5–0. (Touchdowns were worth just five points in those days.) Later, the Orangemen recovered a fumble on the Indians' 33-yard line. They marched smartly down the field for the touchdown and converted the extra point to go up by one. The Orangemen scored again in the second quarter after a 35-yard touchdown run by Thorpe was nullified by a holding call. The Indians were forced to punt, and Lewis Castle secured the wet ball and didn't stop running until he had reached the end zone. The kick made it 12–5 SU. The Indians finally cut the deficit back to one late in the game as Thorpe scored once more; this time, he made good on the conversion, but it was too little too late as 11,000 shivering fans witnessed what remains one of the biggest upsets in Orange football history.

"Jim was inconsolable after the game," wrote Robert Wheeler in his book, *Jim Thorpe: World's Greatest Athlete.* "He had kept them in the game, but he blamed himself for the defeat because his celebrated toe failed to convert one of the extra points." Carlisle won its next two games to finish 11–1. The Indians outscored their opponents by a combined total of 298–49, and Thorpe was selected first-team All-American by Walter Camp.

The next summer, Thorpe won gold medals in both the decathlon and pentathlon at the Olympics in Stockholm, after which King Gustav of Sweden dubbed the Native American "the world's greatest athlete." Following that stunning performance, Thorpe returned to the gridiron and earned All-American honors once more. He would also atone for the previous season's loss to Syracuse by scoring three touchdowns in a 33–0 victory at Archbold on October 12, 1912.

Thorpe would go on to play professional football for the Canton Bulldogs and help launch the National Football League. In a 1950 poll of sportswriters, he was voted the greatest athlete of the first half of the 20th century, edging luminaries such as Babe Ruth, Jesse Owens, Jack Dempsey, Joe Louis, and Red Grange.

69 Stephen Crane

He became a heavy hitter in the literary world with the publication of his Civil War masterpiece, *The Red Badge of Courage*, in 1894. But when Stephen Crane enrolled at Syracuse University three years earlier after flunking out of Lafayette College in Pennsylvania, he was more enthused about taking bat to ball than pen to paper. The young man who would write one of America's seminal novels was smitten with the game of baseball—so much so that he expended more energy delivering big hits for the Orangemen's varsity than big papers for his English literature, history, and Latin classes.

Crane later acknowledged as much in a letter to a friend. "I did little work in school, but confined my abilities, such as they were, to the diamond," he wrote in the correspondence. "Not that I disliked books, but the cut-and-dried curriculum of the college did not appeal to me. Humanity was a much more interesting study. When I ought to have been at recitations, I was studying faces on the streets, and when I ought to have been studying my next day's lessons, I was watching the trains roll in and out of the Central Station." Crane seconded these emotions in another letter, telling the editor of *Leslie's Weekly*, "When I was at school, few of my studies interested me, and as a result I was a bad scholar. They used to say at Syracuse University, where, by the way, I didn't finish the course, that I was cut out to be a professional baseball player. And the truth of the matter is that I went there more to play baseball than to study." His Latin professor, Frank Smalley, confirmed these sentiments in a letter to Crane's widow following the author's death from tuberculosis at age 28 in 1900. Wrote Smalley, "He devoted himself to sports with ardor, especially baseball, and was our finest player."

Crane stood only 5'6" and weighed just 125 pounds, but he was a fiery, tenacious performer who, according to a teammate, played "with fiendish glee." After struggling to make the throws to second from a kneeling position behind home plate, Crane shifted from catcher to shortstop. Box scores are hard to come by, but one researcher says the 19-year-old hit about .273 in 1891, his one and only season with the Orangemen.

Though he had never fought in a war, Crane's vivid descriptions of the battles through the eyes of a young soldier were hauntingly accurate, according to Civil War veterans who had read the book. Crane scholars Rick Burton and Jan Finkel believe the author drew his understanding of battle from sports. They wrote, "Despite major differences in the gravity of their outcomes, sports and war share many common attributes: courage, brotherhood, sacrifice, compassion, rescue (salvation as it were), and redemption—plus the opposite qualities. In essence, sports brings out the best and worst in humanity."

One incident near the end of Crane's Syracuse baseball career may have shaped the novel's theme of desertion. On June 6, 1891, his Orangemen traveled to Hamilton to play arch-rival Colgate. However, two players failed to show up, leaving SU short-handed. Crane had to move to first base and the team manager was forced into action in center field, with one position left open. The Orangemen suffered an embarrassing loss, and Crane was said to have been furious with the teammates who failed to travel for his sacred game. Upon his return to campus, he took his final exams and then headed to New York City to pursue his writing career in earnest.

He obviously didn't receive his degree, but he did receive an education. Lessons from the diamond rather than the classroom would help shape a novel that remains a classic more than a century later.

70 Rent a Copy of *The Express*

If you are a fan of college football and tearjerkers, then you should see *The Express*, a biopic about the short but profound life of Heisman Trophy winner Ernie Davis, who died of leukemia at age 23. But make sure that, in addition to a box of Kleenexes, you watch it with a grain of salt because Hollywood takes considerable license, and the film generated much debate.

Starring Dennis Quaid as coach Ben Schwartzwalder and featuring former Amherst College wide receiver Rob Brown as Davis, the 2008 Universal Pictures flick is a riveting period piece from the late 1950s and early '60s, and the football scenes are quite realistic. Director Rob Fleder said the structure of *The Express* was influenced by *Seabiscuit*, the highly acclaimed 2003 movie.

"That film was about this incredible horse defying remarkable odds against the backdrop of the Great Depression," Fleder said in a 2008 interview with *Syracuse University Magazine*. "And that inspired me to tell Ernie's story against the backdrop of the civil rights movement of the late 1950s, early 1960s. We hadn't yet reached the boiling point that we would reach after Martin Luther King's assassination in the late '60s. It was still mostly a time of blacks attempting to change things from within the system, and that's what Ernie attempted to do through his remarkable play on the field and his charismatic, color-blind personality away from it."

The Express focuses on the relationship between Schwartzwalder and Davis, and there are several scenes showing the coach and his star player butting heads. Quaid portrays Schwartzwalder as a good-hearted but slightly bigoted football genius who is eventually redeemed through his genuine concern for Davis. Real-life members from the 1959 championship team were not thrilled with the way their coach and teammate were depicted. In fact, they were so upset that several of them said they considered walking out of the movie when it premiered at the Landmark Theater in Syracuse. About a month after viewing the film, Gerhard Schwedes, the captain of the '59 team, wrote a letter to the editor of the *Syracuse Post-Standard*, citing what he and his teammates considered 11 serious errors in the movie. "As a work of fiction, the movie is terrific," he wrote. "But that's not the way it was."

Schwedes said he felt compelled "to set the record straight" after hearing from many of his teammates who were upset by the liberties taken by Fleder. "Ben Schwartzwalder's relationship with Ernie was one of father and son. Ben admired Ernie. Ernie admired Ben. There was never a cross word between the two. Ernie would never talk to Ben as depicted in the film. Ben would have benched him. Ernie respected Ben, as we all did.

"The portrait of Ben by Dennis Quaid was off. Ben did not have a racist bone in his body. He treated everyone the same, even when we made miscues, or history. No one on this team wanted to let him down, which fostered our success on and off the field."

Fleder admitted that a long talk with Davis' predecessor, Jim Brown, helped him decide to use racial discord as a backdrop. This irked many of the '59ers. "Jim Brown's influence in the film throws Ernie's character off base," Schwedes wrote. "Jim and Ben had their differences; Ben and Ernie did not."

The Express shows powerful images of a racially divided America in 1959. During one seven-minute sequence, SU's racially mixed team faces an angry white crowd at West Virginia, where fans shout slurs and throw garbage and even the referees are corrupt. Quaid's character warns his team to stay helmeted to protect themselves from tossed beer bottles. The movie sets the date at October 24, 1959. Trouble is, it never happened. That year, SU played the Mountaineers at Archbold Stadium in Syracuse, and Davis had a breakout game with 141 yards rushing. There were no reports of racial incidents, though such issues rarely made their way into newspaper stories in those days. The exception was the Cotton Bowl game after that season, in which racial conflicts were well-documented. West Virginia critics of the movie said their school was used unfairly in the movie as a composite for racial problems in America at the time.

Despite the inaccuracies and license taken, the movie has many redeeming qualities. The essence of Davis' charisma and courage is captured by actor Rob Brown. John Brown, an African American teammate of Davis', was also upset with the portrayal of Schwartzwalder as racially insensitive and agreed with Schwedes that Ben loved Ernie like a son and that the two never locked horns. But Brown said he was also thrilled that Davis' story had finally made it to the silver screen. For years, he fretted that his late classmate, teammate, and friend was destined to become a forgotten hero.

"I worried that Ernie was eventually going to end up like yesterday's newspaper," Brown said. "You know, read once then tossed away. No, [the movie] wasn't entirely accurate, but it did my heart good, knowing that people throughout America were awakened to what a truly marvelous person Ernie was. It's a story that has parallels to Jackie Robinson's quest to break the color barrier in Major League Baseball. Ernie's winning of the Heisman was a watershed event and paved the way for so many African American football players who followed. It's a story that should be told and needs to be told."

If you are a Syracuse fan, you should see it. But if you want a more accurate accounting of Davis' life, you also should read the book on which the movie is loosely based—*Ernie Davis: The Elmira Express*, by SU alumnus Robert Gallagher.

71

The Legend of 22

While No. 44 is considered *the* number in SU sports history, it's not the only significant number. In lacrosse, the legacy of greatness belongs to No. 22. And unlike football's 44, lacrosse's 22 is still in circulation and still churning out All-Americans.

The legend of No. 22 began with Gary Gait, a four-time All-American who, along with twin brother Paul, led the Orangemen to three NCAA championships while revolutionizing the game with moves never before seen on a lacrosse field. "Gary was such a phenomenal talent that even if we never issued the number again, it would have been legendary," said Roy Simmons Jr., who coached Gait and a total of 130 All-Americans during his nearly three decades running the SU program. "Like Jim had in football, Gary set the bar very, very high. You obviously had guys like Ernie Davis and Floyd Little who followed Jim and nudged the bar even higher. The same thing happened with No. 22 after Gary graduated."

Charlie Lockwood put on No. 22 the year after Gait's college career ended, and all he did was earn All-America honors four times, including first-team selections during his junior and senior years. After Lockwood graduated in 1994, the Powell brothers—Casey, Ryan, and Mike—would own the number for the next dozen seasons. Each of them became four-time All-Americans, with Mike becoming the first lacrosse player in SU's storied history to be a first-team selection all four years (2001–04). Mike also twice won the Tewaaraton Award, college lacrosse's version of the Heisman. And several of his predecessors would have won it, too, had it been awarded before the 2001 season.

Coach John Desko, who took over after Simmons retired following the 1998 season, decided there would be way too much pressure on whoever succeeded the Powells, so he put the number in storage for one season. Dan Hardy was awarded the jersey in 2006 and was named honorable mention All-American three times while leading the Orange to two national championships. Attackman Cody Jamieson wore No. 22 for just one season (2010) and carried on the tradition by earning honorable mention All-American honors a year after delivering the winning goal in the championship game. JoJo Marasco earned All-American honors twice in the three seasons he wore No. 22. In 2014, it was awarded to Jordan Evans, who was rated the top high school player in America by *Inside Lacrosse* magazine.

So here's a tally of the numbers behind the No. 22: 26 All-American selections, 10 NCAA championships, and two Tewaaraton Awards. The double-deuce is also significant because it represents the number of consecutive seasons the Orange reached the Final Four. The streak ended in 2005 when SU was knocked out in the first round of the NCAAs. It's a record that most likely will never be equaled.

72 Ouch, That Smarts

Greg Monroe, one of the most deadly accurate outside shooters in SU history, sighed when asked to reflect on the Orangemen's 1987 NCAA championship matchup with Indiana in the New Orleans Superdome. "Everybody expected it to be a great game," he said. "And it was—until the final four seconds."

As far as SU fans are concerned, Monroe provided a nothing-but-net assessment. Up to that point, it appeared the Orangemen were going to win their first NCAA basketball title. Then Keith

Smart swished a drifting 16' baseline jumper over defender Howard Triche's outstretched arms to propel the Hoosiers to a 74–73 victory in front of 64,959 spectators in the Superdome and millions more on CBS' national telecast. And by doing so, the native of Baton Rouge, Louisiana, who once worked as an usher in the Superdome, had stuck not only a jumper but a collective dagger into Orange hearts.

"Decades later, I still don't like hearing the words, 'Keith Smart,'" Monroe said. "The mere mention of his name is a painful reminder." Smart understands completely. "From time-to-time, I run into Syracuse people and they'll say, 'Geez, Keith, why couldn't you have been a little off with that shot?'" Smart said. "And I tell them, 'It wouldn't have mattered if your boys had made their free throws.' But I do feel for them. It has to be extremely difficult to come that close and lose."

The truth hurts. Smart is right. Had SU converted 13 instead of 11 of their 20 free throw attempts, the team would have won the championship and Smart's name wouldn't be remembered with such pain in Syracuse.

The Orangemen's woes at the line were particularly costly down the stretch. With 41 seconds remaining and Syracuse ahead 72–70, Indiana fouled Triche. The senior hit his first shot but missed the second and the Hoosiers got the ball out to Smart, who eluded two defenders for a basket to cut the 'Cuse lead to one. Indiana immediately fouled Derrick Coleman on the inbounds and the confident freshman, who had already put together a sterling performance with 19 rebounds and eight points, headed to the foul line with 28 seconds remaining.

"I thought, *There it is*," SU center Rony Seikaly recalled. "I thought Derrick was going to sink both ends of that one-and-one and we were going to win the national championship." On the SU bench, Stevie Thompson, a freshman who had predicted an NCAA championship at the start of practices five months earlier, had the same thoughts. After bouncing the ball at the foul line a few times, Coleman released his free throw attempt. He knew immediately it was going to bounce off the right side of the rim. "My hands were sweaty," he explained after the game. "And as I threw it up, I knew it was off right. I said, 'Damn! It's off.'"

Indiana grabbed the rebound, brought the ball up the floor, and worked the clock down to about seven seconds. The Hoosiers' first option was Steve Alford, but Sherman Douglas stuck to him like a coat of paint. They passed the ball inside to Daryl Thomas, who was covered closely by Coleman and Seikaly. Instead of attempting a difficult shot over his two taller defenders, Thomas threw the ball out to Smart who dribbled toward the baseline and let loose with his game-winning shot. Douglas tried to get a timeout immediately, but SU wasn't granted one until just one second remained.

"I tried to get [the referees] to look at the monitors, but they refused," Douglas said. "Smart took the shot with five seconds to go. The difference between three seconds and one second is huge. With three seconds, which we should have had, you can set up a play. With one second, you have no chance." Coleman's desperation heave was intercepted at half court by Smart, and the buzzer sounded on the most disheartening loss in Syracuse sports history. "It was like somebody had stabbed you in the heart," Monroe said. "And it all happened so fast. One second, you're ready to celebrate. The next second, you're saying to yourself, *What just happened?*"

The 1986–87 Orangemen were arguably the most talented and balanced team in school history. Three players—Coleman, Seikaly, and Douglas—went on to have long, productive NBA careers. All five starters averaged in double figures in scoring. Coleman and Seikaly were dominating forces inside. Douglas was a superb floor general who ranked among the nation's assists leaders and was also a potent scoring threat. Monroe was a dead-on three-point shooter who had experience playing the point, too, which enabled him to average 4.1 assists per game and take some of the ball-handling pressure off Douglas. Triche was a shut-down defender, a dependable rebounder, and a good fifth scoring option (11.8 points per game). Guard Stevie Thompson averaged 5.1 points a game off the bench, center Derek Brower could bang the boards and spell Seikaly, and forward Herman "The Helicopter" Harried could fill in for either Coleman or Triche.

Syracuse finished 31–7 and was dominating during the NCAAs that year, knocking off a very good Florida team and second-ranked North Carolina on its way to the title game. "The only thing missing from us making that claim as the best 'Cuse team of all time was that championship," Coleman said. "Damn, if I could only step to that free throw line and shoot that shot again. Or if that buzzer had only sounded four seconds earlier."

They would have been champions instead of the best SU team not to win it all.

73 Memorable Nicknames

Here is a list of some of the most memorable nicknames in Syracuse University history:

Pearl	Dwayne Washington
Coach Mac	Dick McPherson
The Louie and Bouie Show	Louis Orr and Roosevelt Bouie
Rocket Man	Chris Sease
The Zoo	Student section in Manley Field House
G-Mac	Gerry McNamara

The Sizeable Seven	Linemen on SU's 1959 national championship football team (Fred Mautino, Maury Youmans, Bob Yates, Bruce Tarbox, Al Bemiller, Roger Davis, and Gerry Skonieczki)
Roy's Runts	Name for coach Roy Danforth's vertically challenged basketball teams of the early 1970s
Melo	Carmelo Anthony
Otto, Saltine Warrior, and The Dome Ranger	Mascots
Sweet D	Dennis DuVal
The Elmira Express	Ernie Davis
The General	Sherman Douglas
Air Gait	Revolutionary lacrosse shot invented by Gary Gait
The Helicopter	Herman Harried
Otto's Army	Student section in Carrier Dome
Bullet	Billy Gabor
Bill Orange	Nickname for SU teams in newspaper articles
Poetry in Moten	Lawrence Moten
Red	Tony Bruin
Slugger	Roy Simmons Jr.
Fast Eddie	Eddie Moss
Sour Citrus Society	SU Pep Band
Simmie	Roy Simmons Sr.
The Loud House	Carrier Dome
The Kangaroo Kid	Vaughn Harper
Four-Wheel Drive	Defensive line of the mid–1980s (Tim Green, Blaise Winter, Bill Pendock, Jamie Kimmel)
Bug	Jimmy Williams

Archie or Old Archie	Archbold Stadium
Kid	Greg Kohls
Pride of the Orange	SU Marching Band
Coach P	Paul Pasqualoni
Ol' Ben	Ben Schwartzwalder
Four Furies	SU's backfield on the 1959 national championship team (Ernie Davis, Dave Sarette, Gerhard Schwedes, and Art Baker)
DC	Derrick Coleman
Buffalo Bill	Bill Hurley
Money	Greg Monroe
The Braintree Butcher	Tom Stundis
The Blond Bomber	George Hicker
Burgermeister	Derek Brower
Fab	Fabrizio Melo
Shack	Dale Shackleford
Z or Z-Man	Lazarus Sims

74 Al Davis

Al Davis left Syracuse University in the spring of 1950 with a degree in English. However, it was what he didn't leave campus with that gnawed at him and motivated him for the rest of his compelling, non-conformist, often mysterious life.

A frustrated jock who wound up becoming the influential, maverick owner of the three-time Super Bowl–winning Oakland Raiders, Davis had hoped to leave SU with a varsity letter in football. The man who would become associated with the Silver and

Black badly wanted to become an Orangeman. Alas, it was not to be. Davis wound up playing junior varsity football, basketball, and baseball at SU but was never quite talented enough to make the big squads. "I didn't do as well at Syracuse as I dreamed or hoped to," he told his old Syracuse buddies at a New York City reunion in 1992. "I just didn't do it."

What he did do well at Syracuse was acquire a wealth of football knowledge that would serve him greatly, first as a coach at the college and pro levels and then as a talent evaluator when he became the Raiders owner in the early 1960s. At SU, Davis lived with the jocks in the temporary Quonset-hut barracks known as "The Shacks" that sprung up on campus to accommodate the influx of G.I. Bill students after World War II. When it became apparent that he wasn't going to make it as an athlete, Davis became a student of football, often attending classroom strategy sessions taught by SU assistant coach Bud Barker. Legend had it that some of Davis' best lessons occurred outside the classroom.

After being cut from the varsity, he reportedly still attended practices. He would observe intently from the stands or on Hendricks Hill just above Archbold Stadium and take copious notes about coach Ben Schwartzwalder's revolutionary unbalanced-line, wing-back offense. Although some of Davis' classmates corroborated the story, Davis dismissed it in a 1992 article by *Syracuse Post-Standard* columnist Sean Kirst. "Why would I do that?" Davis asked. "I could look at the playbook any night I wanted back in the prefabs."

Davis developed a passion for literature at SU, but he had no intention of putting his English degree to use as either a writer or teacher. "I majored in English, but it was pointless," he said. "I remember thinking, *What am I studying English for when all I want to do is coach?*"

After graduating, the Brooklyn native landed his first job as the offensive line coach at Adelphi College. He would later work as a scout for the Baltimore Colts and as the offensive line coach

Al Davis, general manager and head coach of the Oakland Raiders, signs a new five-year contract as E.W, McGah (left) and Wayne Valley, general partner in the American Football League club watch in Oakland, California, on March 30, 1965. The 35-year-old graduate of Syracuse signed a three-year contract with the Raiders in 1963 and immediately improved their last-place position to second place with a 10–4 record. (AP Photo)

at The Citadel and the University of Southern California. In 1960, he returned to pro football as the receivers coach for the Los Angeles Chargers of the newly formed American Football League. After three seasons with the Chargers, Davis became the youngest head coach and general manager in professional football when the Oakland Raiders hired him at age 33. He earned the league's Coach of the Year honors that year, and three years later, as commissioner of the AFL, he helped broker the merger with the established NFL. He then returned to the Raiders as owner, a position he held until his death at age 82 in 2011.

During his nearly five-decade reign, Davis' Raiders established themselves as the winningest franchise in all of sports...and one of the most polarizing. Davis relished his renegade role, as did many of the unsavory characters who played for him. As former Oakland linebacker Duane Benson said, only partially in jest, "We used to say, 'You don't have to have a criminal record to play on this team. But it really helps.'"

Davis' Raiders teams came to be known for their fearless, and some would say dirty, tactics. He would prove to be a thorn in the side of his fellow owners and former commissioner Pete Rozelle, going so far as to sue the league on several occasions. But Davis also proved to be an innovator and ahead of his time in many ways. He was the first man to draft a black quarterback in the first round (Tennessee State's Eldridge Dickey in 1968), the first man to hire a Hispanic coach (Tom Flores in 1979), the first man in the modern era to hire an African American coach (Art Shell in 1988), and the first man to hire a woman as CEO (Amy Trask in 1997). His ground-breaking hires resulted, in part, from the sensitivity he developed at SU, where he roomed with Bernie Custis, one of the first African American quarterbacks in major college football.

For a long time after graduating, Davis had nothing to do with his alma mater. The hard feelings, he said, were the result of his former coaches not being helpful during his job searches.

But thanks to the intervention of former classmate and former SU football standout Luke LaPorta, the fences were mended. Davis eventually donated several hundred thousand dollars to renovate the football locker room. And in 1985, Davis returned to campus and received something that had eluded him during his undergraduate days—he was finally named a LetterWinner of Distinction.

75 Tyler Ennis Takes His Best Shot

Tyler Ennis spent just one season with Syracuse before bolting to the NBA, but the unflappable point guard won't ever be forgotten. The high-arcing, buzzer-beating, victory-grabbing shot that Ennis heaved in at Pittsburgh on February 12, 2014, earned him a permanent place in the hearts and memories of SU basketball fans. "He came up with a play to go down in history," teammate C.J. Fair said after Ennis' 35' toss secured a 58–56 victory. "I think I got hoarse from being so excited and happy."

Here was the situation. The Orange trailed by one with 4.4 seconds remaining and were inbounding near Pitt's basket, meaning they would have to go the length of the floor in order to attempt the winning shot. Jerami Grant had been instructed to throw the ball long to Fair. But when Fair couldn't break free, Grant went to his second option, Ennis, who was also being tightly covered. The instant Ennis got his hands on the ball, he raced up court in four dribbles. After the last dribble—a wicked crossover that enabled him to split Pitt defenders Cameron Wright and Josh Newkirk—Ennis leaped into the air and released his shot just before the buzzer sounded. "I don't think those shots are going to go in, really, I never do," SU coach Jim Boeheim said. "But when

Other Memorable SU Basketball Buzzer-Beaters

- Jim Lee vs. North Carolina in the 1975 NCAA East Region semifinals
- Leo Rautins' tip-in vs. Villanova in the third overtime of the 1981 Big East title game
- Pearl Washington vs. Boston College during a 1984 regular season game
- Dave Johnson vs. Georgetown in the 1992 Big East championship game
- Conrad McRae vs. Villanova during a 1993 regular season game
- Jason Cipolla vs. Georgia in a 1996 NCAA tournament game
- Ryan Blackwell vs. St. John's in a 1998 Big East semifinal game
- Marius Janulis vs. Iona in a 1998 NCAA tournament game
- Gerry McNamara vs. Georgetown in a 2004 regular season game
- Terrence Roberts vs. Rutgers in a 2006 regular season game
- Gerry McNamara vs. Cincinnati in a 2006 Big East tournament game

he shot it, I saw his release. And when I saw the ball, I thought it was going in."

It did, and Boeheim thrust his arms into the air as many of the 12,935 spectators in the Petersen Events Center looked on in stunned disbelief. Some students in the "Oakland Zoo" smacked their fists against their seatbacks, and a few flipped off Ennis. But the point guard was too busy celebrating to notice.

In the locker room, after he finished his interview with ESPN, Ennis received a phone call from his father, Tony McIntyre. "I pretended like I didn't watch the game," McIntyre told the *Daily Orange*. "I just said, 'Hey, did you guys win?' He was like, 'Oh, shut up. Don't tell me you missed that?' It was actually funny. I just asked how it felt and he said, 'As soon as I let it go, I knew it was good.'"

McIntyre wasn't the only one to phone him. Ennis also received a call from Vice President Joe Biden, who is a Syracuse

University law school graduate and a huge Orange basketball fan. "He was kind of shocked by that," McIntyre recalled. "He sent a text, like, 'Hey, can you believe I just got a phone call from the vice president of the United States?' He was in shock a little bit."

The victory extended SU's win streak to a school record 24 consecutive games. The Orange would tack on one more win with yet another cardiac finish before watching their season wind down in disappointing fashion, with six losses in their final nine games and a second-game exit from the NCAA tournament. Ennis earned All-ACC freshman honors after leading the league in assists (5.5 per game) and steals (2.1) while averaging 12.9 points per contest. Less than a week after the season ended, Ennis announced he was entering the NBA draft.

76 A Trip to Lockerbie

When people ask Roy Simmons Jr. to name the biggest thrill of his lacrosse career, they're usually surprised by his response. Most people would expect him to talk about his Hall of Fame induction, or his six national championships as a coach, or the thrill of playing on an undefeated team for his father and with legendary teammates Jim Brown, Oren Lyons, and Jim Ridlon.

But in his mind, none of those experiences can match the one that occurred at the end of 1989. That's when he and his players traveled across the Atlantic to Lockerbie a year after Pan Am Flight 103 exploded above that Scottish village. Two-hundred-fifty-eight passengers were killed when a terrorist's bomb was detonated. Among the dead were 35 SU students who were returning home after a semester in London. The wreckage also killed several residents of the village when the fuselage and wings came crashing down.

The spring following the tragedy, the SU lacrosse team wore special "103" patches on their uniform sleeves, but Simmons wanted to do more. And that's when he got the idea of taking his team to Great Britain to, as he told his players, "soften the sorrow."

"Native Americans regard lacrosse as a medicine game, a healing game, and I was viewing our trip that way," Simmons said. "I wanted the village to know that we felt for them, and I wanted them to know that there would always be a special connection between our university and Lockerbie. But I didn't want that connection to just focus on a tragedy. I wanted to build a positive relationship, so they would think good thoughts, not just sad thoughts, when they heard the words *Syracuse University*. I thought we as a lacrosse team could be the ambassadors to do that by teaching them our game."

Though no funding was available for the trip from the financially strapped SU athletic department, Simmons and his players were able to raise enough money from car washes, bake sales, and generous donations from people near and far, wealthy and not so wealthy. "I think the idea of this trip really struck a chord with a lot of people," Simmons said.

The legendary lacrosse coach also was able to convince a number of sporting goods manufacturers to donate balls and sticks to give to the Scottish kids during the clinics and exhibitions staged by SU. While in Lockerbie, Simmons and his team paid a visit to Dryfesdale Cemetery and the memorial to Pan Am Flight 103. Near the collage of photos, flowers, and cards of remembrance, Simmons placed a stick that had been carved by a member of the Onondaga Nation. He would later be told by villagers he kept in touch with that the stick remained at the memorial for many years.

To add to his players' educational and cultural experience, Simmons arranged for them, as well as himself, to stay in the homes of villagers rather than a hotel. The visit made an indelible impression on all of them. "We were young and maybe didn't realize it fully at the time we went," said former All-American Gary Gait. "But as the years go by, you realize it was a life-changing experience, especially to see the looks on those kids' faces as we were showing them how to play the game."

A year after their visit, Simmons received a phone call from a man he had befriended in Scotland. "He says in his thick brogue, 'Roy, we got a problem here. Everyone wants to play your game,'" Simmons recalled. "We couldn't afford to bring the entire team again, so I got a couple of my assistants and we gathered up more sticks and balls from the manufacturers and we headed back to Scotland and replenished their supplies. It was a great feeling. We felt a little like Johnny Appleseed. We got lacrosse going there, and all these years later, the Scots field a very fine national team, and there has been a ripple effect that has carried over to England and Wales. It's all so very gratifying."

It's the highlight of a lacrosse career that has known many.

Tie-Dyed by Auburn

The undefeated and fourth-ranked Syracuse football team headed to the Sugar Bowl in New Orleans on January 1, 1988, hoping to lay claim to another national championship. They dreamed about celebrating a 12–0 record on Bourbon Street. Thanks to Auburn coach Pat Dye and a kicker inappropriately named Win Lyle, the Orangemen left the French Quarter fit to be tied.

A little background is in order. In SU's regular season finale against West Virginia, the Orangemen preserved their unbeaten record when they went for and converted a two-point conversion as time expired to nip the Mountaineers 32–31. Those were the days before college football decided tie games in overtime. After SU had pulled to within a point on a Don McPherson touchdown pass to tight end Pat Kelly in the waning seconds, coach Dick MacPherson opted to go for the win. Running back Michael Owens delivered the victory when he took an option pitch and scored the decisive two-pointer. "I don't think you should do that," Coach Mac said afterward, in reference to kicking for the tying point.

Too bad Auburn coach Pat Dye didn't subscribe to the MacPherson theory that you play for the win, not the tie. Six weeks later in the Sugar Bowl in New Orleans, Auburn trailed SU 16–13 with the ball on the Orange 13 and enough time for one last play. Rather than going for the victory, Dye sent on his kicker, Win Lyle, to boot the tying field goal. MacPherson went from being incredulous to angry. As Lyle's kick sailed through the uprights, Coach Mac flung his game plan—three rolled-up sheets of paper—to the Louisiana Superdome turf. "I was mad at myself," he said.

Minutes earlier, when his team had to decide to go for it on fourth-and-inches from the Auburn 22, he sent in kicker Tim Vesling, who put SU up by three. "I told my guys a field goal was like a touchdown," he said. "I told them if we made it, Auburn would have to go for the touchdown. If I had thought in my wildest imagination he'd go for a field goal, we would have gone for that first down."

Dye said afterward that his Tigers had played "with too much character and class" to risk going for a 13-yard touchdown in the final seconds against the fourth-ranked Orangemen. Coach Mac thought that was a bunch of malarkey, noting that Auburn didn't make a single throw toward the end zone during that final drive. "What the hell was [Dye] thinking?" he fumed afterward. "What hell did they come here for in the first place?"

A Syracuse radio station, angered by Dye's passive decision, encouraged angry fans to send the Auburn coach the ugliest ties they could find. An estimated 2,000 ties flooded the school's athletic department. Dye signed each one with the 16–16 score, and they were sold for $100 apiece. Reportedly $20,000 was raised for the Auburn scholarship fund.

The 11–0–1 Orangemen retained their No. 4 ranking in the final polls, but the blemish of the tie cost them a chance to make a claim for the title. Forevermore, Auburn's legendary coach would be known in Syracuse as Pat "Tie" Dye.

78 Bill Smith's Two Unforgettable Games

He jokes that he's the forgotten Orangeman, that his achievements "have been kind of lost in the mists of time." And there's some truth to that because although Bill Smith's name is still all over the SU basketball record book, few fans remember him.

The 6'11" center still holds the single-game scoring mark with 47 points, which he put up against Lafayette's overmatched 6'6" center Ron Moyer in front of 2,015 fans at Manley Field House on January 14, 1971. He's also one of only two SU players who played at least two varsity campaigns to post a career scoring average in excess of 20 points per game (20.7). He owns the second-best career rebounds per game average (12.9) and field goal percentage (.596) in school history. He was an academic All-America his senior year and started for the Portland Trail Blazers his rookie season, scoring 17 points in a quarter against Lew Alcindor. His 47-point night—which included 17 field goals and

Eye-Popping Numbers

On November 5, 1904, on the Oval gridiron on the Syracuse University campus, the Orangemen destroyed Manhattan College 144–0. It's the most points ever scored by an SU football team and was preceded that season by 69–0 victories against Clarkson and Allegheny. That high-scoring SU club, coached by Dr. Charles P. Hutchins, averaged a school-record 45 points per game but still managed to lose three of nine games, including an 11–0 shutout vs. arch-rival Colgate.

The 1998 Orangemen, quarterbacked by Donovan McNabb and coached by Paul Pasqualoni, almost matched the 1904 squad's per-game output with a 42.5 average. The McNabb-led team beat Rutgers 70–14, Cincinnati 63–21, and Miami 66–13 en route to an 8–4 record. Interestingly, 144 is also the single-game record point total for the SU hoopsters. That came in a 144–92 thrashing of Siena on January 17, 1979, in Manley Field House midway through Jim Boeheim's second season as coach.

Here are some other eye-popping team and individual numbers from SU sports history:

- 42 tackles, including 22 solo stops, by linebacker Jim Collins in a game vs. Penn State (October 20, 1979).

13 free throws—was one point better than Dave Bing's record. Smith also had a 41-point game in 1968, but no one noticed because Calvin Murphy scored 68 for Niagara University in the same contest.

But the most memorable and bizarre night of Smith's college career came on February 14, 1970—his 21st birthday. The Orangemen were playing at West Virginia that night and, with 61 seconds remaining, Smith was slapped—literally, he claims—with his fifth foul by referee Herb Young. Smith said he voiced his displeasure with the call, and Young slapped him across the face. Smith retaliated by punching the referee, and a donnybrook ensued as players and fans joined the fray. Once order was finally restored

- NCAA-record 29,919 per-game average basketball attendance during the 1989–90 season.
- 43 points scored by Jim Brown in a 61–7 football victory against Colgate (November 17, 1956). Big Jim scored six touchdowns and kicked seven extra points.
- NCAA record-tying 67 minutes played in a single game by Jonny Flynn in a six-overtime contest vs. Connecticut in the Big East Tournament (March 12, 2009).
- Nation-leading 99 points per game average by the 1965–66 Syracuse basketball team. The Orangemen exceeded the century mark in fourteen games that season and finished one basket shy of averaging 100.
- NCAA-record 262 consecutive extra points converted by SU placekickers from 1978 through 1989.
- 34 rebounds by Frank Reddout in a game against Temple (February 9, 1952).
- NCAA record-tying 22 assists by Sherman Douglas in a game vs. Providence (January 28, 1989).
- National best 7.83 yards per carry by Ernie Davis in 1960 (877 yards on 112 carries).

after several free-for-all minutes, the Mountaineers were awarded a 94–84 victory. The Orangemen had to stay holed up in their locker room for almost 90 minutes before it was safe enough for police to escort the team bus off campus.

"I'll never forget [SU Coach Roy] Danforth," Smith recalled in the book, *Tales from the Syracuse Hardwood*. "He said, 'Smitty, you hit the ref.' And I said, 'Yeah, but he slapped me.' And he said, 'Smitty, you hit the ref.' And I said, 'Yeah, but he slapped me.' We just kept going back and forth like that."

Smith was kicked off the team for the rest of the season. But he returned the following year for his senior season and led the Orangemen in both scoring (22.7) and rebounding (14.5). He was chosen by Portland with the 42ⁿᵈ pick of the 1971 draft. His NBA career lasted just 30 games over two seasons. He stayed in Oregon after his career was through and landed a job with Smith Barney.

"You know, each year the people at Syracuse send a copy of the press guide to me," he said. "And every year I look through it and check out the records. I see that, all things considered, I'm still one of the school's better players. But I think I've been kind of overlooked. I'm not bitter about it, but it's true. I don't know. Maybe it's because of the fight at West Virginia."

79 Catch the Pride of the Orange Marching Band

If you want to experience true school spirit before home football games, head over to the quad and listen to the Syracuse University marching band put on a rousing mini concert, replete with a baton twirling show by the Orange Girl.

The quad, a grassy rectangular area the size of several football fields, is usually a beehive of activity on game days, with food and drink tents set up all over the place and people tossing around footballs and Frisbees. The 200-member band, known as the Pride of the Orange, gets fans in the mood for that day's contest by playing snippets from several of the songs they'll be performing during pregame and half-time shows in the Carrier Dome. After finishing their montage, band members gather on the steps of Hendricks Chapel and belt out the SU fight song before delivering a soft version of the alma mater in which fans often join along in the singing. The band then lines up in parade formation and marches completely around the quad, which is bordered on all sides by academic buildings, some of which date back to the 1870s and 1880s. As they play their way down a wide sidewalk to the Dome, throngs of spectators follow. While walking past a life-sized, bronze statue of Ernie Davis, many touch the late Heisman Trophy winner's cleats for good luck.

The pregame concert is a good warm-up. It allows people to listen to a world-class marching band that's been performing at SU football games since October 9, 1901. It is also an opportunity to be outdoors on what are usually gorgeous autumn days, and it enables people to appreciate the campus' architectural diversity and the numerous mature trees and colorful changing leaves.

The Syracuse University marching band performs before Super Bowl XLVIII at Metlife Stadium on Sunday, February 2, 2014, in East Rutherford, New Jersey. (AP Photo/Ben Liebenberg)

80 Vinnie Cohen and the Hoops Title That Wasn't

There was an unwritten and unspoken rule in the 1950s that former Orange basketball star Vinnie Cohen believes cost Syracuse a national basketball championship in 1957.

"Before Texas Western came along [in 1966 and won the title with an all African American lineup], the understanding was that teams would not start more than two blacks," Cohen said in Bud Poliquin's book, *Tales from the Syracuse Hardwood.* "After [Texas Western's upset of Kentucky], real integration came into the sport. But it was too late for us. I've always believed that Syracuse would have won the national championship in my senior year if not for that funny rule."

The Orangemen had a team that contended for a national title that season. Led by two African Americans—Cohen, a 6'1" guard who earned All-America honors, and Manny Breland, the first black to receive a basketball scholarship to SU—Syracuse went 18–7 and lost to North Carolina 67–58 in the NCAAs in a contest that denied the Orange a trip to the Final Four. The unbeaten Tar Heels would go on to beat the Wilt Chamberlain–led Kansas Jayhawks in an epic national championship game that went three overtimes. SU was outscored by 23 points at the foul line in that East Region finals loss to North Carolina. But the referees didn't cost Syracuse the opportunity—that funny rule did. It resulted in Jim Brown, who had been a dynamic basketball player for the Orangemen during his sophomore and junior seasons, to skip hoops as a senior.

"Jim quit the team because of that rule," Cohen said. "He would have brought at least 15 points and 10 rebounds with him every game that season, and that would have been enough to get us to the finals and the national title. But Manny and I were the two black starters, and Jim saw the unfairness and he just wouldn't accept it."

Without Brown, a talented SU team that included Cohen, Breland, Jon Cincebox, Gary Clark, Jim Snyder, and Larry Loudis came up one man short. "It wasn't so much [Coach] Marc Guley's fault," Cohen said. "It was the way of America then. I always thought sports were sort of pure. If you can run faster than me, then you win the 100-yard dash, you know? But that's not the way it was in basketball. It hurt the university, and I think the university knows that now. But it was the custom in those days, the practice. Syracuse just went along to get along, I guess."

Cohen, who came to Syracuse from Brooklyn's Boys High School, averaged 24.2 points per game that season, a figure topped only twice in school history—by Dave Bing in 1965–66 (28.4) and Greg Kohls in 1971–72 (26.7). But Cohen, who arrived on campus the same year as Brown did, in the summer of 1953, almost didn't hang around SU long enough to make his mark there. Like Brown, he showed up at Syracuse without a scholarship.

"Funny isn't it?" he said. "The guy who would become the star of the football team doesn't have a scholarship. And the guy who would become the star of the basketball team doesn't have a scholarship. And both are told that if they "prove" themselves, they'll get scholarships. Interesting, huh?" Even after Cohen led the Syracuse freshman team in scoring, Guley hemmed and hawed about whether to give him a scholarship. Cohen was so angry about it that he prepared to transfer. And Brown considered leaving, too. But both were persuaded to stay after the scholarships were finally awarded.

Cohen attended Syracuse Law School after graduating and became a prominent attorney in Washington, D.C., practicing law for 40 years. He rejoiced when his alma mater won it all in 2003. He just wished that "funny rule" had not existed back in his day because he believes it robbed him, his teammates, and the school of a national championship.

81 "Now Kicking for the Orange, Ted Koppel"

Ted Koppel made a name for himself as the longtime anchor of *Nightline*, ABC's highly regarded late-night news interview show. But if he had his druthers, and if Syracuse football coach Ben Schwartzwalder had been a little more visionary, Koppel might have gotten his kicks from football rather than journalism.

The British born and raised Koppel was weaned on soccer and became an excellent striker for the Orangemen in the late 1950s—good enough to garner a few All-American votes. Convinced the Orangemen's placekicking needed improvement, Koppel approached Schwartzwalder to offer his services. In those days, football was far less specialized, and no coach in America had a guy on his roster who did nothing but kick. The kicking chores were usually handled by a position player, which is why, in addition to playing running back and defensive back, Jim Brown kicked extra points for the Orange. When Koppel, who had immigrated with his family to New York City when he was 13, floated the idea to the coach, Schwartzwalder looked at him as if he was crazy.

"I still had an English accent, and I was not the imposing figure I am today," the 5'9" Koppel joked in a 2005 interview with *The Washington Post*. "He took one look at me and said, 'We don't have an extra position.' And that was that."

Koppel claims that he—not future Buffalo Bills and New York Giants standout Pete Gogolak—came up with the idea of soccer-style placekicking. Booting the ball with the side of your foot rather than with your toe is far more accurate, and before long every team in college and the NFL was making room for soccer-style kicking specialists. "I was the first to think of it," Koppel said. "I was ahead of Gogolak. It would have been a big deal."

Koppel obviously shook off Schwartzwalder's rejection quite well and made a career out of being able to think fast on his feet rather than using his feet. During his senior year in 1959–60, Koppel was forced to choose between soccer, which he had played since he was old enough to walk, and a job as program director of the campus radio station, WAER. "I had to weigh my chances of a career as a professional soccer player in the United States against

Ted Koppel, the host of ABC's Nightline, *is pictured in this 1987 photo.*
(AP Photo)

broadcasting," he said. "I thought about it for, oh, maybe 30 seconds." After a brief pause, he added with a chuckle, "I made the wrong choice. I coulda been a contender."

Koppel spent 42 years with ABC, including 25 as *Nightline*'s anchor and managing editor. After leaving the network in 2005, he worked various jobs with The Discovery Channel, NBC News, BBC World News America, and National Public Radio.

82 Lon Keller and the New York Yankees Logo

After graduating from Syracuse University with a degree in fine arts in 1929, Lon Keller embarked on a career as an illustrator that would see him design more than 5,000 program covers for sporting events. He was so prolific and so respected among his peers that he became known as "the Norman Rockwell of sports." Of his numerous designs, none was more recognizable than the Uncle Sam hat-on-the-bat emblem of the New York Yankees. It continues to be used by the team today and is arguably the most famous and familiar logo in sports history.

Keller was reportedly commissioned by Yankees co-owner Larry MacPhail in 1946 to design a logo to strengthen the team's advertising opportunities following World War II. Keller had been hired because of his reputation for designing hundreds of major college football program covers as well as his work with World Series programs. His first drawing used the word "Yankees" in script with a top hat placed above the "k." It was first seen on the cover of the team's spring training roster in 1946.

MacPhail was pleased with the outcome but wanted Keller to develop it a bit more. The artist added a baseball to surround the "Yankees" script, changed the "k" to depict a baseball bat, and positioned the top hat directly above the bat. The new logo premiered on the team's spring training roster in 1947 and was an instant hit. From that point on, the logo has been used in virtually every Yankees correspondence and publication, and it has remained unchanged.

Keller, who was inducted into the New York State Sports Museum and Hall of Fame in 1991, died at age 87 in 1995. Interestingly, not long after Keller's death, the family of another illustrator, Sam Friedman, disputed reports that the former SU student had created the Yankees logo. According to Friedman's family, their "Uncle Sam" was the true originator. They claim that former Yankees owner Dan Topping told Friedman that he desired a patriotic-themed logo for the team, but the ad agencies he had worked with produced nothing satisfactory. The story goes that Friedman then swiftly pulled out a pen and began sketching a design on a cocktail napkin.

Jack Friedman, Sam's nephew, eventually wrote a letter to Yankees owner George Steinbrenner after reading a Keller obituary that credited him with the logo. Friedman received a response from the team's media relations department, noting that Keller has long been given credit. "Since Dan Topping is no longer living, it is not possible to verify the informal input other people may have contributed to the design," the response said.

In 2011, another person claimed that her uncle had designed the logo in 1936. She filed a copyright infringement suit that was dismissed by a federal judge in 2012. The Yankees continue to list Keller as the official designer of the logo in their annual media guide.

83 Marquis Franklin "Big Bill" Horr

Not long after 6'2", 240-lb. Marquis Franklin Horr showed up for his first Syracuse football practice in the summer of 1905, he was given the nickname "Big Bill." It fit because Horr was considered enormous for his day, and his legend as both a football and track & field star quickly became Bunyan-esque.

Horr was a four-time letterman in both sports, and in 1908 he became the first SU football player to earn All-American honors when he was named a first-team selection on the All-Star team chosen each year by pigskin pioneer Walter Camp. Earlier that same year, Horr won two medals in the discus at the Summer Olympics in London.

Sportswriters marveled at the big lineman's strength. As one wrote in the florid prose of the day, "Horr had enormous girth of chest and waist, with limbs like the trunks of trees, yet there was no superfluous pounds upon his great physique. His flesh was hard as iron...and after a week or two of preliminary training, he would go into a game and play through two long halves without the semblance of any trouble with his bellows. To show his strength it may be mentioned that, while fooling with his mates, he would frequently grab a 'little fellow' of 160 lbs., or thereabouts, by the waist band, and with one hand elevate him above his head to the length of his arm, as one would shove up a weight. And, like most such giants, he was the soul of good nature. Upon the football field he was known as one of the fairest of opponents, though he was business from the word go."

Horr was also blessed with the ability to run the 100-yard dash in under 11 seconds, an extraordinary time for a man of that size from that era. To take advantage of Horr's rare combination of size, strength, and speed, SU's coaches occasionally shifted Big Bill from the line, where he was a punishing blocker, to the backfield so he could carry the football. Though individual statistics from the time are sketchy, there is record of Horr christening Archbold Stadium on September 25, 1907, with a 75-yard touchdown run in a 28–0 thumping of Hobart College. The Orangemen experienced a football revival during Horr's four varsity seasons, going 25–12–2 and becoming competitive against national powerhouses Yale and Princeton.

As good as Horr was in football, however, he might have been even better in track & field, where he excelled in tossing the discus, shot put, and hammer. He established a world record in the discus and won a silver medal in the Greek discus competition and a bronze in the freestyle discus event at the 1908 Summer Games in London. Winner of two national titles in the discus and two more in hammer throwing, Horr added to his gigantic legend by defeating Jim Thorpe, who was regarded as the world's greatest athlete, in the discus during a dual meet.

Horr received his undergraduate and law degrees from Syracuse and had a successful career as an insurance attorney in central New York. He also returned briefly to his alma mater, serving as the line coach for several seasons. Big Bill became a LetterWinner of Distinction in 1969.

84 Ya Gotta Regatta!

If Syracuse University's first chancellor had his way, the school never would have fielded a crew. In fact, every other sport would have been dead in the water, too.

According to author Malcom Alma's book, *Mark of the Oarsmen*, chancellor Alexander Winchell was opposed to muscular sports of all kinds and refused to allow students to form a crew when the idea was first broached by two freshmen back in 1873, just three years after the school was founded. When Winchell heard that SU students Charles Holden and George Hine were going to hold a regatta on Onondaga Lake and offer prize money donated by downtown Syracuse merchants, Winchell had a snit. He wrote letters of displeasure to friends and community figures, but his attempts to torpedo the idea were too late because Holden and Hine had already captured the imagination of the community and interest from crews from Rochester, Buffalo, and New York City. Thousands of spectators showed up to watch the races. The daring duo thought the enormous success of the regatta would change Winchell's mind, but it didn't.

Rowing wouldn't be taken seriously until a more forward-thinking chancellor, James Roscoe Day, embraced the idea in 1900. Day convinced benefactor Lyman Cornelius Smith, a local typewriter tycoon, to provide financial assistance, and SU football coach Edwin Regur Sweetland offered to take on the additional duties of coaching the team in order to earn a little extra money. The first organized crews would become known as the Syracuse

A Team of Distinction

Led by legendary crew coach Bill Sanford, SU's Varsity Eight won the 1978 Intercollegiate Rowing Association Championship on Onondaga Lake. It was SU's first national rowing title in 58 years. Members of the crew were Gerald Henwood, Andy Mogish, Bill Purdy, Bill Reid, John Shamlian, Art "Skip" Sibley, Ozzie Street, and David Townsley. Several of the rowers would go on to compete in international competitions. Purdy wound up qualifying for the 1980 Olympics in Moscow but was not allowed to compete because of the Olympic boycott.

University Navy, but they didn't get off to an auspicious start and Sweetland resigned in 1902.

James A. Ten Eyck, a professional sculler and coach of the U.S. Naval Academy's first crews, took over the program, and a golden era of SU rowing ensued. During Ten Eyck's 34 years as coach, the Orangemen won the Intercollegiate Rowing Association's regatta—regarded as the national championship—five times. A year before Ten Eyck's death at age 87 in 1938, the university built and dedicated a boathouse in his honor.

Another seminal moment in the program's rich history would come in 1959 when Loren Schoel coached SU, the U.S. representative in the Pan American Games, to victory. That same year, Schoel recruited a superb rower named Bill Sanford, who would become varsity captain in 1963 and go on to coach for 34 years, producing an IRA Varsity Eight champion in 1978 and a Varsity Four champ in 1980. Through the years, the men's and women's teams churned out a number of Olympic rowers, most recently Natalie Mastracci, who won a silver medal at the 2012 Summer Games in London, and Mike Gennaro, who was an alternate on the U.S. men's team.

From 1952 through 1992 and again in 1994, SU served as hosts of the IRA on Onondaga Lake, staging huge regattas that undoubtedly would have made Holden and Hine burst with pride and Chancellor Winchell explode with anger. Crowds in excess of 15,000 people would gather on the shores and in the park for the three-day event. Over time, the partying and boozing of the spectators overshadowed the races themselves. One scribe described the scene as "rowing's Woodstock." By the early 1980s, race officials stopped allowing alcohol to be brought into the park. Flooding forced the races to be moved in 1993. After returning to Onondaga the following year, the regatta was moved to Cooper River in Pennsauken, New Jersey.

85 Turning Down the Rose Bowl

On at least two occasions, officials from the Rose Bowl invited Syracuse's football team to come to Pasadena, California, to participate in "the granddaddy of them all." And both times the Orangemen's hopes were sacked by chancellors who told the bowl committee, "Thanks, but no thanks."

The first invite was extended after the 1915 Orange squad outscored the opposition 331–16 en route to a 9–1–2 record. SU's only blemishes were a 3–0 loss to Ivy League powerhouse Princeton, a scoreless tie with Dartmouth, and a 6–6 tie vs. Montana in a game that was played in a blizzard. Led by All-American, two-way linemen Christopher Schlachter and Harold White, the Orangemen pitched a school-record nine shutouts, including an 82–0 evisceration of upstate rival Rochester. SU played an ambitious schedule that saw it become the first Eastern school to embark on a West Coast swing. The Orange traveled by train to Montana for a November 25 game. They continued west for a December 1 contest with Oregon State and then went south to Los Angeles for a game five days later vs. Occidental College.

After returning to campus, SU coach Frank J. O'Neill received a letter from the Tournament of Roses director inviting the Orange to play Washington State in Pasadena in what would later become known as the Rose Bowl. The invitation was a huge deal because, unlike today where there are nearly 40 Division I bowl games, the Rose Bowl was the only postseason game in 1916. O'Neill and his players were excited for the opportunity, but chancellor James Roscoe Day immediately put the kibosh on it. He said the football team's three-week, West Coast road trip depleted the school's athletic budget. Brown, which was blanked 6–0 by SU in the regular season, went in place of the Orangemen and lost 14–0 to Washington State.

Seven years later, under coach John "Chick" Meehan, Syracuse fielded another football juggernaut that caught the eyes of the folks from Pasadena. And once again, the Orange didn't wind up smelling like a rose. Led by quarterback Roy Simmons and two-way All-American end Evander "Pete" MacRae, Syracuse went 8–1, its only stumble being a 16–7 loss to arch-rival Colgate. The Orangemen recorded seven shutouts—including blankings of Alabama (23–0), Pitt (3–0), and Penn State (10–0)—and outscored the opposition 237–19. A week after having its perfect season ruined by the Red Raiders, SU traveled to Lincoln, Nebraska, to play a Cornhuskers team that two weeks before had stunned Knute Rockne's unbeaten Notre Dame "Four Horsemen" team for the second straight season. The Orange knocked off Nebraska 7–0, becoming the first visiting team to win a game in the Cornhuskers new stadium.

"There was only one bowl game in those days—the Rose Bowl—and their people were at the Nebraska game, ready to give

Digging Graves

Quarterback Marvin Graves is one of just a handful of players in college football history to have won Most Valuable Player awards in three different bowl games. The native of Washington, D.C., earned those honors after guiding SU to a 28–0 victory against Arizona in the 1990 Aloha Bowl, a 24–17 victory vs. Ohio State in the 1992 Hall of Fame Bowl, and a 26–22 victory vs. Colorado at the 1993 Fiesta Bowl.

Graves threw for 8,466 yards in his career, second all-time at SU behind Ryan Nassib (9,060). Graves also led the Orange to a 31–12–3 record (.707 winning percentage) in games he started. His greatest statistical game occurred on October 10, 1992, when he threw for 425 yards and three touchdowns in a 50–28 blowout of Rutgers.

the Cornhuskers a bid," Simmons Sr. said in a 1985 interview. "But we changed those plans. We beat Nebraska, and the Rose Bowl committee decided to invite us instead." Simmons remembered the joyous train ride back to Syracuse and the heartbreaking news that followed. "Our chancellor [Charles Wesley Flint] turned down the bid," Simmons recalled. "He was opposed to exploiting a college team for financial gain. Most of us were in a state of shock."

Three decades later, Syracuse received another bowl bid. This time its chancellor didn't intervene, but it might have been better if he had. The 7–2 Orangemen played Alabama in the Orange Bowl on New Year's Day 1953. The Crimson Tide was so loaded with talent that season that future Hall of Fame quarterback Bart Starr couldn't crack the starting lineup. He eventually made it into the game that day—as did every other player wearing crimson—and tossed a couple of touchdown passes. 'Bama annihilated Syracuse 61–6, at the time the largest margin of victory in bowl-game history.

There had been reports, never substantiated, that Alabama had spied on SU's practices leading up to the game. "Coach [Ben] Schwartzwalder told us about it at a team meeting," said Pat Stark, who quarterbacked SU that day and later served as an Orange assistant. "I don't know if it was accurate or a figment of his imagination, but it did get you a little paranoid. I remember looking around every so often during practice to see if there were any suspicious characters hanging around."

That game would mark the first of 25 bowl appearances by Syracuse. The Orange are 15–9–1 in those games.

Tom Coughlin

Floyd Little and Larry Csonka already have busts in the Pro Football Hall of Fame. And if Little's football fantasy comes true, their old Syracuse University backfield mate, Tom Coughlin, will one day be immortalized in Canton, too.

"It would be me on one side and Larry on the other, with Tom right there between us," Little said of the enshrinement ceremony he envisions. "And we'd be wearing our yellow jackets. And I'd be saying, 'Welcome to the Hall of Fame, Tom Coughlin.' For me, that would be the greatest thing in the world."

It's not a farfetched vision, considering Coughlin has guided the New York Giants to two Super Bowl titles and ranks among the top 14 winningest coaches in NFL history. And if it comes true, SU would have the distinction of being the only school to have its entire backfield—halfback, fullback, and wingback—represented by sculpted busts in the Hall.

In retrospect, Little never expected Coughlin to be in the discussion for football immortality. After first laying eyes on Coughlin in the mid-1960s, he thought the young man would wind up being a bust, not receiving one. "The first time I saw Tom, I thought he was a kicker," said Little, who was a sophomore at the time. "He couldn't have weighed a buck-eighty, if he was that. And he didn't have a whole lot of speed. I was a track man, and Tom obviously wasn't. He ran with a different intent, a different style. But he came to Syracuse to compete at the highest level he could, and you had to respect that."

With halfback Little and fullback Csonka forming arguably the greatest one-two combination in college football history, touches were few and far between for Coughlin. But the Waterloo, New

New York Giants coach Tom Coughlin smiles as he leaves the field after the Giants beat the Washington Redskins 20–14 on Sunday, September 19, 2004, at Giants Stadium in East Rutherford, New Jersey. (AP Photo/Bill Kostroun)

York, native made the most of his opportunities, limited though they might have been. During his senior season in 1967, he averaged 6.1 yards on 42 carries and caught a then-record 26 passes for 257 yards and two touchdowns. He also completed 3-of-4 passes for 35 yards and one score. The Orangemen went 23–8 and made an appearance in the 1966 Gator Bowl during his three varsity seasons. An outstanding student, Coughlin received SU's Joseph Alexander Award for excellence in football, scholarship, and citizenship. He graduated in 1968 with honors in history.

While living in Sadler Hall, Coughlin's resident advisor was Jim Boeheim, who was working on his master's degree at the time. The two were familiar with one another because when Boeheim was a senior at Lyons High School, his team defeated Waterloo, which included Coughlin, who was a sophomore. "I figured he'd become an eighth-grade math teacher. That seemed to be the kind of personality he had: pleasant, low-key, comfortable," Boeheim recalled.

However, as was the case with Boeheim, Coughlin wanted to remain involved with the sport he loved, so he began a coaching career as a graduate assistant at SU in 1969. After a four-year stint as the coach of Division III Rochester Institute of Technology, he returned to his alma mater, working as an assistant on Frank Maloney's staff for seven seasons. In 1994, after three successful seasons as the head coach at Boston College, Coughlin was named the head coach of the Jacksonville Jaguars, an NFL expansion team that would begin play a year later. By his second year, Coughlin had the Jags in the AFC Championship Game.

Other NFL Head Coaches with SU Ties

Jim Ringo: An All-America center at SU in 1952, Ringo went on to a Pro Football Hall of Fame career with the Green Bay Packers and Philadelphia Eagles. He became a highly respected offensive line coach but went 3–20 in his two seasons (1976–77) as head coach of the Buffalo Bills.

Doug Marrone: An All-Big East tackle at Syracuse in the mid-1980s, Marrone spent nearly two decades as a college and pro assistant before becoming the head coach of the Orange in 2009. He led SU to a 25–25 record and two Pinstripe Bowl victories before becoming head coach of the Bills. He was 6–10 in his first season in Buffalo in 2013.

Dick MacPherson: Coach Mac ignited the football revival at Syracuse, leading the Orangemen to a 66–46–4 record and three bowl victories in 10 seasons. He left to coach the New England Patriots in 1991 and received NFL Coach of the Year consideration after the Pats made a five-game improvement from their 1–15 mark a year before his arrival. MacPherson was fired following a 2–14 record his second season.

Bud Wilkinson: Before guiding Oklahoma to three national championships, Wilkinson spent the 1938–41 seasons as an assistant at SU. The Orangemen went 16–12–4 in those four seasons. In 1978, he became head coach of the NFL's St. Louis Cardinals, going 9–20 in his two seasons before stepping down.

In 2004, he took over the Giants and has led them to Super Bowl titles in 2007 and 2011. Interestingly, his first Lombardi Trophy was secured in large part when former SU special teams star David Tyree made his famous ball-against-his-helmet reception during the winning drive. The 2013 season was Coughlin's 42nd year as a coach. Through 2013, he had a 170–137 record (including postseason) with five divisional crowns and two championships in his 18 NFL seasons, good for 14th all time.

87 Arachnophobia

Paced by the multi-talented Billy Owens and featuring a solid lineup that included guards Adrian Autry and Michael Edwards, the 1990–91 Orangemen won nine of their last 10 to finish the regular season with 26–4 record and a No. 4 ranking in the polls. Unfortunately for the team known as "Billy and the Beaters," their spectacular regular season would be sullied by arguably the most disappointing and shocking postseason in program history.

The Orangemen were knocked off by Villanova 70–68 in the first round of the 1991 Big East tournament. The NCAA selection committee didn't put much stock in the loss, chalking it up to one of those things that happens in conference playoffs, and they installed Syracuse as the No. 2 seed in the East. That meant the Orangemen would face the 15th-seeded Richmond Spiders in the first round in College Park, Maryland. Everybody expected Syracuse to cruise into the second round, but Richmond had other ideas. For the first time in NCAA tournament history, a 15 seed upset a second seed as the Spiders won 73–69 in a game that is still painfully known in Syracuse as "Arachnophobia."

"That was the worst day of my life," Owens told *Syracuse Post-Standard* beat reporter Mike Waters. "I was mad. I was mad at me. I was mad at the team. It really hurt me a lot."

Boeheim believes the NCAA's investigation of the basketball program at the time contributed to that monumental loss by sapping the team of its energy. "The circumstances that surrounded the game and the turmoil were really the reasons we lost, rather than Richmond out-playing us," he said. "Mentally, we were beat at the end of the day." Owens concurred, saying, "You could just tell on the court. You could see that game slipping away, and we didn't do anything. They were setting simple cross picks, and we were acting like we didn't know how to defend. I remember Boeheim screaming, 'We've got to fight through the picks,' and it didn't happen."

The loss would mark the end of Owens' college career. A few weeks later, the first-team All-American forward announced he was skipping his senior year to turn pro.

88. The Case for More Heisman Winners

The Heisman Trophy won by Ernie Davis in 1961 is prominently displayed in the Iocolano-Petty Football Complex adjacent to Manley Field House on SU's South Campus. There are those who believe there should be at least two more Heismans residing there—one bearing the name of Jim Brown and the other the name of Don McPherson.

Not only didn't Brown win the award in 1956, he somehow finished fifth in the balloting. That election remains one of the most controversial in the 80-year history of the Heisman for a number of reasons. Notre Dame's Paul Hornung wound up winning the trophy, despite playing for a 2–8 football team. Johnny Majors, who led Tennessee to a 10–0 record, finished second, followed by Oklahoma's Tommy McDonald and Jerry Tubbs, who finished three and four, respectively.

Hornung was clearly a superb all-around player, but his achievements in the autumn of '56 were dwarfed by Brown's. Hornung played quarterback on offense and in the secondary on defense. He also kicked extra points and returned kickoffs. That season, he rushed for 420 yards and six touchdowns. He completed 53 percent of his passes (59-of-111) for 917 yards and three scores, but he also threw 13 interceptions. He had three receptions for 26 yards and had a 95-yard kickoff return for a touchdown vs. USC. Defensively, he finished second on the team in tackles and interceptions (3).

Contrast those stats with Brown, who was also a two-way player who handled the kicking chores. Brown rushed for 960 yards, which was third-best in the nation. (It should be noted he played in one less game than the two players who finished ahead of him.) He led the nation with 13 rushing touchdowns. Brown also had five receptions for 56 yards and a touchdown. He completed 3-of-4 passes for 76 yards and one score, and he kicked 31 extra points for a total of 105 points. As a linebacker, he was second on the team in interceptions (3), and although there aren't tackle figures available, he made several key stops, including three at the goal line to preserve a 7–0 victory vs. Army. Additionally, he set an NCAA record that season by scoring 43 points in a single game vs. Colgate.

Theories abound for Brown's poor showing in the balloting. Some say it reflected the low esteem in which Syracuse and Eastern football was held. Some say it was an indictment of SU's schedule, which was weaker than Notre Dame's. "What voters failed to take into account is that Jim Brown single-handedly made Syracuse football relevant again," said Jim Ridlon, a teammate of Brown's in football and lacrosse who went on to play several seasons in the NFL. "Without Jim, we would have been lucky to win two to three games. With him, we became a bowl team back in a time where there were only four or five bowls."

Others believe racial prejudice played a significant role. "Hornung didn't deserve it; not with three touchdown passes and 13 interceptions, and not on a 2–8 team," wrote Steve Delsohn of ESPN.com, who co-wrote Jim Brown's best-selling autobiography, *Out of Bounds.* "The Heisman should have gone to Jim Brown. But, in 1956, Jim Brown had the wrong color skin."

Dick Schapp agreed with that assessment. He was an assistant sports editor at *Newsweek* at the time and cast his first-place vote for Brown. "At that time, no black athlete had ever received the Heisman, and I swore that I would never vote again," he wrote. "I waited a quarter of a century—till I voted for Marcus Allen in 1981. Times had changed. Allen's Heisman was the eighth in a row for a black running back."

Race clearly was not an issue in 1987 because both McPherson and the man who beat him out—Notre Dame's Tim Brown—were African American. In the Hornung election, many criticized the voters' infatuation with Irish football. Similar complaints were lodged 31 years later. Like Hornung, Brown was a superb all-around player, though his primary position was wide receiver. That year, for a Notre Dame team that went 8–4, he caught 39 passes for 846 yards and three touchdowns, rushed 34 times for 144 yards and one score, and returned three punts for touchdowns.

McPherson, meanwhile, played at the most influential position on the field—quarterback—and he guided the Orangemen to an 11–0 record, an improvement of six wins from the year before. He also led the nation in passing efficiency, completing 56 percent of his throws for 2,341 yards and 22 touchdowns. He was picked off just 11 times. He also rushed for 230 yards and five touchdowns, and he even caught a seven-yard touchdown pass. His statistics, though excellent, might have been even gaudier had he played more, but he often left games by the end of the third quarter because the Orangemen were usually were so far ahead.

"The argument I would make is that if you took Don McPherson and his stats and his won-lost record from that year and put him in a Notre Dame uniform, he would have won by one of the biggest landslides in Heisman Trophy history," said Daryl Johnston, who played fullback on SU's 1987 team and went on to win three Super Bowls with the Dallas Cowboys before becoming a respected NFL analyst. "Conversely, if you took Tim Brown's stats and his team's record and put him in a Syracuse uniform that year, he probably wouldn't receive many votes. That's by no means a condemnation of Brown—he was a great player. It's just meant to illustrate the politics involved."

In the history of the Heisman voting, three other Orangemen cracked the top five. Floyd Little finished fifth both in 1965 and 1966, and when you add punt return and kickoff return skills to his running back skills, you could make an argument for him, too. Fullback Larry Csonka finished fourth in 1967, and quarterback Donovan McNabb finished fifth in 1998.

89 Notable Women Sports Figures

Kayla Alexander was the first Syracuse University player to be selected in the first round of the WNBA draft (2013). A 6'4" center, Alexander is the school's all-time leader in points (2,024 points) and blocked shots (350). The Milton, Ontario, native led the Orange to a record 96 wins in four seasons, earned All-Big East honors three times, and was an honorable mention All-American during her senior year. She was drafted eighth overall by the San Antonio Silver Stars.

- Beth Record was the first female Orange hoopster to be drafted, as the 65th pick by the Los Angeles Sparks, in 2001.
- Swimmer Liz Vilbert was the first Orangewoman to be selected All-American four times. Vilbert ultimately chose Syracuse over several of the nation's top swimming programs because her coaches believed she could handle the rigors of pursuing a nursing degree and a competitive swimming career. She earned her All-American honors in 1978, 1979, 1980, and 1981. In 1981, she also earned her nursing degree.
- Doris Soladay was the first and only director of women's athletics at SU. She served in that capacity from 1975 through 1995. She helped establish athletic scholarships for women and increase budgets for their programs so they would have equipment, training facilities, and practice and game schedules on par with men. Upon her retirement, an award was established in her name and is presented annually to the top female and male student-athletes at the university.
- Ice hockey player Stephanie Marty is the first SU athlete to compete in the Winter Olympics and also the first athlete to medal. She skated for the Swedish hockey team in the 2010 Games in Vancouver and the 2014 Games in Sochi, helping the Swedes to a bronze medal in Russia.

    Between indoor and outdoor track, shot put and discus thrower Cheree Hicks earned first-team All-American honors four times during her final two seasons.
- Rower Anna Goodale was a three-time All-American, and she also won a gold medal in the women's eight crew at the 2008 Summer Olympics in Beijing. She was named a National Scholar Athlete her senior year and graduated with a degree in illustration in 2005.

- Katie Rowan is the most decorated women's lacrosse player in Syracuse history. The program's only three-time first-team All-American, Rowan led the nation in scoring in 2008. She is the Orange women's career leader in points (396) and assists (164). She won the Soladay Award in 2009.

- Katharine Sibley was SU's first instructor of women's physical education and athletics; she spent 47 years at the University. In 1905, she established the Women's Athletic Association, which was a club sport program that enabled women to participate in tennis, field hockey, soccer, archery, gymnastics, basketball, swimming, fencing, rowing, bowling, skiing, and volleyball.

- Basketball player Felisha Legette earned honorable mention All-American honors as a sophomore and junior and had a good shot of becoming a three-time honoree before she injured her knee during her senior season. She played from 1985 to 1989 and remains SU's fifth all-time leading scorer (1,526 points) and third all-time leading rebounder (927). She was named Big East Rookie of the Year in 1985.

- Rower Natalie Mastracci was a first-team All-American in 2013. The Welland, Ontario, native won a silver medal for Canada's women's eight crew at the 2012 Olympics in London.

- Lucille Verhulst, a former director of women's physical education, submitted a proposal in 1971 to chancellor Melvin Eggers for five club sports—basketball, swimming and diving, fencing, tennis, and volleyball—to receive varsity status—and he approved, laying the groundwork for the women's intercollegiate sports programs that would blossom after the passage of the Title IX legislation the following year.

- Erin O'Grady is the most prolific scorer in the history of the women's soccer program. She owns six career and single-season scoring records and led the team to its first NCAA tournament appearance in 1998, just the third year of the program.

- Lauren Penney made SU history by becoming the first Syracuse female cross-country runner to be honored as an All-American. Penney led the Orange in every race she participated in and punctuated her 2011 season with a second-place finish at the NCAA Northeast Regional.

Kayla Alexander (40) takes a shot over Rutgers' Monique Oliver during the first half of a game in Piscataway, New Jersey, on Tuesday, January 3, 2012.
(AP Photo/Mel Evans)

- A 1998 Academic All-American, Keri Potts was the first volleyball student-athlete in school history to complete her undergraduate degree in three years and enroll in graduate school. She was a team co-captain as a senior and won the 1999 Soladay Award.

- Tennis All-American Jana Strnadova is Syracuse's all-time leader in career wins with 202. Her 58 overall wins and 35 singles wins as a freshman still stand as SU single-season records.

90 A Fine Mess and Probation

On November 17, 2011—just weeks after the Jerry Sandusky child sex abuse scandal rocked the Penn State football program and the sports world—ESPN reported that longtime SU assistant basketball coach Bernie Fine had molested former ball boy Bobby Davis when Davis was between the ages of 12 and 27. The story, according to the network, had been corroborated by Davis's stepbrother, Mike Lang, who told ESPN that Fine had also molested him. Fine denied the allegations, and SU officials said they conducted an investigation when the accusations were first brought to their attention in 2005 and could not find anyone—including Lang—to corroborate Davis' claims.

Shocked by the news, Jim Boeheim came to the defense of Fine, whom he had known since their undergraduate days. The SU coach called Davis and Lang liars and said they were attempting to capitalize on the timing of the Penn State scandal. Davis and Lang later sued Boeheim for defamation of character, a suit that was rejected by a State Supreme Court judge. Syracuse police and federal investigators searched Fine's house for several hours, seizing file cabinets after the U.S. Attorney's Office issued a search warrant. After nearly a year of scouring more than 100,000 pages of seized documents and interviewing 130 witnesses, the investigation concluded without Fine or anyone else being charged. Fine, who had been fired by SU chancellor Nancy Cantor shortly after the initial ESPN report, became a recluse and put up his suburban Syracuse home for sale.

Another major sports scandal occurred in 1992 when the NCAA placed the basketball program on two-year probation for widespread violations involving recruits and student-athletes. The Orangemen were banned from the 1993 NCAA men's basketball tournament and lost two scholarships. The sanctions came after a two-year investigation, which was triggered by a book, *Raw Recruits*, which claimed SU had benefited from its relationship with a New York City street agent who steered several prospects to Syracuse. It also alleged that SU players had been provided with money and free sneakers as well as use of discounted cars and airline tickets. The book prompted an exhaustive investigative series by the *Syracuse Post-Standard*, which in turn prompted the NCAA to conduct its own investigation. The men's lacrosse, football, and wrestling programs, and the women's basketball program, were also cited for minor violations and were penalized.

91 Billy Gabor

Billy Gabor was quicker and faster than just about everyone he played with and against on the basketball court, which explains how he became known as "Bullet."

"I really don't know who gave me the nickname," Gabor said in the 2004 book, *Legends of Syracuse Basketball*. "But it stuck."

His swiftness would serve him well and enable him to excel, despite his slight build (5'11", 175 lbs.). During the 1940s, Gabor established SU records (since broken) for most points in a game (36), a season (409), and a career (1,344), and he earned All-America honors after averaging 16.3 points per game his junior season. He would also become the only player in school history to lead the Orangemen in scoring four consecutive years. SU went 61–33 and earned two postseason invitations during his career. Gabor's speed enabled Syracuse to play an up-tempo style of basketball during a pre-shot-clock era when most teams walked the ball up the floor and worked the ball around methodically before taking a shot.

"We were ahead of our time because of our fast-breaking style of play," said Royce Newell, a lanky 6'8" center/forward on those teams. "Our job as the youngsters was to get the rebound, get it to Billy, and he was gone."

There was more to Gabor's game than just speed, however. He was a superb outside shooter whose two-handed set-shot was deadly accurate from as far away as 30'. And his quickness made him a pesky defender who often created his own offensive opportunities with steals. His dibbling skills, combined with his agility, also enabled him to create scoring chances for teammates.

Gabor's endurance was the stuff of legend, too. Early in his freshman year, he often logged basketball doubleheaders, playing an entire game with the freshmen team, then toweling off and seeing action in the varsity game that followed. After leading the varsity in scoring with a 12.1 average in 1942–43, Gabor was drafted into the Army Air Corps and spent two years as a bombardier in World War II before returning to campus. Despite not having touched a basketball in 30 months, he picked up where he left off, averaging 15.2 points per game during the 1945–46 season. The following campaign, he became the first player in school history to exceed 400 points in a season as the Orangemen went 19–6. He and his teammates had great expectations for the 1947–48 season, but Gabor was hampered most of the year by a nagging toe injury, and SU slipped to 11–13.

Gabor spent six seasons in the NBA with the Syracuse Nationals. He made the league's All-Rookie team in 1949, was an All-Star in 1953, and was a member of the Nats championship team in 1955. His career scoring record would stand for nearly two decades before being broken by Dave Bing. On May 1, 2009, Gabor became the ninth player in program history to have his jersey number retired.

92 Sheldon Leonard

He would go on to become one of the most influential writers, producers, and directors in the history of television. But long before making a cannonball splash in Hollywood with immensely popular programs such as the *Dick Van Dyke Show*, *I Spy*, and *The Andy Griffith Show*, Sheldon Leonard was splashing around in the pool on the Syracuse University campus as a member of the varsity swim and water polo teams. In fact, the Brooklyn native actually came to SU in 1925 on an athletic scholarship. He would leave with a degree in sociology and a love for the dramatic arts.

After graduating with high honors in 1929, Leonard began work as a stockbroker on Wall Street. His first day on the job did not go very well. It fact, it was the same day as the infamous stock market crash that would plunge America into the Great Depression. Quickly out of work, Leonard decided to go for broke and pursue his true passion—acting. He began landing parts in Broadway productions before heading to Hollywood where he

SU LetterWinners of Distinction

Each year, Syracuse honors several former varsity athletes, coaches, and contributors "who have gained distinction in their community or profession and brought honor to themselves and the University." The first LetterWinners of Distinction were honored in 1965 and included John Connor, a former Orange football player who became the United States Secretary of Commerce; Gordon Hoople, a member of the crew team who became a prominent physician and surgeon; and Vic Hanson, a three-sport letterman and three-sport captain who is the only person to be inducted into the basketball and college football halls of fame.

Since that first class, more than 300 male and female athletes and contributors have been honored. Here are a few highlights:

F. Story Musgrave: A varsity wrestler and a 1958 mathematics graduate, Musgrave went on to become a physician and an astronaut. He flew on the first five space shuttle missions for NASA.

Melissa "Emme" Entwistle Aronson: A four-year women's rowing letter-winner who was invited to the U.S. Olympic trials in 1985, Aronson became a world-renowned supermodel known simply as Emme.

Duffy Daugherty: A rugged lineman, the affable Daugherty became the winningest coach in Michigan State football history and earned induction into the College Football Hall of Fame.

Americo Woyciesjes: An intercollegiate boxing champion and a decorated World War II hero, Woyciesjes (pronounced Woy-SEE-jis) became a scientist who helped discover Gentamycin, an antibiotic that has saved thousands of lives.

Virginia Guilfoil Allen: A 1940 graduate and one of New York's top amateur golfers, Allen became the first woman to be named a LetterWinner of Distinction.

Thomas Lombardi: A football letterman and 1933 graduate, Lombardi joined the U.S. Navy and survived the sinking of the battleship *West Virginia* in Pearl Harbor. He later commanded the main gun battery on the same re-floated ship.

John Hordines: A letter-winner in track, football, wrestling, crew, and rugby, Hordines became a teacher, coach, and writer who coached the only blind crew in the world.

appeared in more than 150 films, often playing the roles of snarling, underworld figures. One of his most memorable supporting roles was as the bartender who threw Jimmy Stewart out of the bar in *It's a Wonderful Life.*

Leonard would become better known for his work behind the camera as a writer, producer, and director. He joined Danny Thomas' TV show in 1953, and the two collaborated on a number of productions before Leonard branched off on his own. His timing proved impeccable because he became involved with television just as it was ascending into an immensely popular form of entertainment in America.

"Sheldon was one of the pioneers of situation comedy in television," said Chuck Wren of the Directors Guild of America. A winner of five Emmys who was nominated for 18 more, Leonard had a hand in an important television milestone, producing the comedy-adventure *I Spy*, which made Bill Cosby the first black star of a program on a major network. Leonard was so successful at taking the pulse of American audiences that he became known as "the King Midas of television programming."

His influence continues to be felt nearly two decades after his death on January 11, 1997. The characters Sheldon Cooper and Leonard Hofstadter on CBS' *The Big Bang Theory* are named in his honor.

Leonard returned to his alma mater several times through the years, including in the fall of 1968 when he was feted as a LetterWinner of Distinction. He established two fellowships at Syracuse for the study of television audiences, something for which Leonard clearly had great instincts. He traveled far since his days in the SU pool.

"I always said there must have been something in that water in Syracuse that helped me get to where I am today," he once joked. "They must have used just the right amount of chlorine."

93 Ron Luciano

Long before he became arguably the most popular and funniest umpire in Major League Baseball history, Ron Luciano made a name for himself as a hulking, two-way lineman for the SU football team. In fact, the 6'4", 260-lb. tackle was so good that he earned first-team All-American honors during his senior season (1958) and was drafted by the Detroit Lions in the third round of the NFL draft the following spring. A shoulder injury in the annual College All-Star Game prevented him from playing a single down for the Lions. The Buffalo Bills of the competing AFL picked him up in 1961, but a knee injury forced the unlucky Luciano to retire.

Football's loss was baseball's gain. Luciano began umpiring in the Florida State League in 1964. He slowly climbed the minor league ladder and in 1969 received the call-up to the American League. Known for his flamboyant calls and humorous quotes, Luciano quickly became an umpire that fans actually liked. However, managers such as the pugnacious Earl Weaver weren't amused by Luciano's antics. Luciano, who umpired for 11 big-league seasons, once ejected Weaver from both games of a doubleheader. The feud between the two became so heated that Weaver's players on the Baltimore Orioles would stage friendly wagers as to what inning their manager would get tossed by Luciano.

Luciano's relationship with feisty New York Yankees manager Billy Martin wasn't much better. "Billy came up to me with the lineup card before a game and began complaining to me about an umpire," Luciano recalled in a 1984 interview with the *Utica*

Observer-Dispatch. "He says, 'Ron, can you believe that call that jerk made at first base last night? Can you believe that anyone could be so dumb, so blind?' I said, 'Billy, now wait a minute. That umpire was me.'"

Although he majored in mathematics at SU, Luciano always had a soft spot for the theater and was a voracious reader of Shakespeare. After retiring from baseball before the 1980 season, he collaborated on five books, including two best-sellers—*The Umpire Strikes Back* and *The Fall of the Roman Umpire*—and became a popular speaker on the banquet circuit.

According to several of his former SU teammates and coaches, Luciano was extremely popular, in large part because of the pranks he pulled and his quick and often self-deprecating sense of humor. His ability to laugh at himself was on display in an interview with the Rochester (NY) *Democrat & Chronicle* years later, when he recalled his final college game—a 21–6 loss to Oklahoma in the Orange Bowl on New Year's Day 1959. "Our coach, Ben Schwartzwalder, was so happy to see me go that he wanted to have a parade," Luciano joked. "Who could blame him? I still maintain that the reason Syracuse won the national championship the next year was because I wasn't there. I was the missing ingredient, or rather, the ingredient that should have been missing."

Unbeknownst to many, Luciano battled depression for many years and was hospitalized for treatment in 1994. The following year he was found dead, at age 57, in his garage at his home in Endicott, New York, a victim of suicide due to carbon monoxide poisoning.

Dr. Fred Lewis

While unfortunate, it's understandable why Dr. Fred Lewis is as forgotten as Zoo kazoos, the two-handed set shot, and that rubbery wrestling-mat-like court the SU hoops team used to play on in the Carrier Dome.

See, Lewis coached Orange basketball for just six seasons (1962–68), the shortest tenure of any head basketball coach in SU annals. And like every other coach in school history, he wound up being lapped several times by his former walk-on who eventually followed in his footsteps—a guy named James Arthur Boeheim. But make no mistake. Lewis' role in re-launching a program that had become the dregs of college basketball was monumental. At a time when JFK was asking our space program to take us to the moon, Lewis was asking the Orange basketball program to shoot for the stars. Had the good doctor not made a (Manley Field) House call back in the day, this half-century run of hoops success on the Hill far above Onondaga's waters would not have happened.

His legacy includes:

- Out-recruiting the nation's top programs for Dave Bing's services
- Taking a chance on Boeheim, who blossomed into a good player and a Hall of Fame coach
- Giving assistant and eventual successor Roy Danforth the opportunity to develop the coaching skills necessary to guide SU to its first Final Four and lay the foundation for Jimmy B's magnificent career
- Recording a 91–57 record and three postseason appearances (one NCAA, two NITs) in six years.

To fully appreciate Lewis' impact, one must journey back to the 1960–61 and 1961–62 seasons. Those forgettable campaigns, under Coach Marc Guley, had produced 4–19 and 2–22 records as well as a 27-game losing streak, which was the Division I sub-standard for sustained hoops futility at the time. The *Daily Orange* pulled no punches summing up the dire situation by writing that Syracuse "basketball wasn't a sport—it was a crime against humanity." Students and people in the community were so turned off by the mediocrity that crowds for SU home games at the 7,000-seat Onondaga War Memorial, routinely numbered in the low 100s.

A month before the 1961–62 season ended, Guley announced he would be retiring after the final game. A search committee, headed by athletic director Lew Andreas, reviewed the credentials of more than 50 candidates. For the first time in the 60-year history of the program, an outsider was hired as coach.

Lewis arrived on campus with a long and impressive basketball resume. After earning All–New York City basketball honors in high school and a brief stint at Long Island University under legendary coach Clair Bee, Lewis transferred to Eastern Kentucky University where he finished second and third in the nation in scoring while earning All-American honors his junior and senior years. Drafted in 1947 by the Sheboygan Redskins of the National Basketball League (a forerunner to the NBA), he finished second in the league in scoring and earned Rookie of the Year and All-Star honors. He later played with the Baltimore Bullets before hanging up his sneakers to begin his coaching career.

After four years coaching at the high school level, Lewis took the University of Hawaii job and led the Rainbows to a 21–2 record in 1956. He then headed to Southern Mississippi University, where his Golden Comets went 89–38 in five seasons. Lewis' success there, along with his reputation as a disciplinarian and an offensive innovator, as well as his recruiting connections in

New York City, convinced Andreas that he was the right guy to rebuild SU basketball.

The cornerstone of Lewis' first recruiting class, of course, was Bing, who hailed from Washington, D.C.'s Spingarn High School. That Lewis was able to convince Bing to spurn scholarship offers from more than 200 other schools—including national basketball powerhouses UCLA and Maryland—in order to play for a program that had won just six of its previous 47 games, ranks as one of the greatest recruiting upsets of all time. Lewis and Bing hit if off immediately. "I told him about how Syracuse basketball had been struggling, but between the two of us, we could turn it around," Lewis recalled.

The coach's impact was felt immediately as the Orangemen improved to 8–13 in 1962–63, his first season. Bing was eligible for varsity play the following season, and SU went 17–8 and earned an invitation to the National Invitational Tournament, where it lost in the first round. After a disappointing 13–10 showing in 1964–65, the Orangemen rebounded with a vengeance the following season as Bing averaged 28.4 points and 10.8 rebounds per game for a Syracuse team that went 22–6 and reached the NCAA East Region Finals, where it lost to Duke 91–81. Those fast-breaking Orangemen featured four players (Bing, Boeheim, George Hicker, and Rick Dean) who averaged double-digit scoring figures, and a fifth (Vaughn Harper) who just missed at nine points per game. Syracuse shot 50 percent from the field that season and averaged an NCAA record 99.9 points per game—a remarkable figure in an era before the shot clock.

Despite the graduation losses of Bing and Boeheim, Lewis' team turned in another solid campaign in 1966–67. Hicker (18.6 points per game) and Harper (14.3 rebounds per game) guided SU to a 19–2 record and a No. 8 ranking, but three losses in their final four regular season games cost them another NCAA berth. They ended up in the NIT where they fell to New Mexico in the first round.

The following season would be Lewis' last at Syracuse, and it wasn't a pleasant experience. The coach had several publicized disputes with players and the administration, and the result was an 11–14 record punctuated by a seven-game losing streak in the middle of the season. After it was over, Lewis left Syracuse to become the athletic director at the University of California at Sacramento. "It's not worth the aggravation to remain at SU," he told reporters at his final press conference. Lewis coached one year at his new school, posting a 7–28 record before giving it up for good. He finished with a very respectable 208–125 record in 12 seasons at the college level, but his best work was done at Syracuse. He helped revive a dead program, laying the foundation for Danforth, and then Boeheim, to take the Orange to heights never realized before.

95 1970 Football Boycott

In May 1970, nine African American football players at Syracuse University boycotted spring practice to protest what they considered racial discrimination and insensitivity in the program, headed by longtime coach Ben Schwartzwalder. The players— Gregory Allen, Richard Bulls, John Godbolt, Dana Harrell, John Lobon, Alif Muhammad (then known as Al Newton), Clarence McGill, Duane Walker, and Ron Womack—became known as the "Syracuse Eight." (The news media was unaware that an injured player was also part of the boycott.)

Dave Meggyesy and *Out of Their League*

In 1970 Dave Meggyesy spent four months writing his memoir at Jack Scott's Institute for the Study of Sport and Society in Oakland, California. The end result was a scathing, best-selling expose of the dehumanizing aspects of football titled *Out of Their League.*

Meggyesy wrote that his disillusionment with football began during his days as an All-American linebacker at Syracuse in the early 1960s. He criticized coaches for being authoritarian and unconcerned with their players' academics and physical well-being, often pressuring them to return to action before they were healed. The book also contains allegations of regular payments under the table by alumni and boosters—allegations that were denied by school officials, coaches, and several players.

Published a year after Meggyesy finished a seven-year career with the St. Louis (now Arizona) Cardinals, the book received critical acclaim and officially launched Meggyesy's career as a social activist. He would go on to teach sociology of sport courses at the college level and work with the NFL's Players Association to improve salaries and working conditions.

Among the changes they wanted implemented were stronger academic support for student-athletes, better medical care for injured players, assignment of starting positions based on achievement rather than race, and the integration of the all-white coaching staff. Schwartzwalder saw the demands as a challenge to his authority and refused to act. The protesting players felt they had no choice but to sit out the season, and the story drew national media coverage. Former SU All-American Jim Brown returned to campus to speak with the nine players and act as a peacemaker between them and Schwartzwalder, but Brown said his old coach "didn't have a clue what the protest was about and refused to budge. It dearly cost the men who protested and really set the university and the program back. Fortunately, though, positive changes were made, and steps were taken to heal old wounds."

A huge step occurred the weekend of a home football game against Louisville in late October 2006 when Syracuse University invited the nine players back to campus, where they were honored during halftime ceremonies in the Carrier Dome. Chancellor Nancy Cantor issued a formal apology from the university and presented each of the players with chancellor medals and SU lettermen jackets. During her remarks she lauded their "act of courage in standing up for what they believed."

Lobon, a defensive lineman on that team, was especially emotional. "This was the beginning of a new day," said the man who became a senior vice president of the Connecticut Development Authority and would be appointed to that state's Commission on Human Rights and Opportunities. "People really don't know the sacrifices that black athletes and other black students made during this period. I think we laid the groundwork for Syracuse to become one of the leading schools regarding the graduation of black athletes. I'm proud to wear my Syracuse gear today."

Emperor of the Empire State

Like rock balladeer Billy Joel, Jim Boeheim has always enjoyed being in a New York state of mind. You'd like being there, too, if you racked up the wins against your upstate and downstate basketball opponents the way Boeheim's Syracuse teams have.

Through the 2013–14 season, his teams have recorded a 205–23 mark against teams based in New York state. The numbers become even more mind-boggling when you subtract SU's record vs. longtime Big East Conference rival St. John's. Syracuse was

In the Garden

Through the years, Madison Square Garden has become SU's home away from Dome. Even when the 'Cuse plays St. John's there, the crowds are more pro-Orange because of the large number of SU alumni in the New York City metropolitan area.

Here's a look at how SU has fared at its favorite Big Apple building. (Records are current through the 2013–14 season.)

Overall	93–74
Regular season	43–38
Big East Tournament	46–27
NIT	3–9
NCAA	1–0
Under Jim Boeheim	75–46

162–3 against all other New York colleges during Boeheim's first 38 seasons as head coach. That's a .982 winning percentage. The only Empire State teams other than the Johnnies to beat the 'Cuse during his era are Fordham once and St. Bonaventure twice. And you have to go all the way back to December 12, 1981, for Fordham's 79–78 win and March 1, 1978, for the Bonnies' last victory (70–69) in the series.

SU currently has a 38-game win streak vs. New York foes and has won 84 of the last 85. Of these so-called rivals, none has fared worse than Syracuse's neighbors Colgate and Cornell. The Orangemen have won 48 straight against Colgate and are 121–45 all-time vs. the Red Raiders. The last time Colgate prevailed was a 67–63 victory on February 24, 1962. Cornell has not made out much better, losing 34 straight to trail 88–31 in its series. Canisius has lost 17 straight and trails 46–24, Niagara has dropped seven in a row and trails 53–28, and the Bonnies have a 13-game losing streak and trail 23–3. St. John's has lost nine straight but has been competitive with the Orange through the years and trails its series 51–37.

97 1951: National Cross-Country Champs

Tom Coulter chuckled when he recounted the crowd's reaction to those P.A. announcements at Syracuse University home football games during the autumn of 1951.

"When there was a break in the action, they would give the results of that morning's cross-country meet," the former All-American runner recalled in a 2011 interview with *Syracuse University Magazine*. "The announcer would say, 'Earlier today, it was Syracuse 15, so-and-so 45.' And you'd hear this collective groan fill Archbold Stadium. People would be saying things like, 'Oh, no, we got killed,' not realizing that in cross-country, like in golf, the low score wins. It went on like that throughout the '51 season, and my teammates and I would just laugh about it. It took some time before people learned that we were doing the clobbering rather than the other way around."

The lesson of Syracuse's dominance in the sport was driven home on November 26 that year on a snow-covered, four-mile course at Michigan State as five Orange runners combined to win the NCAA championship. Sophomore sensation Ray Osterhout paced SU with a third-place finish. He was followed across the finish line by senior captain Bill Irland (sixth), sophomore Coulter (12th), sophomore Don Fryer (27th), and freshman Steve Armstrong (32nd). The combined 80 points by SU's Fab Five enabled Coach Bob Grieve's Orange to easily defeat runner-up Kansas (118) and 16 other schools in the meet. Based on their finishes, Osterhout, Irland, and Coulter were named All-Americans. "It was," said Irland, "a very special achievement."

A somewhat improbable one, too, because Irland, the team captain and an Army veteran, was the only experienced varsity runner on a squad featuring three sophomores and one freshman. "That kind of inexperience isn't exactly a recipe for success," Fryer said. "But we had some pretty talented guys, and Bill was a fine leader."

The youthful Osterhout and Coulter quickly established themselves as two of the swiftest runners in the country, teaming with Irland to form a potent triumvirate. After losing by two points to powerful Army in the first meet of the season, SU won its next four dual meets and appeared to be peaking at the right time. At the IC4A championships in New York City a week before the nationals, the Orange finished a respectable third behind Penn State and Army as Osterhout took second, Irland fifth, and Coulter seventh.

"Unfortunately, the rest of our runners suffered off-days," Irland said. "Otherwise I think we would have won that title. But it did give us confidence heading to Michigan State for the NCAAs. We figured if Ray, Tom, and I could continue our strong running and Don and Steve just had solid days, we'd have a good shot at winning the whole thing." And that's what happened.

The funny thing is that Armstrong originally wasn't supposed to compete at the nationals, but Coach Grieve decided to play a hunch and use the freshman in place of a veteran runner who had underperformed in New York. "I thought I was just going along for the ride and that I wouldn't finish high enough to figure into the scoring," Armstrong said. "I'm glad I thought wrong."

Upon their return from East Lansing, Michigan, the victorious harriers received a big spread in the pages of the *Daily Orange* and were invited to dinner by chancellor William Tolley. "It wasn't a huge deal on campus, like football or basketball, and we understood because it wasn't particularly exciting watching a bunch of guys run four miles," Irland said. "But I do believe we boosted the spirits on campus a bit because football was down at the time, and a national championship is a big deal, regardless of the sport."

Coulter also excelled in boxing and track & field, earning 10 varsity letters, which is believed to be a school record. He made a name for himself in pugilism as the coach of the 1988 U.S. Olympic boxing team, which captured eight medals, including three golds, at the Olympic Games in Seoul. He ran the Syracuse Friends of Amateur Boxing Club, a non-profit, and he continued to oversee boxing clinics around the world into his eighties.

98 Calvin Murphy's 68 Points

As a freshman basketball player during the 1965–66 season, Bob Kouwe took 30-second showers after games so he could get back out into the stands in time to watch Syracuse legend Dave Bing play.

"That's how great I think Bing was," Kouwe said in the book, *Tales from the Syracuse Hardwood*. "But as great as he was—and I guarded him a lot in practice, so I know Dave Bing was absolutely great—watching him play was nothing, I mean *nothing*, compared to watching Calvin Murphy play." Kouwe should know because he twice played against Murphy, and in those two games, all the Niagara University All-American did was score 50 the first time and 68 the second time. "And remember," Kouwe said, "there was no three-point line back then." If there had been, Murphy probably would have had an 80-point night.

SU has logged close to 3,000 games since its hoops program began back in 1900, and Murphy is the only opponent who has scored more than 41 points in a game against the Orange—and he did it twice.

The 68-point performance came in a 118–110 Niagara home win on December 7, 1968. Talk about a date that will live in

Other Other-Worldly Performances vs. the Orange

Julius Erving's 32 rebounds. During a game on February 22, 1971, the Massachusetts sophomore who would become known as Dr. J hauled down the most caroms ever by an Orange opponent.
Brian Brohm's 555 yards passing. In a game on September 22, 2007, the Louisville quarterback shredded SU's secondary for a record number of yards, but the Orange prevailed 38–35.
Eddie Meyers' 298 yards rushing. On November 7, 1981, Navy's star back ran for more yards than any Orange opponent in history. He also scored four touchdowns.

infamy. The 5'9", 165-lb. dynamo was faster with the ball than most of his opponents were without it. And he had springs in his legs that enabled him to dunk over defenders a foot taller. As if that wasn't enough, he had a deadly accurate jump shot from 25' to 30' from the basket. On his record-setting night, he shot 24-of-46 from the field and 20-of-23 from the line.

"We had Ernie Austin guard him," Kouwe said. "We had John Suder guard him. We had Ray Balukas guard him. I guarded him. But there was no way to stop him. None. We picked him up as soon as he crossed center court. We tried a box-and-one. We double-teamed him. We triple-teamed him. We'd play defense on him when we had the ball on the offensive end, and I'm serious about that. But it was fruitless. There was no playing Calvin Murphy. It was a total loss even trying." The Orangemen futilely attempted to stop him the season before, too. Guess you could say they had better success during that January 31, 1968, game because Murphy scored "just" 50 points.

SU was hardly the only team Murphy went off on. In his three varsity seasons, he averaged 33.1 points per game, so he pretty much had his way against everybody.

99 Father Charles

For nearly three decades, players and coaches came and went while venues changed from Archbold and Manley to the Dome. But the one constant on the sidelines and bench at SU football and basketball games was the jovial priest in the orange sweater and the "Go Orange" cap.

Father Charles Borgognoni, known to everyone at SU simply as Father Charles, served as team chaplain from 1962 to 1991. But he was much more than a chaplain to the players and coaches. "He was a friend," said Floyd Little, who got to know Father Charles during Little's All-American football career in the mid-1960s. "It didn't matter if you were Catholic or Baptist or Jew or an atheist, Father Charles just had this way about him that enabled him to connect with everybody. And he had a way of making you believe that no matter what happened out there, win or lose, everything was going to be okay."

Little likes to tell a story about his first varsity football game at Syracuse. It was at Boston College, and the debut didn't go so well. The running back struggled mightily, and the ninth-ranked Orangemen were upset. "I told Father Charles that we never had a chance in that game because we were outnumbered 100 to one," Little said. "He said, 'Floyd, what are you talking about?' And I told him, "There were about 100 priests behind the BC bench and, no disrespect respect to you Father Charles, but there was only one of you on our side. Who's God going to listen to? One priest praying? Or a hundred?' He had a good laugh over that."

Tim Green vividly remembers the pep talk Father Charles delivered before SU played top-ranked and 24-point favorite

Nebraska in the Carrier Dome in 1984. "He told us about David and Goliath," Green recalled. "But it wasn't the story, it was his energy. It filled the room. It helped us believe." The Orangemen scored a 17–9 upset that day. "I thanked Father Charles for arranging the divine intervention," SU coach Dick MacPherson joked. "I think somebody up there definitely liked us that day."

Father Charles often would hold a service at the team dinner the day before a football game. "We weren't there to pray to win the game," he said. "I wanted them to know God gave them a talent and to make sure they were using it." Before kickoff, he would lead the team in singing the SU alma mater and reciting the Lord's prayer. And after the game? "If we lose, we cry. If we win, we sing, 'Amen, Amen.'"

Father Charles was known for his booming baritone, and on several occasions he sang the "Star Spangled Banner" before SU basketball and football games. One of the shining achievements during his 50 years in the greater Syracuse area was directing the nationally recognized Pompeian Players amateur theatrical group.

When he announced he was stepping down as the university's Catholic Chaplain, his friends held a farewell banquet for him at Drumlin's Country Club on south campus. The sellout crowd of more than 700 included a number of SU sports luminaries. Father Charles, who had been named a LetterWinner of Distinction in 1984, was presented with numerous gifts.

Perhaps no one was more choked up about Father Charles' retirement than Orange basketball coach Jim Boeheim, who had also just received the news that his star, Billy Owens, was forgoing his senior year to become eligible for the NBA draft. "It's been a great day so far," Boeheim told the audience. "I lost my best player, and now I'm going to lose my best pray-er. It's the hardest thing I've had to say in the city of Syracuse. There just aren't words.... He cannot be replaced."

Those sentiments were echoed by many that evening. It would not be the same without the jovial priest in the orange sweater and the "Go Orange" hat on the sidelines and the bench.

100 Duking It Out with Duke

The first tent had been pitched outside the Carrier Dome 12 days earlier. By the morning of February 1, 2014, about 50 tents had sprouted in the area dubbed "Boeheimburg." The temporarily insane Syracuse students camping outside the Dome in the depths of the polar vortex were hoping to get prime tickets for that night's first Atlantic Coast Conference clash between the Orange and the Duke Blue Devils.

"Hey, we're talking about a front-row seat to history," a shivering young man explained when asked why anyone in his right mind would risk frostbite and hypothermia to attend a basketball game. "The sacrifice is worth it." Apparently, neither wind nor rain nor snow nor the threat of pneumonia was going to keep these deliriously dedicated young people from their appointed rounds. They were taking school spirit to the nth degree—or maybe to the minus-10th degree, which is how low the temperature plunged on one of the nights leading up to the game.

As it turned out, the sacrifice proved worthwhile as this much-anticipated showdown between the fourth- and fifth-winningest programs in college basketball history did something hyper-hyped sporting events rarely do—it exceeded expectations. From the rousing rendition of the national anthem by SU alumna and former Miss America Vanessa Williams to Rakeem Christmas' spectacular

Boeheim and Coach K

The two men got to know each other when Jim Boeheim started playing in Duke University charity golf tournaments in the late 1980s, but they didn't become friends until he started working with Mike Krzyzewski on the coaching staff of USA Basketball a decade later.

"I was good friends with P.J. Carlesimo and Mike was good friends with P.J., so they kind of brought me in to work with them when Mike was looking to add to his staff for the Goodwill Games," said Boeheim. "That's when we really started to hit it off and our friendship began to blossom."

So, too, did their respect for one another's basketball acumen, which resulted in Coach K asking Boeheim to join his U.S. Olympic team staff before the 2008 Games in Beijing. The collaboration resulted in an Olympic gold medal there as well as in London four years later, and the duo will attempt a three-peat at the 2016 Games in Rio de Janeiro. In the meantime, they'll continue their friendly head-to-head battles in the Atlantic Coast Conference. Each time they meet, one of the story lines will be the matchup between the coach with the most victories in the history of men's college basketball (Krzyzewski at 983) vs. the coach with the second-most victories (Boeheim at 948).

"Neither Mike nor I like to lose, and neither of us likes to see the other one lose," Boeheim said. "Once the game gets going, you do forget about your friendship because you're concentrating on doing what you need to do to help your players win the game. But all is forgotten afterward, and you go back to being friends."

blocked shots to the chainsaw-to-the-ear decibel levels generated by an NCAA on-campus record crowd of 35,446, this game hit all the right notes as SU scored a 91–89 overtime victory against Duke. As advertised on thousands of orange T-shirts, a rivalry was indeed born that first night of February, a rivalry that promises to be as entertaining as SU's long-time matchups with Georgetown and Connecticut.

"I don't think I've ever been involved in a better game in here that I can remember, where both teams played at such a high level,"

USA head coach Mike Krzyzewski (right) gestures as assistant coach Jim Boeheim (left) looks on during their first round game at the world basketball championships on August 23, 2006, against Italy in Sapporo, northern Japan. (AP Photo/Mark J. Terrill, File)

Jim Boeheim said afterward. "Both teams just went after it. We've had a lot of games here that have been great. There's never been one as good as this one." And that was saying something, considering there had been about 600 basketball passion plays staged in the Dome up until that point.

Syracuse, fueled by C.J. Fair's career-best 28 points, appeared to have the game sewn up in regulation, but Duke's Rasheed Sulaimon beat the buzzer with an off-balance three-pointer that tied the game at 78. The Blue Devils then took an 87–84 lead with 80 seconds left in overtime before Syracuse rallied. Sophomore forward Jerami Grant was the hero, scoring eight of his 24 points in the extra session as the unbeaten Orange set a school record for the best start to a season with their 21st consecutive win. Three weeks later, at Duke's Cameron Indoor Stadium, they played a rematch. The sequel would also live up to the hype. With courtside seats going for $2,000 and the Cameron Crazies screaming so loudly that some media members and security guards wore earplugs to protect their ears, Duke won 66–60. Unlike the first game, this one was more like a heavyweight boxing match than an Olympic track meet.

Emotions ran so high that Boeheim came unhinged and was escorted off the court by police after being tossed with 10.4 seconds remaining. It was the first time in his 38-year career that he had been ejected from a regular season game. Boeheim's meltdown started after Fair drove the baseline and collided with Duke forward Rodney Hood before making an acrobatic layup that was waved off when an offensive foul was assessed by official Tony Greene. Boeheim tried unsuccessfully to rip off his jacket before sprinting onto the court and showering Greene with expletives more suited for HBO than ESPN. The outburst led to a double technical that put the game out of reach. Interestingly, Hood had been at the center of a controversy near the end of the first meeting at the Dome. Trailing by two with seconds to play, Hood missed a dunk on a play in which there was body contact with Christmas. No foul was called.

After the loss at Duke, Boeheim said that it was "the worst call of the year." Blue Devils coach Mike Krzyzewski refused to get into it with his longtime friend and Olympic team assistant. He instead lauded the intensity of both games. "I love the NBA to death, but this is something they can't do," Coach K said. "That's our product."

It took just two games for a rivalry to be in full swing.

Sources

Books

Brown, Jim and Delsohn, Steve. *Out of Bounds*. New York: Zebra Books, 1989.

Fisher, Donald M. *Lacrosse: A History of the Game*. Baltimore and London: The Johns Hopkins University Press, 2002.

Gallagher, Robert C. *Ernie Davis: The Elmira Express*. Silver Spring, MD: Bartleby Press, 2008.

Galvin, Ed, Margaret A. Mason, and Mary M. O'Brien. *Syracuse University: The Campus History Series*. Charleston, SC: Arcadia Publishing, 2013.

Keeley, Sean. *How to Grow an Orange: The Right Way to Brainwash Your Child into Becoming a Syracuse Fan*. Bloomington, IN: Wordclay, 2010.

Mullins, Michael. *Syracuse University Football: A Centennial Celebration*. Norfolk, VA: The Donning Company/Publishers, 1989.

Pitoniak, Scott. *Color Him Orange: The Jim Boeheim Story*. Chicago: Triumph Books, 2011.

Pitoniak, Scott. *Playing Write Field: A Collection of the Works of Scott Pitoniak*. Rochester, NY: CASS Publications, 1997.

Pitoniak, Scott and Sal Maiorana. *Slices of Orange: Great Games and Performers in Syracuse University Sports History*. Syracuse, NY: Syracuse University Press, 2005.

Pitoniak, Scott. *Syracuse University Football*. Charleston: Arcadia Publishing, 2003.

Poliquin, Bud. *Tales from the Syracuse Hardwood: A Collection of the Greatest Stories Ever Told*. Champaign, IL: Sports Publishing, 2003.

Rappoport, Ken. *The Syracuse Football Story.* Huntsville, AL: The Strode Publishers, 1975.

Schapp, Dick. *Flashing Before My Eyes: 50 Years of Headlines, Deadlines and Punchlines.* New York: HarperCollins, 2001.

Snyder, Bob. *Syracuse Basketball: A Century of Memories.* Champaign, IL: Sports Publishing, 2004.

Snyder, Bob, Hart Seely, Tom Flemming, and Mike Greenstein. *Syracuse University Basketball Trivia.* Boston: Quinlan Press, 1988.

Waters, Mike. *Legends of Syracuse Basketball.* Champaign, IL: Sports Publishing, 2004.

Waters, Mike. *The Orangemen: Syracuse University Men's Basketball.* Charleston, SC: Arcadia Publishing, 2002.

Youmans, Gary and Maury. *'59: The Story of the 1959 Syracuse University National Championship Football Team.* Syracuse: Syracuse University Press, 2003.

Magazines
Central New York Sports magazine
Eastern Basketball
ESPN: The Magazine
Inside Lacrosse
People
Pursuits
Sporting News
Sports Illustrated
Syracuse University Magazine
Upstate magazine

Newspapers
Boston Globe
Chicago Tribune

Finger Lakes Times
Hartford Courant
Los Angeles Times
Lyons Republic
Newsday
New York Daily News
New York Post
New York Times
Philadelphia Daily News
Rochester Business Journal
Rochester (NY) *Democrat & Chronicle*
Rochester Times-Union
Rome Daily Sentinel
Syracuse Herald-Journal
Syracuse Post-Standard
The Daily Orange
The National
USA Today
Utica Daily Press
Utica Observer Dispatch
Washington Post

Websites

www.syracuse.com
www.cuse.com
www.nunesmagician.com
www.archives.syr.edu
www.sportsillustrated.cnn.com/vault
www.espn.go.com
www.cbssports.com
www.newspaperarchive.com

www.profootballresearcher.org
www.orangefizz.net
www.sujuiceonline.com

Miscellaneous
Syracuse University basketball media guides, 1972–present
Syracuse University football media guides, 1970–present
Syracuse University lacrosse media guide, 2014
Heisman Trophy banquet program, 2008
Syracuse University Game Day Programs, 1980–present
The Onondagan, 1977

DVDs
Archbold Stadium: The Story of '78. A documentary by SU grad
students Gordon Brookes and Erick Ferris, 2009.
Orange Glory: The 20 Greatest Moments in Syracuse Basketball.
Sharp Entertainment, New York, 2010.